Benjamin Ward Richardson

Ten Lectures on Alcohol

Benjamin Ward Richardson

Ten Lectures on Alcohol

ISBN/EAN: 9783743313774

Manufactured in Europe, USA, Canada, Australia, Japa

Cover: Foto ©ninafisch / pixelio.de

Manufactured and distributed by brebook publishing software (www.brebook.com)

Benjamin Ward Richardson

Ten Lectures on Alcohol

TEN LECTURES ON ALCOHOL

BY

BENJAMIN W. RICHARDSON, M.A., M.D., F.R.S.,

FELLOW OF THE ROYAL COLLEGE OF PHYSICIANS, AND HONORARY PHYSICIAN TO
THE ROYAL LITERARY FUND.

NEW YORK:

National Temperance Society and Publication House,

58 READE STREET.

1883.

CONTENTS.

I.
ON ALCOHOL, ... 190
    A COURSE OF SIX CANTOR LECTURES, DELIVERED BEFORE THE SOCIETY OF ARTS.

II.
ACTION OF ALCOHOL ON THE BODY, ... 30

III.
ACTION OF ALCOHOL ON THE MIND, ... 28

IV.
MODERATE DRINKING, FOR AND AGAINST, . . 47

V.
THE MEDICAL PROFESSION AND ALCOHOL, . . 33

VI.
THE LIBERTY OF THE ABJECT, ... 12

VII.
THE EFFECTS OF ALCOHOL, ... 8

VIII.
TWENTY-ONE HISTORICAL LANDMARKS, . . . 24

              TOTAL PAGES, . . . 372

ON ALCOHOL.

A COURSE OF SIX CANTOR LECTURES DELIVERED BEFORE THE SOCIETY OF ARTS.

INTRODUCTORY NOTE.

THE course of Cantor Lectures on Alcohol here published were prepared at the request of the Council of the Society of Arts, and were delivered before the Society in the months of November, December, January, and February last.

I do not remember to have delivered any Lectures that have attracted so much earnest public attention, and in publishing them in this cheap form I am responding to a request too general to admit of hesitation or delay on my part. With the exception of the transference of the tabular matter into an Appendix, the introduction of a few minor and verbal corrections, and the addition of a page of learned and interesting passages kindly communicated to me by Mr. Stanford, M.A., F.R.S., the Lectures are published as they were spoken.

In this form I found them favorably received by the large audiences who honored me with their attention, and I am, therefore, led to hope for them equal favor with the larger public to whom they are now addressed.

It remains for me only to add,, that though I have spoken out freely the lessons I have learned from nature, no pledge binds me, and no society banded to propagate particular views and tenets claims my allegiance. I stand forth simply as an interpreter of natural fact and law.

    12 HINDE STREET W.
      May 1, 1875.

CONTENTS

	PAGE
Preface, by Dr. Willard Parker,	9

I.

On Alcohol, in relation to some of its varied services to Mankind, ... 13–40

II.

The Alcohol Group of organic Bodies—Actions of different Alcohols, ... 41–68

III.

The Influence of Common or Ethylic Alcohol on Animal Life—The primary physiological Action of Alcohol, . 69–63

IV.

The Position of Alcohol as a Food—Effects of Alcohol on the Animal Temperature—Hygienic Lessons, . . 94–122

V.

The Secondary Action of Alcohol on the Animal Functions, and on the Physical Deteriorations of Structure incident to its Excessive Use, ... 123–148

VI.

Physical Deteriorations from Alcohol (*continued*)—Influence of Alcohol on the Vital Organs—Mental Phenomena induced by its Use—Summary, . . . 149–179

APPENDIX, ... 181–190

PREFACE.

I AM very glad to learn that the "Course of Cantor Lectures on Alcohol," delivered by B. W. Richardson, M.D., F.R.S., before the Edinburgh Society of Arts, is about to be presented to the American public. They are clear, scientific, and couched in language free from technicalities and easily understood by all. I have seen no work on this subject so satisfactory as these lectures, which present it without "special pleading"; I hope they will be carefully read in every household. Aiming as they do to impart knowledge based on sound scientific principles, to the public mind, they cannot fail to awaken it to a realization of the evil that is being wrought by this agency, most destructive to human life and usefulness.

Alcohol has no place in the healthy system, but is an "irritant poison," producing a diseased condition of body and mind. Statistics show that ten per cent. of the annual number of deaths in this country are due to alcohol; that fully thirty-five per cent. of our insane, are so either directly or indirectly from its use; and that from seventy-five to ninety per cent. of the inmates of our penal and pauper institutions owe their condition to its influence. Besides this, we find that forty-five per cent. of the inmates of our asylums for idiots, are the offspring of parents addicted to drink.

Destroying as its use does, the will, the judgment, and the moral sense, may we not with propriety consider it a cause of that low state of public and private integrity which permits, even in our very midst, the formation of those shameful combinations to defraud and steal commonly known as "rings"?

Now the question meets us, how can this destruction of lives valuable to the state in their productiveness, be arrested, and a better condition of things be brought about, so that the burden of our taxation be lightened—taxation of which the great proportion goes to support our drinking-classes and their offspring. Let public intelligence and public morals be so educated that the *cause* of these things be appreciated, and so appreciated that they shall insist on laying the axe at the root of the tree, instead of lopping off the branches, by *preventing* a traffic in alcohol, instead of punishing the unfortunate victims of its use.

In Pennsylvania, in the year 1867, for every fourteen dollars received from license fees, the State expended one hundred in the support of the victims of alcohol; on principles of political economy, is this sound legislation?

If the habitual use of distilled liquors increase as rapidly within the opening century as it has during the one just ending, how sad the outlook! I can discern nothing in the future but a wreck of national honor, and the sinking to a lower standard of civilization and morality, unless public sentiment in this regard be changed. As a means to this end, let me again express the hope that these lectures may be carefully read in every home in the land.

WILLARD PARKER, M.D., etc.

ON ALCOHOL.

CANTOR LECTURES.

LECTURE I.

ON ALCOHOL, IN RELATION TO SOME OF ITS VARIED SERVICES TO MANKIND.

WE had before us a few weeks since an interesting national event. It was that of an archbishop and a minister of the Crown speaking almost at the same time, on one of the most important subjects of the day, viz., the part performed by alcohol on the national stage as it is set forth and played upon at this period of our history. The distinguished prelate took naturally for his view of the subject the moral influence of alcohol, and from this point denounced alcohol, in whatever form it presents itself for human consumption, in terms as eloquent as they were persuasive and forcible. The statesman took for his view of the subject the financial influence of alcohol; he gave a clear and by no means exaggerated estimate of the importance of an agent which, in these kingdoms, rests on an invested capital of not less than one hundred and seventeen millions of money; and submitted in conclusive terms, an argument, which, contrasted with that of the prelate, means that an agent so commercially potential cannot be materially interfered with in the present stage of our civilization, whatever may be the result of its influence on the community for good or for evil.

To the utterances of the church and of the legislative chamber we are accustomed to listen with such regard, that when any representative of either body speaks, we turn an ear almost automatically, and accept what is said as commanding respect, even though we dissent from the opinions that are expressed. No one therefore who stands out of these spheres can hope to obtain a hearing extended so far and wide, and equally authoritative.

And yet there is scope for honest utterance on another side of the alcohol question. The prelate and the legislator can hardly have more intimate conversance with the influence of alcohol than the physician and man of science. To the moral view of the question and to the legislative may well therefore be added the physical, and it is to this I shall try to direct public attention in these discourses, conscious, fully, of the disadvantages under which I should labor were it not for the countenance and support I shall hope to receive from you.

The strain running through all these lectures, in however diverse a manner the subject-matter of them may be pursued, will then be simply this: **Of what physical value has alcohol been to man?**

of what value is it to man? We know it is of no value to any other animal, and thus we limit our inquiry at once to the highest order of the animate series of natural development, or of natural creation.

In the studies that are in this sense to be undertaken, I will not fail to remember the injunction placed upon me to speak simply and plainly; not to offend pride of learning by too great simplicity of statement, nor yet to embarrass humility by a display of technical language and of the abstruse technical reasoning, for which the subject in hand affords so much opportunity. As far as possible I will strive to be plainness itself, and that, not only in mode of expression, but in matter of it; I mean in truthfulness of expression, as far as I am guided by the light that enables me to see what is nearest to the truth.

I shall propose in this description to glance first at the value of alcohol to man in a general sense; that is to say, to its value as an agent useful for other purposes than as a fluid to be imbibed. From this I shall be naturally led to consider its action, physically, on man, and its use as a fluid consumed with, and, according to common acceptation, as a food. Lastly, I shall be brought to treat upon its secondary action on the vital functions, physical and mental, i.e., on the deteriorations of structure and derangements of function, which may follow its use.

THE TERM "ALCOHOL."

The first employment of the word alcohol is obscurely recorded. Bartholomew Parr, one of the most learned of our scientific classics, taking the usual derivation of the word as from the Arabic *A'l-ka-hol*, a subtile essence, says it was originally employed to designate an impalpable powder, used by the Eastern women to tinge the hair and the margins of the eyelids. As this powder, viz., an ore of lead, was impalpable, the same name was given to other subtile powders, and then to the spirit of wine exalted to its highest purity and perfection.

The earliest systematic and truly scientific use of the term that I can discover is in Nicholas Lemert's 'Course of Chemistry,' published in 1698. There the word is used as a verb, "to alcoholize," and the definition of this is said to be "to reduce to alcohol, as when a mixture is beaten into an impalpable powder." The word, says Lemert, is also used to express a very fine spirit; "thus the spirit of wine well rectified is called the alcohol of wine."

The word employed in this sense merely tells us of a refined fluid substance obtained by a subtile process of separation from a grosser substance. But it was not applied to the special fluid now under our consideration until long after that fluid had actually been separated. Then it was used as a supplementary term to the earlier terms, *Vinum adustum*, *Vinum ardens*, *Spiritus vini*, *Spiritus ardens*, by which a spirit obtained from the grosser fluid, by the action of fire, was known and described.

FERMENTATION OF WINE.

We must now go back to a much earlier study, viz., to the study of the primitive fluid, from which the subtile spirit was derived. In the history of the production of alcohol we gather, in fact, the use of two of the most prominent words of our modern language: fermentation and distillation. They each mark distinct progressive epochs in natural science.

The term fermentation brings us in contact with the primitive fluid. It leads us to ask how, from the vegetable world, by change or mutation of its matter, a new product was evolved? The origin of this procedure is so old we have no possible means of tracing it. Before ever the word chemistry, or the science which that word implies, was dreamed of, this process of obtaining the crude liquor, from which alcohol was ultimately extracted, was in active operation. By some accidental discovery it had been started by human hands, and the act of first lighting and reproducing fire was hardly a less wonderful development of the higher faculties resident in man, than was this discovery. The operation itself, originally, was, we may presume, very simple. As there is a spontaneity in nature to produce fire, as for instance, when a metal like iron strikes a stone, so there is a spontaneity of fermentation in vegetable matter—especially in the juices of fresh ripe fruits in warm weather—which fact being observed, first, from the motion induced in the fluids, and secondly from the crude products that were left, would lead naturally to the contemplation of the steps of the process, to its easy, artificial, and more perfect development, to a method of separating and purifying the products, and afterwards of tasting and using them.

The products of fermenting fruits were limited to four : an active air which escapes freely ; a froth or yeast which floats above as a crust; a heavy mass or lees which sinks to the bottom ; and a fluid which remains apart. These portions, each readily separable, indeed, separable of themselves, were soon understood in respect of their virtues. That invisible air, which escapes so actively, is a deadly vapor or miasm ; that froth, unpleasant to the taste, is an active promoter of the motion that springs from the fruit; those lees are like sediment from muddy water, excrementitious, to be cast away ; but that remaining subtile fluid, to the palate so grateful, to the senses so exhilarating, to the heart so forcing, to the intellect so exciting or so deadening:—let it be brought forth in the daintiest cups the handicrafts can fashion from the rude earth! It is not, to the savage, a mortal thing at all. Water flows in open streams, a common liquid, at which cattle and creeping things may drink; this must be the drink of the superior intelligences from whom the savage came! It lifts the man who takes it into a higher sphere of life, or it degrades him to the lowest. It introduces him, as it were, to a new human organization that is not to be a passing phenomenon, but, for good or for evil, is to remain for ages.

The fluid is wine.

The discovery is an epoch surpassed by none

other, in the history of one portion of mankind, and the early dawning civilizations show their wonder at it in their mythology. Egypt claims the invention for her god Osiris, Greece for Bacchus, and Rome for Saturn. The Greeks, most ambitious to be connected with the origin, assert that the very name belongs to them, for the drink was first discovered in Ætolia by Orestheus, the son of Deucalion, whose grandson, Oeneus, was so called from Oinos, which was the old name of the vine. Or else the discovery was by Oeneus himself, who first pressed the rich grapes. Thus Oinos—oinon—vinum—wine. Then by these nations the praises of wine and of the wine gods, one and all, were sung into the later times. The first of the Roman poets, excited to his labor by Mæcenas, the friend of Augustus, who would that the vineyards should flourish, is thus prompted to invoke Bacchus, under the name of Pater Lenæus—

> "Hither, oh, Lenæus—Father Lenæus, come.
> By thee with heavy viny harvest crowned,
> The pasture flourishes. In the full vats
> The vintage foams.
> Hither Lenæus, Father Lenæus come,
> And, with thy buskins off, in the new wine,
> Stain, thou, thy naked legs even with me."

And thus on until our own era, in which—alas for the mutability of even god-like virtues!—under the title of "The Worship of Bacchus," our veteran artist, George Cruikshank, has turned the praises of his brother artist, Virgil, into scorn, and has transformed Pater Lenæus the wine giver, into the destroyer of every civilization over which he has become enthroned.

It is worthy here of special remark that the invention of wine was local on the planet, and that it came from some centre of the ancient world lying near to those points from whence our modern civilization took its rise. For when that civilization concentrated itself into bands or armies, or navies, for the purpose of discovering new portions of the earth, where other savage nations, as they are called, dwell, it found the wine god, the wine cup, and the wine equally unknown. A good three-quarters of the old world knew no more of wine than of the people who invented it, until they were taught to know it—then they learned about it fast enough.

The practice of exciting fermentation and of obtaining the coveted fermented liquor once known, the knowledge was extended, until from varied vegetable substances wine became a product extracted by an art that was successful, however rude. The discovery of the ferment, that is to say of the body that would produce fermentation, was sufficient to set in mutation or intestine motion a whole series of fermentable vegetable substances, and to extend the manufacture of various vinous fluids to an unlimited degree. From the expressed juice of the grape the transition was easy to other juicy fruits, such as the mulberry, the apple, the pear, the peach: from these again to those juices which exude from trees, as from the Eastern palm-tree; and from these again to such similar looking substances as manna and honey. From fruits, moreover, it was an easy transition to seeds, and from seeds that were soft and succulent to seeds that were hard and of the character of what we now call grain.

From all these varied sources of fermentable substances there was produced for ages the fluid containing the basis of alcohol. Its most common name was wine, though the term was modified by adjective additions signifying sometimes its color, sometimes the place where it was made or marketed. Thus were introduced the white and red wines, the Vino Tinto and the golden unctuous Vino Greco. Even after the discovery (of which I shall soon again speak) of the existence of a distinct essence or spirit in wine, the original fluid held pre-eminence over all other strong drinks, and in the early and middle stages of civilization in Europe the number of wines that were used exceeded anything we now have in common use. In the Appendix to these lectures, there will be found, in a table—Table I.—lists of ancient Roman wines arranged in nine groups.

As a matter of some historical interest, it is worth a moment or two to touch on the special qualities of a few of those vinous drinks.

Certain of the ancient Roman wines of the first group were home wines. The Falernian, one of these, was, it is believed, something like our modern Madeira, and was not commonly used until it was ten years old. After it was twenty years old it affected the body unfavorably, causing headache. This was the experience of Galen.

Other wines were foreign. Chian, also called

the Ariusian, of which there were three varieties—austere, sweet, and intermediate—and the Lesbian, considered to be a diuretic, were of this kind.

Some wines were named after their color, as white, dark, and red. The white were thought to be the thinnest and least heating; the dark-colored and sweet the most nourishing; the red the most heating.

Some, again, were named after qualities, of age, and the like: as old (Vetus); new (Novum); of the present year (Hornum); of three years (Trimum); mellow (Molle, Lene, Vetustate edentulum); rough (Asperum); pure (Merum); strong (Fortius).

Certain wines, named Myndian, Halicarnassian, Rhodian, and Coan, were made with salt water. They were considered not to be intoxicating, but to promote digestion.

Two wines, Cnidian and Adrian, were also medicinal wines. The first, it was believed, engendered blood and was at the same time a laxative; the second was diaphoretic.

Mustum was a term applied to wine newly made, or the fresh juice of the grape. Protropum was the juice which runs from the grapes without pressing. Mulsum was a mixture of wine and honey. Sapa was Mustum boiled down to a third. Defrutum was Mustum reduced to half, and Carenum was the same reduced to a third.

Passum was a sweet wine, prepared from grapes that had been dried in the sun. Passum creticum, also a sweet wine, is believed to have been the same as the wine which our own forefathers called Malmsey; the wine in which the Duke of Clarence brother of Edward the Fourth, elected to be drowned.

A wine called Murrhina, placed in the last group in the Appendix, has a curious history. The Greeks had a wine of this kind, which consisted of pure wine perfumed with odorous substances. The Romans had a wine similarly named, which is supposed to have been wine mingled with myrrh. It was administered to those who were about to suffer torture, in order to intoxicate them and to remove the sense of suffering.

The ancient wines retained their place probably until the end of the Middle Ages, but we have no reliable evidence bearing upon this point, if we except an occasional reference by some poet or physician to the subject of wine. Very slowly the names, rather than the wines, changed generally. The Roman conqueror who built his villa on our islands, and fitted it with so much taste and means of luxury, added to it his wine-cellar, in the manner he had been instructed by his forefathers, and from it took out his red and white and old wine, as we do now; boasting possibly of the vintage from which it was grown, and eloquent as to its age and perfect ripeness. If he had no old port, he had old Falernian or Passum; his rough and his sweet, his light and his heavy wines, the same as our connoisseur of to-day. But, perhaps, he knew a great deal more, in the way of fact about the vintages, than his modern follower.

How the wines changed in name through the centuries will be gathered from the lists of the wines of Europe in use in the last century, collected by the distinguished chemist Neumann, and detailed in the Appendix, Table II.

Some of the wines mediæval and later derive additional names from peculiarities in themselves. Sec, from which we derive the name of the wine Sack, on which Sir John Falstaff so keenly enjoyed himself, means dry; the wine being made from half dried grapes. Malmsey was called by the Italians "Manna alla bocca e balsamo al cervello"—"Manna to the mouth and balsam to the brain."

From the chemist of last century, Neumann, who has collected for us such a long list of wines, we are supplied with a very instructive table of analyses showing the amount of spirit present in the different specimens. The wines he analysed are tabulated in alphabetical order. I believe his to be the first true chemical analyses that were ever made, on an extensive and comparative scale, of different wines, and if they indicate all the spirit in the wines named, it is clear that the amount of spirit in them was exceedingly small, when compared with what is present in the wines of the present day. Malmsey, the strongest of them, contained but about twelve per cent. of spirit, and sack a little more than half that amount. Falstaff might readily drink at a draught a pint of sack that contained rather less than seven and a half per cent. of spirit.

BEER.

The only other diluted rival of wine obtained by fermentation was the liquid derived from corn. Tradition, active again in giving celestial origin to strong drinks, has assigned the introduction of the art of making this product first to Osiris, the divinity of Egypt, and afterwards to the goddess Ceres. The fluid thus produced became, in Saxon language, known as beer, bere, from barley, or perhaps from the Hebrew, *bar*, corn. Tacitus calls it Zythum. The Egyptians, it is said, made it first for the common folk that they too might receive the gift of Osiris. In its original state beer was what we would now call the sweet fluid or wort fresh from the vat, and untinctured with any additional substance. So it continued probably until the ninth century, when it began to be treated with the *lupulus*, or hop. The first mention of this plant is made by an Arabian, named Mesue, of about the year 850, but he does not refer to it in relation to beer. The hop not only flavored but tended to preserve the beer, and in a few centuries it became of general use. In the reign of Henry the Sixth the use of hops was for a time forbidden, on the ground that they spoiled the beer and rendered it dangerous. An order prohibiting hops and sulphur for beer was also made in the reign of Henry the Eighth. But the hops at last won their way. It is worthy of notice that Neumann, who analysed the beers of last century, as well as the wines, found that the beers contained an amount of spirit varying from 5 per cent. in the weakest, to 10.90 per cent. in the strongest kinds. The malt liquors of the last century were, it appears from this, of much the same strength as those of the present.

Thus in the history of alcohol the first step of

discovery was that of its production from vegetable matter by the process of fermentation. As so produced it was a mixture of that which we now call pure spirit, or alcohol, with water, and with small quantities of other extraneous substances of minor moment.

On the nature of the fermentative change by which the juice of the fruit, or the exuded fluid of the plant or tree, or the seed or the sweet sugar, is transformed into the new product, speculation has been rife for a hundred years at least. In this day the atomic constitution of water, of alcohol, and of the substances which yield alcohol are known, and the atomic change of constitution that takes place is known; but the reason of the process is, according to my judgment, as little understood as it was when the discussion began. Probably, indeed, the latest theories that have been advanced are rather a retrogression, by a line of learned subtleties, from the earlier views, than an approach to simplicity of truth. I do not, therefore, venture to trouble you with any description on this head. One word I would add in the way of a guard against misuse of terms from assumed analogies. We often hear processes described as fermentative, which in truth have no relation, by any proved physical argument, with the true process of fermentation of vegetable matter connected with the production of wine. To take one example; we speak commonly of the zymotic or fermentative diseases, applying the term to those maladies which, in the form of contagious fevers, become epidemic. Hence many are led to believe that in these diseases there is in the body an actual fermentation like that in wine or beer; a comparison no closer, according to our knowledge as it now actually exists, than might be instituted between the same process and the so called ferment of a mob when it assembles to give vent to its turbulent rage.

DISTILLATION.

I have said that for many centuries there was nothing known to mankind beyond the formation of a vinous fluid. At length a new process was brought to bear on wine, which simple as it is to us now, was in its early days, and for many long days afterwards, a wonder and a mystery. This was the simple act of distilling wine, and of obtaining from it by distillation a fine spirit containing no water. The discovery of distillation of wine has been attributed to Albucasis, or Casa, an Arabian chemist and physician of the eleventh century. The evidence on this point is not very convincing. It is true that the refined body called spirit of wine began to be known in alchemical and Arabian schools about or soon after the time of Casa, and from that circumstance, rather than from direct evidence derived from his works, the discovery has probably been imputed to him. However, it is historically correct that from the school of Albucasis the discovery sprang. The alchemists or adepts were conversant with pure spirit, and, says Boerhaave, when they had reduced it to the utmost subtlety, they made use of it in the preparations of all their secret menstruums.

Distillation itself was probably an imitation of nature, for nature is ever distilling and condensing. In the cold, water condenses on the leaf and on the grass, as dew, and ascends as vapor in the sun. This process of raising water into a state of vapor by heat, and condensing it by cold, the simplest of immediate imitations of nature, would by easy transition pass to other liquids, and with special ease to that liquid which has rivalled water as a drink for man—wine.

The pure spirit of wine in its earlier use was applied mainly to chemical and medicinal purposes, and indeed many centuries elapsed before the process of distillation became active for the production of those stronger drinks, which, under the name of "spirits," are now in such common use in daily life. Brandy from *brennen*, to burn; thus *Branntwein*, brandy, is a comparatively late term in European literature. Gin, contracted from Geneva, is not to be found as signifying a spirituous drink in our vocabularies of two hundred years ago. The term rum is assigned to the native American peoples, who so designated the vinous spirit distilled from sugar; and whiskey (Celtic *uisge*, water), though it may have been known as a distilled drink as long as Branntwein, has not been Anglicised, I believe, for more than a century and a half. Some further notes on this subject by Mr. Stanford will be found in the Appendix.

In the earlier modes of distillation the instruments used were simple but effective. They consisted of the furnace, the receptacle to the furnace, the receiver which stood within the receptacle, and the alembic or condenser, which was made of tin or other metal.

The ancient alembic, the use of which is still valued, was, in truth, a very scientific instrument, and caused a perfect collection of the distilled fluid. The spirit from the crude wine ascended from a heated reservoir into a conical tube, and then downwards through a returning exit tube into a receiver.

The adepts were, indeed, marvellously mechanical, and when we recall that they neither had cork nor elastic tubing, nor gas, we wonder by what clever devices they were so successful. They had many useful arts, I am sure, which we have improperly forgotten, and which might with advantage be revived. Some of their instruments, for a long time thought to be fanciful and useless, are being again considered of value. One of these was called a cohobator, and another called a circulator, in which they caused spirits to boil and distil, and condense and distil again, for months at a time. The fluids went round and round in the circulator like the wheel of fortune, and many an adept has looked upon his fortune as spinning in that wheel, from which the elixir of life and the philosopher's stone were, in his ardent imagination, to be evolved.

To sum up, let us remember the four stages in the general history of alcohol, from the first to the time when it came strictly under analytical chemical observation; and, in regard to common knowledge, to the present time.

(*a.*) The stage of manufacture of wine or beer by fermentation. A stage extending from the earliest history until the time of the adepts, say about the eleventh century of the Christian era.

(*b.*) A stage when there was distilled from the wine a lighter spirit called, first, spirit of wine, and afterwards alcohol.

(*c.*) A stage when this subtile or distilled spirit from wine was applied in its refined and pure state to the arts and to the sciences.

(*d.*) A stage when this same process of distillation was applied to the production of alcoholic spirits for the use of man as spirituous drinks, under the names of brandy, gin, whiskey, rum,—a stage comparatively modern.

USES OF WINE.

We will, if you please, leave now, for a time, the consideration of wine and alcohol as drinks, and dwell briefly on the uses to which these fluids have been applied for other purposes. The study is peculiarly interesting, and I could easily carry you on during the whole course of these lectures with the narration of it. Unfortunately every word I have to say must be introduced into this hour, so that I can refer only to the salient points, and to a few only of these.

From the first, the preservative or antiseptic quality of wine was recognised, and the fluid was employed for the preservation of animal and vegetable substances. The Roman butchers, who, like our modern butchers, sold their fresh and their salted meats, prepared their salted flesh in the following manner:—The animals they intended to preserve were kept from drinking any fluid on the eve of the day on which the killing took place. After the killing the parts to be preserved were boned and sprinkled lightly with pounded salt. Then, having well dried off all dampness, the operators sprinkled more salt, and placed the pieces so as not to touch each other, in vessels that had been used for oil or vinegar. Over the whole they poured sweet wine, covered the contents of the vessel with straw, and, when they could, kept down the temperature of the room in which the vessel was placed by sprinkling snow around. When the cook wished to remove the salt from the meat, he took it out of the wine and boiled it first in milk and afterwards in rain water.

Long previous to the Roman era this preservative process of wine had been recognised and applied. Palm wine was used by the Egyptians in their most costly processes of embalming the bodies of the dead. This same application of wine, or spirits of wine, for the preservation of animal and also of vegetable substances, has been maintained up to our time. In our museums the specimens therein preserved, in the moist state, are immersed in spirit, and the modern art of embalming is not perfected without the employment of the same antiseptic agent.

Early after the discovery of the properties of wine the fact must have been observed that from a change in it another substance was produced, to which, in these days, we give the name of vinegar.

To prevent the formation of vinegar in wine, the ancients boiled the wine, and to remove the acidity arising from vinegar they added gypsum to sour wine, and thus rendered it palatable. Vinegar itself they employed for purposes precisely the same as we in this day; they partook of it with vegetables, they employed it for preservation of animal and vegetable substances, and they applied it for numerous medicinal purposes. After the process of distillation was discovered by the adepts, the distillation of vinegar was also carried on, and in this way was obtained that strong vinegar, which enters so largely into various uses as an acid, called aromatic vinegar.

Very early in history wine was employed for another purpose, that, namely, of extracting the active principles from plants and other substances possessing, or supposed to possess, medicinal virtues. Dioscorides, one of the fathers of medicine, and particularly of that part which pertains to the use of curative substances, or medicaments proper, is full of descriptions of vinous tinctures, some of which were sufficiently potent even for our present use. A vinous tincture of this kind has a very singular and, I had almost said, romantic history. This is the wine of Mandragora. In the Isles of Greece there has grown for ages a plant called mandrake; it belongs to the same family of plants as our belladonna, or deadly nightshade. From the root of this plant the Greeks extracted, by means of wine, a narcotic, and what in this day we should call an anæsthetic. Some, says our learned Dioscorides, boil the root in the wine down to a third part and preserve the decoction, of which they administer a cyathus (about what would now be a common wineglassful), for want of sleep, or for severe pains of any part, and also before operations with the knife or cautery, that these may not be felt. Again, he says, a wine is prepared from the bark without boiling, and three pounds of it are put into a cadus (about eighteen gallons) of sweet wine, and three cyathi of this are given to those who are cut or cauterised, when, being thrown into a deep sleep, they do not feel any pain. Again, he speaks of a preparation of mandragora called morion, which causes infatuation and takes away the reason. Under the influence of this agent the person sleeps, without sense, in the attitude in which he took it, for three or four hours afterwards. Pliny, the Roman historian, bears evidence, much later, to the same effect, and adds the singular remark that some persons have sought sleep from the smell of this medicine. And again, Lucius Apuleius, the author of the book called the 'Golden Ass,' who lived about 160 A.D., and of whose works eleven editions were republished in the fourteenth and fifteenth centuries, says that if a man has to have a limb mutilated, sawn, or burnt, he may take half an ounce of mandragora in wine, and whilst he sleeps the member may be cut off without pain or sense.

It is unquestionably to this same anæsthetic wine our own Shakespeare refers in his half-imaginary, half-legendary Middle Age history. This is the wine of that insane root, which, says Macbeth, "takes the reason prisoner." This is the wine that Juliet drinks, and the action of which the Friar Lawrence describes—

> "Through all thy veins shall run
> A cold and drowsy humor, which shall seize
> Each vital spirit; for no pulse shall keep
> His natural progress, but surcease to beat:
> No warmth, no breath, shall testify thou liv'st;
> The roses in thy lips and cheeks shall fade
> To paly ashes; thy eyes' windows fall,
> Like death when he shuts up the day of life;
> Each part, deprived of supple government,
> Shall stiff, and stark, and cold appear like death:
> And in this borrow'd likeness of shrunk death
> Thou shalt remain full two and forty hours,
> And then awake as from a pleasant sleep."

It follows therefore from the history of scientific discovery that our modern great advance of removing pain during surgical operations is in fact, if not as old as the hills, as old almost as wine. But is the story true, you say? I answer Yes, and the answer is from experiment. Thinking it a subject of very great interest, I instituted, a few years ago, an inquiry into the matter. Through the kindness of my friend, the late Mr. Daniel Hanbury, F.R.S., I obtained a fine specimen of mandragora root, and I made once again, after a lapse of probably five centuries, Mandragora wine. I tested this, and found it was a narcotic having precisely the properties that were anciently ascribed to it. I found that in animals it would produce even the sleep of Juliet, not for thirty or forty hours, a term that must be accepted as a poetical licence, but for the four hours named by Dioscorides easily, and that in awakening there was an excitement which tallies with the same phenomenon that was observed by the older physicians.

Thus, one of the first uses of wine to man was amongst the most noble and beneficent that man by his ingenuity can confer on his kind, and if wine had ever been used in this way and in none worse, Pater Lenæus might have retained his supremacy in the good opinion of all the world.

Besides using wine for extracting the virtues of the vegetable kingdom, our ancient chemists tested it on metals and made it here subservient to their purpose. What they called the extract of Mars was a solution of iron, made with an astringent wine, and reduced into a thick consistency by fire. Eight ounces of the rust of iron, powdered very fine, were put into an iron pot and covered with four pints of strong red wine. The iron crucible was then set on the fire, and the mixture, stirred with an iron rod, was boiled to a third: then it was strained through a cloth and evaporated into an extract. To this extract wonderful curative powers were ascribed, and indeed it was a very useful medicine. The metal antimony also was subjected to the action of wine. The so called liver of antimony was treated with white wine and dissolved in it, and to this day we retain the remedy. It was originally called the emetic wine.

USES OF SPIRIT OF WINE OR ALCOHOL.

After the process of distillation of wine was discovered, the use of the new spirit rose rapidly into application in a variety of ways. The adepts, the

Middle Age chemists of whom I have spoken, kept this distilled spirit long a secret. They found in it a solvent for many things that before were insoluble. Oils, resins, gum resins, balsams were now brought into a medium that acted towards them as a menstruum, and straightway they were dissolved. The East Indian Styrax Benzoin yielded a balsam which, dissolved in the distilled spirit, was a fortune to the chemists. The Commander's balsam, or balsam for wounds, or Friar's balsam, was soon the reputed heal-all of every injury.

The useful extracted first out of the new distillate, beauty was next remembered. Alas for the female face divine, the cosmetic and the subtile wash that should veritably make young faces old and assumably make old faces young, were soon in process in the laboratory of the adept who could distil wine. Again, the artist came in for a share in the discovery. The once insoluble and the useless resins and ambers were dissolved for his brush, and gave him coatings, preservatives, and washings, of which previously he had no conception.

This spirit of wine burns. It does not touch oil for the light it gives, but how strange! it burns away without a trace of smoke, and with an excellent heat. So the spirit lamp in due time is invented. A trifle, say you? Nay, it was as great an advance to the chemist who first used it as the gas in the Bunsen burner is to us.

Once more: this subtle spirit has in it the virtue of preserving all organic substances with which it is brought in contact. It masters putrefaction itself; perchance the elixir of life is therefore found.

It dissolves insoluble bodies; perchance it will by careful study and experiment reveal the grand secret of transmutation. In this way reasoned its first masters.

I must not dwell longer over these details of minor things of major usefulness. I must turn to some applications of our refined spirit which are major in fact as well as in use, in theory as well as in practice, in science as well as in art. In this regard we have to consider alcohol as the basis of other essences not less potent than itself.

The process of distillation of essences from liquids and from vegetable substances once established, it was but natural that some adept should turn his hand to mineral bodies and try if they would not yield some new product that should be of effective and novel quality. Into the distillatory soon pass, therefore, all manner of things, from the horn of the stag or hart, to the skull and brain of the dead man. Among other substances there was submitted to distillation the green stony crystal found in the earth, and called green vitriol, in Latin *vitriolum*. The result of the distillation of this *vitriolum* was to obtain as a yield, in the retort, the heavy oily corrosive fluid called, originally, spirit of vitriol, called now oil of vitriol or sulphuric acid.

Many were the fanciful things thought of by the adepts concerning this oil, and even to the letters of which the word *vitriolum* is made up they attached a mystical symbolism. In course of time they began to combine and to distil other fluids with the corrosive sulphurous oil, and amongst the first of fluids used in this manner stood spirit of wine. The experiment did not deceive them, for it gave them as a product one of the most useful and wonderful of liquids. To them this new liquid as it first was taken from the retort was an infinite marvel. They poured it on water and it floated, on spirit and it floated. They poured it into their hands, and, lo! it boiled there. It escaped from them into an invisible state or air before they could well bottle it; it burned and exploded. It caused, when it passed off from the surface of the living body, an intense cold. It dissolved wax, oil, fat, gums, resins, balsams, and yet when it was set free it let them fall again. It was so light that a measure which would hold ten pounds weight of water would only hold seven pounds of this light intangible liquid. What name shall they apply to this substance, the lightest known? They designate it by a term indicating the lightest thing they can conceive: they compare it with the refined medium, with which the philosophers imagine the firmament to be filled, and they give it the same name. They call it *æther*.

Of what strange after-use this magical fluid has been to man we all know. It was introduced early into medicine, and was well studied last century by Dr. Ward, and by Mr. Turner, of Liverpool. In our own time, it has been discovered to have the power of suspending sensation and sensibility after being inhaled by the lungs, and by its means there has been re-introduced to the world that beneficent and long lost art of rendering the body insensible to pain during surgical operations.

More recently by a study of the application of ether for the production of intense cold, I myself introduced that local use of it for benumbing the body, called the ether spray.

The value of this secondary alcohol to man is indeed inestimable. You know how valuable it has been in photography as the volatile solvent of collodion, and in other various departments of the fine and useful arts it has rendered equally good service.

From the distillation of *vitriolum* our adepts soon passed to other solid substances. They distilled saltpetre, and so got the spirit of nitre, which we call now nitric acid; they distilled common salt in combination with oil of vitriol, and so got spirit of salts (marine acid), which we call hydrochloric acid. Again, with these new spirits they distilled spirits of wine to obtain new ethers, nitrous and marine. Then a chemist, the Count de Lauragnais, distilled together acetic acid and spirit of wine, by which process he obtained acetous ether. Thus by these double actions, a numerous series of useful ethers has been obtained, it were too long for me to enumerate.

From the observation of the fermentation of wine we derive, in a certain sense, our first knowledge of gases. Van Helmont gave to the gas which comes from the fermenting of vegetable matter the name of *gas sylvestre*, and from this may be dated the origin of the study of these invisible forms of matter. Priestley made some of his early observations on the gas which escaped from fermenting malt in a brewery at Warrington, and was led step by step to the liberation of gases from mineral and earthy substances, and so to the discovery of oxygen. Upon that discovery, coupled with his method of collecting gases by displacement of water, and of trying their qualities, came the process of distilling and collecting a gas from coal, and thus coal gas.

After the discovery of the element known as chlorine, and of the compounds of that element with other elements, another new era was opened in the history of alcohol. By passing chlorine through alcohol, Liebig obtained that narcotic substance which we call chloral hydrate; and by treating alcohol with chloride of lime, the same great experimentalist produced for us chloroform, an agent which has rivalled ether in its service as a soother and saver of pain. A glance at the table—No. IV. of the Appendix—of anæsthetics or sleep producers will show by the names in italics those substances which come from alcohol. All that have proved of most use excepting one, nitrous oxide or laughing gas, have this common origin.

Had the time not been expended, I could have brought before you further illustration upon illustration of these secondary uses of alcohol to man; but I must stop, content in having recalled to your minds some of the more striking facts in the history of the curious and important agent which is now the subject of our studies.

LECTURE II.

THE ALCOHOL GROUP OF ORGANIC BODIES—ACTIONS OF DIFFERENT ALCOHOLS.

IF before a chemist of a hundred years ago you could have placed a specimen of spirit of wine or alcohol, and could have asked him of what it was composed, he would have told you that it was the element of water combined with elementary fire, to which elementary fire he would give the name of phlogiston, a name derived from a Greek word signifying to burn or inflame. He would tell you that all bodies that burned were phlogisticated, and that bodies that would not burn were dephlogisticated. The substance that was left behind was, he would probably add, the element with which the elementary fire had previously been combined. Were you to ask him whence he derived this knowledge, he would say, "from the greatest chemist who had ever lived before his time, George Ernest Stahl, Professor of Medicine, Anatomy, and Chemistry in the University of Halle, who had died in Berlin, whither he had gone to be physician to the King of Prussia, forty years ago."

As proof that alcohol was elementary water combined with phlogiston, our ancient chemist would probably show you this experiment:—He would place a portion of the spirit in a cup, would set fire to the spirit, and would invert over the flame a glass vessel, shaped almost like a common globe, which he would call a cucurbit, into which he would allow the flame to ascend. He would indicate that within the glass vessel a vapor, derived from the burning fluid, formed and condensed, as you see it forming and condensing now. Collecting this fluid, he would prove to you that it was water, which water he could show to be nothing else but one indivisible thing, therefore an element. Thus his demonstration would be complete. The element, while it existed as spirit, yielded fire on burning; it was fire water. The fire was condensed with the water. Nothing could be plainer, according to his light of science.

If you had inquired of the chemist whether he had any symbol by which to denote elementary water or spirit, he would give you, as a symbol for water, a sign something like the letter V, with two wavy lines following the letters; and for spirit of wine, a sign like the letter V with the letter S in the centre, as I put it on the blackboard; and if once more you questioned him as to whether his laboratory contained any similar chemical substance, he would answer—none. Spirit of wine stood by itself a pure substance, possessing single and special virtues.

If, passing over the intervening hundred years, you asked the chemist of to-day, "What is alcohol?" he would tell you that it was an organic radical called ethyl, combined with the elements of water. He would explain that water was no longer considered to be an element, but to be composed of two elements, called hydrogen and oxygen, two equivalents of hydrogen being combined in it with one equivalent of oxygen. He would inform you that the radical he had called ethyl was a compound of carbon and hydrogen, and he would add that this radical in alcohol took the place of one of the equivalents of hydrogen of water. He thereupon would give you symbols for water and alcohol, but symbols of a very different kind to those presented by his learned predecessor. He would express the names of the elements composing the water and spirit by the first letters of their names, and add their equivalents, or parts, by figures attached to the letters. Thus his symbol for water would be H_2O; for the radical ethyl, C_2H_5; and for alcohol $(C_2H_5)HO$ or C_2H_6O.

Were you interested about the theory of phlogiston, invented by the illustrious George Ernest Stahl, your modern guide would instruct you that the theory had long since been discarded, and that towards the latter part of the last century the very books of its discoverer had been burned, in derision, by a priestess of science in one of the temples of science in Paris. Then through what a wonderful history of discovery during the hundred years he would, if he liked, lead you. Into this cucurbit in which I burned the alcohol, and which you will observe I closed by placing it with its mouth downwards upon the table, he would pour clear lime water as I do now; he would shake the water round the sides of the cucurbit and see, as he did it, the water would become milky white.

This phenomenon he would indicate was due to the presence of a gas which the old chemist had actually collected but had overlooked. That gas is carbonic acid. It, as well as the water, was the product of the combustion of the spirit, and it now, in combination with the lime water, has united with the lime, forming carbonate of lime or chalk. Following the history of this gas, called once fixed air, because it could thus be fixed by lime and other substances, he would show how it had been proved to consist of carbon and oxygen; how it is given off from the burning of bodies containing carbon; and how a French chemist of the last century, named Lavoisier, traced out by analysis that, in fermentation, the juice of grapes is changed from being sweet and full of sugar into a vinous liquor, which no longer contains any sugar, the inflammable liquor known as spirit of wine. Thence it would be shown that the same illustrious chemist, making an analysis of sugar and studying the effects of yeast in causing fermentation of sugar, collected and weighed the elements produced, determined the elementary composition of spirit as consisting of carbon, hydrogen, and oxygen, and from his research announced the new principle in chemistry, that in all the operations in art and nature nothing is created; that an equal quantity of matter exists both before and after the experiment; that the quality and quantity of the elements remain precisely the same; that nothing takes place beyond changes and modifications in the combinations of the elements; and that in every chemical experiment an exact equality must be supposed between the elements of the body examined, and those of the products of its analysis. Finally, on this head, he would state the theory of Lavoisier, that *must* consists of alcohol combined with carbonic acid, and that the effects of vinous fermentation upon sugar are reduced to the mere separation of the elements of sugar into two portions; one portion oxygenated at the expense of the other, so as to form carbonic acid; the other disoxygenated to form alcohol; so that were it possible to reunite alcohol and carbonic acid the product would be sugar. Bringing you down to a later period, the modern chemist would describe a theory current about between thirty and forty years ago that alcohol is a compound of olefiant gas and water, and that in a state of vapor it consists of equal volumes of these. Or, again, that it was a hydrate of ether; or, again, according to a still later view, that it was a hydrated oxide of ethyl. Thus he would bring you to the latest theory as to composition which I have already supplied.

Lastly, if for the sake of further comparison you asked the chemist of to-day whether alcohol had any ally or congener, he would reply, many. He would give you, for instance, this spirit, which he would call methylic alcohol, and which he would tell you was got also by distillation, only that the distillation was dry, and that the substance distilled was wood; or he would give you this specimen, which he would call amylic alcohol, and which he would tell you was got by distillation, not of wood, but of potato. Again, he would show you other specimens, to which he would give different names as indicated in table No. V. of the Appendix.

Directing your attention to the composition of these alcohols, the chemist would beg you to observe that their chemical construction is throughout the same, that is to say, in all cases, a radical composed of carbon and hydrogen has replaced one of the equivalents of hydrogen of water. The radicals, however, vary in respect to the equivalents of the elements of which they are composed, and to distinguish them they have different names. Essentially each radical, though it is composed of more than one element, acts as if it were one, and is called a base, because it is a root or origin upon which other structures rest. Thus, in the present case, the radicals, as they vary in amount of carbon and hydrogen which they contain, produce, in each case of their combination with water, an alcohol possessing a different property or different properties from the other alcohols. The table No. VI. of the Appendix will give an illustration of the increase of carbon and hydrogen in the radicals of the series.

The first of the radicals, methyl, is composed of one equivalent of carbon and three of hydrogen. The radical ethyl of two of carbon and five of hydrogen. The radical propyl of three of carbon and seven of hydrogen, and so on, the increase in the equivalents of the elements being after a given rule in the whole series, the carbon increasing one, and the hydrogen two with each progressive step. So, as the alcohols progressively change from the first of the series, the methylic, they grow richer in carbon and hydrogen, and proportionately they grow heavier, less soluble, and less volatile.

A very simple experiment suffices to show the increase of carbon in these series. If I take a piece of cotton wool, place it in a glass cup, pour upon it a little methylic alcohol, in which alcohol there is the smallest amount of carbon, set fire to it and hold a white plate over the flame, the plate remains white because the air that reaches the flame is sufficient to consume all the carbon. If I do the same experiment with ethylic alcohol, although the carbon is a little greater, yet the result remains the same. If I move two steps higher, viz., to butylic alcohol, in which there are four equivalents of carbon, the combustion is not quite complete, and therefore a shade or stain of carbon is left on the plate ; and if, going one step further in the series, I use amylic alcohol, then the combustion is rendered so imperfect that a thick layer of carbon, derived from the alcohol, in the destruction of it by the burning, is left upon the white surface. I may digress here for a moment to state,—if the practical fact about to be told be considered a digression,—that this simple mode of testing common alcohol will serve roughly to detect extreme adulteration of it with the heavier alcohol—fusel oil, some of which I last burnt. This heavier alcohol is used in adulteration, and as you will learn when you hear of its effects, it is a dangerous adulterant. I was dining a few months ago with some friends, one of whom produced a small flask of precious liquor he had had presented to him; and which was said to be an unusually choice hollands. On examining it I felt sure it was a gin treated with fusel oil, and on burning a little of it, this suspicion was confirmed by a deposit of carbon upon a white dish. I warned my friends forthwith of the danger of drinking this heavy, though certainly pleasant spirit, and the majority took the warning. Two, less prudent, indulged, to suffer for the next two or three succeeding days to an extent that convinced them that there was no mistake in the scientific and friendly admonition they had received. .

The physical distinctions between the various alcohols now before us are marked by other signs. For example, as we move from the methylic alcohol upwards, we discover that their vapors increase in weight, that as fluids they grow heavier, and that their boiling point, that is to say the temperature required to make them boil, has to be increased. Another table, No. VII. of the Appendix, illustrates these facts in relation to four alcohols of the series: viz., methylic, ethylic, butylic, and amylic.

Thus the vapor density of methylic alcohol is 16 when compared with hydrogen gas as a standard; of ethylic alcohol, 23; of butylic, 37; and of amylic, 44. In respect to the specific gravity of the fluids, that is to say of the weights of the fluids themselves, compared with water estimated as a thousand, the same rule extends, with the one remarkable exception, viz., that the methylic alcohol appears heavier than the ethylic, after which the weights increase, so that amylic alcohol stands as 811, to 792 the weight of ethylic. Again, as to the boiling points, the lightest alcohol boils at 140, that is 72° below the boiling point of water; ethylic at 172; propylic at 205; butylic at 230, or 18° above the boiling point of water; and amylic at 270, or 58° above the boiling point of water, on Fahrenheit's scale.

The analogies between these various alcohols are sustained throughout by other chemical changes relating to them. If we expose diluted common alcohol to the atmosphere under fitting conditions it becomes acidified; in other words, it is converted into vinegar. This is due to its oxydation, in which process there are two steps; one by which the spirit is converted into a substance called aldehyde (dehydrated alcohol—al-de-hyd), and then into acetic acid, or vinegar. In the formation of the aldehyde two atoms of the hydrogen are oxydised, by which water is produced, and the aldehyde has therefore the composition of C_2H_4O. In the formation of the acetic acid another atom of oxygen is added, and the acetic acid has therefore the composition of $C_2H_4O_2$. This same series of changes extends through all the alcohols, as will be seen from table No. VIII. of the Appendix.

I said, in the first lecture, that from common or ethylic alcohol a new compound can be obtained by heating it with sulphuric acid, to which compound the name of ether is applied. In like manner, an ether can be obtained from the other alcohols.

If chlorine be brought to bear upon ethylic

alcohol, the elements of water, that is to say, the oxygen and the hydrogen are removed, and are replaced by chlorine, and there is formed chloride of ethyl. This change can be extended to all the other alcohols, the properties of the products being modified by the base.

The same rule extends to the action of iodine, and to that of nitrous acid. Tables IX. to XII. of the Appendix afford illustrations of these facts. They could be largely extended, but they are sufficient for our purpose.

I have brought for those who are curious to see them, twelve specimens of the different compounds formed on the alcohols. Six of these belong to the ethyl, or common alcohol series, six to the amyl, and they include respectively specimens of the alcohols, of the acids of the alcohols, of the ethers, of the chlorides, of the iodides, and of the nitrites. One of these specimens, I mean the nitrite of amyl, has within these last few years obtained a remarkable importance owing to its extraordinary action upon the body. A distinguished chemist, Professor Guthrie, while distilling over nitrite of amyl from amylic alcohol, observed that the vapor, when inhaled, quickened his circulation, and made him feel as if he had been running. There was flushing of his face, rapid action of his heart, and breathlessness. In 1861-2, I made a careful and prolonged study of the action of this singular body, and discovered that it produced its effect by causing an extreme relaxation, first, of the blood vessels, and afterwards of the muscular fibres of the body. To such an extent did this agent relax, I found it would even overcome the tetanic spasm produced by strychnia, and having thus discovered its action, I ventured to propose its use for removing the spasm in some of the extremest spasmodic diseases. The results have more than realised my expectations. Under the influence of this agent, one of the most agonising of known human maladies, called *Angina pectoris*, has been brought under such control that the paroxysms have been regularly prevented, and in one instance, at least, altogether removed. Even tetanus, or lock-jaw has been subdued by it, and in two instances, of an extreme kind so effectively as to warrant the credit of what may be truly called a cure. I notice this action of nitrite of amyl because it will be referred to again in explanation of certain of the effects of alcohol.

I should have liked, if there had been time, to have dwelt at greater length on many other interesting points bearing on these different alcohols and their derivatives. I should have been pleased to have presented to you a more extended account of the progress of discovery during the past century leading to these modern facts; and I should much have liked to have rendered more complete the description of the alcohol series of bodies, by explaining the differences of what are called monatomic, diatomic, and triatomic alcohols; but I must desist for two reasons; first, because the study would lead me into too great detail, and secondly, because it would introduce to notice a series of compounds, the physiological action of which are not so well understood as are those to which I shall soon direct your attention and the study of which is more than enough for the time that is at our disposal. It must be considered sufficient, therefore, if I have succeeded in showing that the common alcohol is but one of a group of a series of chemical compounds, and that its superior claim to our notice rests upon its antiquity as a discovered substance, and on its enormous distribution in civilised communities, rather than on its special or distinctive properties as a chemical agent.

One other series of facts I would, however, briefly describe before leaving this part of my subject. If into this ethylic alcohol I throw a portion of the metal sodium, a brisk action immediately begins to take place; as you will see, a gas escapes which I easily collect in a glass tube, which burns, and if mixed with air, explodes, as you hear. The gas is hydrogen. A change of substitution has occurred in this experiment. The hydrogen belonging to the water of the alcohol has been replaced by the sodium, and what is called sodium alcohol is produced. The result would have been the same with potassium as the replacing metal.

By acting on common alcohol with strong potash, then with sulphuretted hydrogen, and afterwards with iodide of ethyl, a new alcohol is produced called mercaptan. In this fluid the oxygen of the alcohol is replaced by sulphur, so that the formula for it is (C_2H_5) HS. It is a fluid, whitish in color, and of so offensive and penetrating an odor that it can hardly be approached until it is largely diluted with common alcohol. It is nearly insoluble in water, but imparts to it its peculiar odor; its specific gravity is 832, compared with water as 1,000; it is thirty-one times heavier than hydrogen, and it boils at 135° Fahr.

Sulphur alcohol is very rarely seen, but there is a diluted specimen here which has been prepared with very great care. There is only 5 per cent. of it in the solution, and yet its odor is as strong as can well be borne.

From this point I proceed to dwell on the action of certain of the alcohols which have been brought before us up to the present time, excluding on this occasion the alcohol best known, I mean the common alcohol of commerce, or as we know it chemically, ethylic alcohol. The point I shall aim at will be to show the influence of these alcohols upon animal life, and thereby to lead up to the action of ethylic alcohol pure and simple. The subject is one entirely new, and is limited to a very few bodies of the alcohol group, viz., to methylic alcohol, butylic, amylic, the potassium and sodium alcohols, and sulphur alcohol or mercaptan.

ACTION OF METHYLIC ALCOHOL.

Methylic alcohol, pyroxylic spirit or wood spirit, as it has been differently called, the spirit contained in the liquid got by distilling wood, has been known for about 62 years. It was discovered by Mr. Philip Taylor, in 1812, and was soon applied for lamps and for other purposes as a spirit. It was probably first made commercially by Messrs. Turnbull and Ramsay, of Glasgow. Its properties were investigated and reported upon by Sir Robert Kane, of Dublin, in 1836, and it was also analysed by Messrs. Dumas and Peligot, who determined that it contained 37.5 per cent. of carbon, 12.5 per cent. of hydrogen, and 50 per cent. of oxygen. When it is pure it remains clear in the atmosphere. It has an aromatic smell, with a slight acidity. The specimen I have used for my research had a specific weight of 810, water being 1,000, and it boiled at 140° Fahr.

The spirit has been much used in the arts in the place of alcohol for making varnishes. Having a lower boiling point it is more volatile than common alcohol. It is now also largely used in museums for preserving purposes, and it yields on oxydation a very powerful preservative vinegar. For the sake of economy it is often employed in the manufacture of other compounds called methylated.

Owing to the volatile nature of this alcohol it may be exhibited freely by inhalation in the same manner that chloroform is administered. It then enters the blood by being carried with the air that is inspired into the pulmonary tract, and thus into the air vesicles. Here it is absorbed into the circulation by the minute blood-vessels which make their way from the heart over the lungs, and which ramify upon the vesicles. By administrating the vapor of methylic alcohol in this way its effects are rapidly developed, for it condenses quickly in the blood, is carried rapidly into the left side of the heart, and thence is distributed by the arteries over the whole body as quickly as it is condensed and absorbed.

The alcohol may be administered in the usual way, that is to say, in combination with water, hot or cold. In this way it is not unpleasant to the taste, and in one instance, as I am informed by a veteran member of my profession, this alcohol was invariably drunk by a well-known physician, in preference to common alcohol. He was accustomed to make it into toddy, with water and sugar, and considered that while it was as pleasant to take as ordinary spirituous drinks, it was less injurious than they are. I have myself, of late years, when compelled to allow the administration of alcohol, sometimes recommended this methylic lighter spirit, and I am satisfied, with better results than if the heavier or ethylic spirit had been employed. I have ventured also to suggest that in many instances other physicians might follow the same practice with advantage; for methylic alcohol is much more rapid in its action, and much less prolonged in its effects than is common alcohol, so that it produces its effects promptly, and what is of most importance, it demands the least possible ultimate expenditure of animal force for its elimination from the body. This latter fact, I repeat, is of great moment, for, in the end, all these alcoholic fluids are depressants, and although at first, by their calling vigorously into play the natural forces, they seem to excite and are therefore called stimulants, they themselves supply no force at any time, but cause expenditure of force, by which means they get away out of the body and therewith lead to exhaustion and paralysis of motion. In other words, the animal force which should be expended on the nutrition and sensation of the body, is in part expended on the alcohol, an entirely foreign expenditure.

The lighter the alcohol therefore, *cæteris paribus*, the less injurious its action, and so we may put down methylic alcohol as the safest of the series of bodies to which it belongs. But it is not without potency of effect, and the phenomena it produces are sufficiently demonstrative. Its effects are developed in four distinct stages.

The first stage is that of excitement of the nervous organisation; the pulse is quickened, the breathing is quickened, the surface of the body is flushed, and the pupil is dilated. After a little time there is a sense of languor, the muscles falling into a state of prostration and the muscular movements becoming irregular. Thereupon the second stage follows, if the administration be continued. In this second stage the muscular prostration is increased, the breathing is labored, and is attended by deep sighing movements at intervals of about four or five seconds, followed by further prostration, rolling over of the body upon the side, and distinct signs of intoxication. From this condition the subject passes into the third stage, which is that of entire intoxication, complete insensibility to pain, with unconsciousness of all external objects, and with inability to exert any voluntary muscular power. The breathing now becomes embarrassed and blowing, with what is technically called "bronchial rale," or rattle, due to the passage of air through fluid that has accumulated in the finer bronchial passages. The heart and lungs, however, even in this stage, retain their functions, and therefore recovery will take place if the conditions for it be favorable. Also, if the body be touched or irritated in parts, there will be response of motion, not from any knowledge or consciousness, but from what we physiologists call "reflex action;" that is to say, the impression we have made by irritation upon the surface of the body has travelled by its usual route through the nerves to its nervous centre in the brain, and uncontrolled there by the consciousness has rolled back again, stimulating in its course some muscular fibre to motion. Probably the reason why the heart, which is a muscle, and the breathing muscles, continue to beat while all the other portions are at rest is due to this fact, that the blood which the heart drives to the brain and other nervous centres conveys to the centres which supply the heart a wave of motion that rolls back upon these vital muscles, and sustains them still in their rhythmical motion.

During all these stages there is no violent convulsive action from this alcohol, and no distinct tremor; but one phenomenon has been step by step more marked, and that phenomenon is a reduction of the animal temperature. Even though the body of the subject be exposed to a temperature of 84°, that is summer heat, it will begin to cool from the first, and will continue to cool through all the stages, so that at last the loss of heat will become actually dangerous; for the cold body cannot throw off water freely, and therefore fluid collects in the lungs, and there is risk of what may be plainly considered suffocation like as from drowning. I have seen this decline of temperature from methylic alcohol, in animals narcotised by it, proceed to the loss of eight degrees of heat on Fahrenheit's scale when the insensibility was at its extreme point.

Presuming that the administration of the methylic spirit be continued when the third degree has been reached, there is a last stage, which is that of death. The two remaining nervous centres which feed the heart and respiration cease simultaneously to act, and all motion is over. After the death the blood throughout the body is found charged with the alcohol. The circulation of blood over the lungs has continued to the last, and so the lungs are found containing blood in both sides of the heart; the vessels of the brain are engorged with blood, as are the other vascular organs. The blood itself is not materially changed in physical quality, but coagulates, or forms into clot, rather more slowly than usual.

If at the third stage of insensibility the administration of methylic spirit be stopped, recovery from the insensibility and prostration will invariably take place on one condition, that the body be kept dry and warm. From four to five hours, however, are necessary before the recovery is complete, and under the best conditions the restoration of the animal temperature is not perfected under a period of seven hours.

Happily we have no data to guide us that will show the effects on the animal body of the long continued use of methylic alcohol, for men have not as yet so steadily plied themselves with it as a drink as to induce phenomena of chronic intoxication from it. The above-named facts, however, drawn from careful observations, in which the effects of the agent were seen on the inferior animals, and in one instance where the fluid was taken by accident by the human subject, show that methylic alcohol, though it may be less potent than its allies, is sufficiently potent, and the inference is fair, indeed irresistible, that if the use of it were persevered in for long periods of time, it would lead to structural change in the body, just as all other chemical agents do that modify and pervert the natural mechanism. An agent that causes congestion of the brain cannot be employed many times without destroying the delicate organisation of the vascular structure of the brain, neither can it influence the other vascular organs in the same way without prejudice to their structure; neither can it destroy the function of the nerves, of the muscles, and of the organs of the senses without prejudice to their functions. In many respects this, the lightest and least injurious of the alcohols, resembles chloroform in the ultimate action it produces on the body. It still more closely resembles ether, although recovery from the effects of both these agents is very much more rapid than from the spirit. It may consequently, as a chemical agent possessing a specific power of action over the living organism, be fairly classified with these agents. It is quite as artificial as they are, it is quite as dangerous in the long run, and its effects are more prolonged.

ACTION OF BUTYLIC ALCOHOL.

I pass over the second alcohol of our series, viz., ethylic alcohol, the common alcohol of wines and spirits, because that will of itself engage our attention for the remaining part of the course, after this lecture is concluded. I pass over propylic also for the reason that it is not easily separated as an alcohol, and is less perfectly studied than the other members of the group before us. Thus I am brought to what is called butylic alcohol.

With this spirit we arrive at one of the heavier bodies of the group in which, as our table shows, there is a higher proportion of carbon and hydrogen than exists in those that are placed above it in the scale. Compared with common alcohol the weight of its vapor is as 37 to 23. Its weight, as a fluid, is 803 to 792, and its boiling point 230 Fahr. to 172. It is a heavier fluid; it mixes indifferently with water, but it is not unpleasant to take when diluted and sweetened. Applied to the lips and tongue when in a pure state it creates a sensation of burning, in the same way as common spirit, but with more intensity, and there is this remarkable fact connected with the sensation, that after the burning effect has passed away an extreme numbness of the part, where the fluid was applied, remains. I made this observation originally in 1869, and I have since often applied the knowledge with effect, in relieving, by the application of the agent, local pain. Toothache, for instance, is very quickly soothed by it.

The alcohol is not obtained by a special process of distillation; it is produced with other alcohols in the process of fermentation, and is obtained by what is called fractional distillation, that is, by distillation of it, at certain fixed temperatures, from fusel oil, or from the oil of beet-root, or from molasses after distillation of ethylic spirit.

The action of butylic alcohol on the animal body is divisible into four stages, the same as we have seen in respect to methylic spirit, but the period required for producing the different stages is greatly prolonged; and when the third stage, that of complete insensibility, is reached, there is added a new phenomenon which does not belong to any of the lighter alcohols. In this third degree, after the temperature of the body is depressed to the minimum by the butylic spirit, distinct tremors occur throughout the whole of the muscular system. These come on at regular intervals spontaneously, but they can be excited by a touch at any time, and in the intervals where they are absent there is frequent twitching of the muscles. The tremors themselves are not positively muscular contractions, but are rather vibrations or wavelike motions through the muscles, and are attended with an extreme deficiency of true contractile power in the muscular fibre. An electrical current passed through the muscles, which would, in health, throw them into rigid contraction, will now excite the tremors and keep them proceeding, but will not excite complete contraction. So long as the tremors are present, the temperature of the body is depressed, falling even half a degree; but when they cease the temperature rises again, not to the natural standard, but to or near that which existed before the tremors were excited. After the tremors are once established, they continue without further administration of the alcohol for ten and twelve hours, and so slowly do they decline, they may remain in a slight degree for even thirty-six hours. They subside by remission of intensity and prolongation of interval of recurrence. One fact of singular significance attaches itself to these muscular tremors. They are the tremors which occur in man during the stage of alcoholic disease, when there is set up that malady to which we give the name of *delirium tremens*. An ordinary intoxication with a lighter alcohol is insufficient to produce this extreme perversion of nervous and muscular power, but the introduction of one of these heavier alcohols, or, it may be, the excessive saturation of the body with a lighter spirit, for on this point I am not sure, is sufficient to cause the tremulous motion. What the nature of these muscular movements is, what unnatural relationships exist between the nervous system, the muscles, and the blood, to lead to them are questions still unsolved. Involuntary, developed even against the will, excited by any external touch, attended with great reduction of temperature, and remaining as long as the temperature is reduced, they indicate an extreme depression of animal force: a condition in which all the force of

Action of Butylic Alcohol.

life that remains has to be expended on the more organic acts of life, on the support of the motions of the heart, the muscles of respiration, and the functions of the secreting glands. The voluntary systems of nerve and muscle are indeed well-nigh dead, and recovery rests entirely on the maintenance of the organic nervous power. Still recovery will take place if the body be sustained by external heat and by internal nourishment.

In the extreme stage of intoxication from butylic alcohol the red blood in the arteries loses its rich color, and the blood from the veins, which flows with difficulty, is of a dirty hue. The blood coagulates readily, but the clot is loose, and the fibrine of which it is composed separates in a coarse network or mesh. The little corpuscles of the blood run into each other, forming rolls or columns. Indeed, it is wonderful how the blood circulates through the structures it should nourish. The vascular membranes of the brain are found charged with this tarry blood; the brain structure is softened, and gives the odor of the poison, and the muscles, when divided by the knife, cut without firmness, yielding from numerous points the same tar-like blood. The vascular organs—spleen, liver, lungs, kidneys—are equally changed, and in a similar manner. Their fine structures are infiltrated with the deteriorated vascular fluid which was intended for their maintenance, and even the secretions and cavities of the body are perverted by being charged with fluid derived from the unnatural blood. This is the state of the body of one who dies insensible after the delirium and tremors which characterise the human malady, self-inflicted and terrible, known as *delirium tremens.*

ACTION OF AMYLIC ALCOHOL.

Amylic alcohol, the next of our series, is obtained by the fermentation of potato starch, or starch of grain, and when pure is a colorless fluid. Its weight, compared with water as 1,000, is 818, and it boils at 270° Fahr. It is from this alcohol that the active substance, nitrite of amyl, to which I have before referred, is derived. The odor of amylic alcohol is sweet, nauseous, and heavy. The sensation of its presence remains long. In taste it is burning and acrid, and it is itself practically insoluble in water. When it is diluted with common alcohol it dissolves freely in water, and gives a soft and rather unctuous flavor, I may call it a fruity flavor, something like that of ripe pears. From the quantities of it imported into this country it is believed to be employed largely in the adulteration of wines and spirits.

Amylic alcohol, when it is introduced as an adulterant, is an extremely dangerous addition to ordinary alcohol, in whatever form it is presented, whether as wine or spirit. Its action on the body is the same as that of butylic alcohol. It produces three stages of insensibility, ending in the profoundest narcotism, or coma, followed by reduction of temperature and by muscular tremors. These tremors recur with the most perfect regularity of themselves, but they can be excited at any moment by touching the body, or blowing upon it, or even by a sharp noise, such as the snap of the finger. In all other respects the phenomena induced are the same as are observed from butylic alcohol, except that they are much more prolonged, from two to three days being sometimes required for the complete restoration of the animal temperature. The reason of this prolongation of action lies in the greater weight and the greater insolubility of this spirit; that is to say, the force required to decompose it, or mechanically to lift it out of the body when it has once entered it, is so much greater than is required for the lighter spirits, which diffuse more readily through the secretions, volatilise by the breath or possibly undergo rapid decomposition. The odor of the substance remains for many hours in the animal tissues. Amylic alcohol acts upon some resins and resinous substances, dissolving, I believe, certain of them more easily than the lighter spirits, but its peculiar odor prevents its application on a large scale.

ACTION OF SODIUM AND POTASSIUM ALCOHOLS.

The action of the sodium and potassium alcohols is exceedingly interesting in a physiological, although not in a practical point of view, except in respect to their various uses as chemical re-agents. They act on the living animal tissues as caustics, and will one day be considered of great service to the surgeon. Brought into contact with blood, in solution, there is produced by them an almost instant crystallisation of needle-like crystals spread out in beautiful arborescent filaments. This arborescent appearance is identical with a crystallisation which can be induced in these alcohols themselves, but there are also formed smaller radiant crystals due to the crystallisation of the crystalloidal matter of the blood-cells, and singularly like the forms which, since the time of Dr. Richard Mead, have been described as occurring in the blood after infection by the poison of the viper.

These metallic alcohols are powerful antiseptics, like common alcohol, over which they have an advantage in that they more thoroughly harden soft structures. I have taken advantage of this action to employ them for the preservation of nervous matter, which is rapidly prone to decomposition.

I should add that, by some chemists these alcohols are called ethylates of sodium or potassium, a term which is thought to define more correctly their chemical construction.

ACTION OF MERCAPTAN OR SULPHUR ALCOHOL.

I have already referred briefly to this most curious body of the alcohol series, describing it as an alcohol in which oxygen is replaced by sulphur. In experimenting with it a solution containing 5 per cent. is sufficient, and the vapor of it may be inhaled in order to produce its effects. These are most remarkable.

I found, by direct experiment, that the vapor is not irritating to breathe, but that its influence on the system is speedily pronounced. There is a desire for sleep, and a strange, unhappy sensation, as if some actual or impending trouble were at hand. This is succeeded by an easy but extreme sensation of muscular fatigue; the limbs feel too heavy to be lifted, and rest is absolutely necessary. There is, at the same time, no insensibility to pain, and no intoxication. The pulse is rendered feeble and slow, and remains so for one or two hours: but, in time, all the effects pass off, and active motion in the air helps quickly to dispose of them.

On the inferior animals the action of mercaptan is equally peculiar. Frogs exposed to its vapor fall asleep, and seem to pass into actual death, except that the eye remains bright. They may be left in this apparently lifeless state for half an hour, then, removed into the air, they commence, in the course of an hour and a half or two hours, to breathe again, and gradually recover, precisely as if they were awaking from sleep. The action of this alcohol on the animal body, though it produces these extreme effects, is less injurious than that of the other alcohols. It escapes rapidly by the breath, and in some new form, as a sulphur compound. It communicates to the breath an odor which is by no means uncommon in persons who indulge to a great extent in the use of ordinary alcohol. This observation suggests a most important explanation of certain phenomena connected with the action of common alcohol. It appears to me that in some states there is actually produced in the living organism, by the vital chemistry, sulphur compounds, derived probably from the bile, a substance rich in sulphur, which compounds, distributed by the blood to the nervous matter, create phenomena similar to those I have described as following upon the inhalation of mercaptan. Thus, under unnatural modes of life, the body may actually make its own poisons, and the doctor be often asked to remove what the patient, if he were a better chemist and a wiser man, would never produce for the exercise of the doctor's skil'.

LECTURE III.

THE INFLUENCE OF COMMON OR ETHYLIC ALCOHOL ON ANIMAL LIFE. THE PRIMARY PHYSIOLOGICAL ACTION OF ALCOHOL.

The primary action of ethylic alcohol on animal life forms our next study. This is the alcoholic spirit which enters into wines, beers, and ordinary spirituous liquors.

There are two modes in which this subject must be discussed. One relates to the mere physical action of alcohol upon the body, the other to its action as a food for the body. Of the varied substances which we take into our systems, some, like chloroform, or opium, produce very marked physical effects, which we may call physiological, but which have nothing to do with the nourishment of the organism, nor with the sustainment of its vital power. Other substances act as foods, producing certain continuous phenomena of structural build and of vital function. Alcohol is peculiar in that we are obliged to consider it, at the present time, from each of these points of view, and I now take up the first, I mean the purely physical action of alcohol, reserving the question of its qualities as a food for a future lecture.

A very simple problem lies before us. The sum of £117,000,000 of money is invested in this country on alcohol as a commercial substance. Where does the alcohol go? We know that the larger part of it goes for consumption by human beings. A little—I mean, by comparison, a little—is used for the purposes of art and science, but the greater portion of it, practically all but the whole of it, is consumed by human beings. Thus a question arises, we may almost say, of engineering and commerce, a question, therefore, particularly worthy of this Society, viz., What is the good of this invested capital, and of the substance which it supplies? It is not necessary for any of us to consider ourselves as physicians in studying this matter, but we may all consider ourselves as animal engineers, anxious to know the physical properties of agents which influence the animal life. To put it in a very practical way, suppose that there was no question involved in regard to the influence of alcohol upon the body, but that in the course of the invention of motive engines—common inanimate engines, which can be made to exhibit motive power by the application of heat to water—it had originally become the practice from some circumstance to put into the engines so much spirit with the water, and to work the engines with this mixture. Then suppose somebody said, "This is a very expensive process of working the engines; may be they will work as well without the spirit." You would naturally inquire, "Can such be fact?" And you would seek an engineer to fill the place I have now the honor to occupy, to explain to you the mechanism of the engines. You would also beg him to explain and put before you facts which would bear upon the point, whether the admixture of spirit and water was useful or useless? Now, please, consider me to-night as an engineer, and the animal body as the engine I am to speak upon. I am not going to address a word to you as a physician; I am not going to offer advice. I simply mean to place before you, as far as I know them, the facts relating to the physical effects of this thing, alcohol, when it is put into one of those millions of engines which we call men.

Alcohol will enter the body—the engine of which I am about to speak—by many channels. It can be introduced by injecting it under the skin or into a vein. Exalted by heat into the form of vapor, it may be inhaled by man or animal, when it will penetrate into the lungs, will diffuse through the bronchial tubes, will pass into the minute air vesicles of the lungs, will travel through the minute circulation with the blood that is going over the air vesicles to the heart, will condense in that blood, will go direct to the left side of the heart, thence into the arterial canals and so throughout the body. Or, again, the spirit can be taken in by the more ordinary channel, the stomach. Through this channel it finds its way, by two routes, into the circulation. A certain portion of it—the greater portion of it—is absorbed direct by the veins of the alimentary surface, finds its way straight into the larger veins, which lead up to the heart, and onwards with the course of the blood. Another portion is picked up by those small structures which proceed from below the mucous surface of the stomach, which are called *villi*, and from wnich originate a series of fine tubes that reach at last the lower portion of a common tube known as the thoracic duct, the tube which ascends in front of the spinal column, and terminates at the junction of two large veins on the left side of the body, at a point where the venous blood, returning from the left arm, joins with the returning blood from the left side of the head on its way to the heart.

Thus in whatever way the alcohol is introduced it enters the blood; the shortest way is that by inhalation, the longest and most ordinary way is by the stomach. Indeed, except for experimental purposes, the introduction is always by this latter and longest route, and we may, for our practical purposes, only think of alcohol as a fluid taken by the mouth into the stomach, and absorbed like a food or a drink from the surface of the alimentary canal.

Suppose, then, a certain measure of alcohol be taken into the stomach, it will be absorbed there, but, previous to absorption, it will have to undergo a proper degree of dilution with water, for there is this peculiarity respecting alcohol when it is separated by an animal membrane from a watery fluid like the blood, that it will not pass through the membrane until it has become charged, to a given point of dilution, with water. It is itself, in fact, so greedy for water, it will pick it up from watery textures, and deprive them of it until, by its saturation, its power of reception is exhausted, after which it will diffuse into the current of circulating fluid.

To illustrate this fact of dilution, I perform a simple experiment. Into a bladder is placed a mixture consisting of equal parts of alcohol and distilled water. Into the neck of the bladder a long glass tube is inserted and firmly tied. Then the bladder is immersed in a saline fluid representing an artificial serum of blood. The result is, that the alcohol in the bladder absorbs water from the surrounding saline solution, and thereby a column of fluid passes up into the glass tube. A second mixture of alcohol and water, in the proportion this time of one part of alcohol to two of water, is put into another bladder immersed in like manner in an artificial serum. In this instance, a little fluid also passes from the outside into the bladder, so that there is a rise of water in the tube, but less than in the previous instance. A third mixture, consisting of one part of alcohol with three parts of water, is placed in another little bladder, and is also suspended in the artificial serum. In this case there is, for a time, a small rise of fluid in the tube connected with the bladder; but after a while, owing to the dilution which took place, a current from within outwards sets in, and the tube becomes empty. Thus each bladder charged originally with the same quantity of fluid contains at last a different quantity. The first contains more than it did originally; the second a little more; the third a little less. From the third absorption takes place, and if I keep changing and replacing the outer fluid which surrounds the bladder with fresh serum, I can in time, owing to the double current of water into the bladder through its coats, and of water and alcohol out of the bladder into the serum, remove all the alcohol

In this way it is removed from the stomach into the circulating blood after it has been swallowed. When we dilute alcohol with water before drinking it we quicken its absorption. If we do not dilute it sufficiently it is diluted in the stomach by transudation of water in the stomach until the required reduction for its absorption; the current then sets in towards the blood, and passes into the circulating canals by the veins.

All the returning veins end in the large trunks which terminate in the central organ of the circulation—the heart. The heart, a moving muscular organ, has four cavities; two above called the auricles, two below called the ventricles. The cavities on the right side are called respectively the right auricle and right ventricle; the cavities on the left side are called respectively the left auricle and the left ventricle. The right auricle receives all the venous blood of the body, and transmits it to the right ventricle; the right ventricle drives the blood over the lungs where the blood is arterialised; the left auricle receives the blood from the lungs, and transmits it to the left ventricle, which in turn drives it through the arterial tubes over the whole of the body, whence it returns again by the veins to the right side of the heart, and so on, in continuous circuit.

Alcohol, therefore, entering the veins, makes its way in the course I have described through the right heart, through the lungs, through the left heart, through the body at large by the arteries. This is the course of its travel in the organism. What does it do as it makes the round?

As it passes through the circulation of the lungs it is exposed to the air, and some little of it, raised into vapor by the natural heat, is thrown off in expiration. If the quantity of it be large this loss may be considerable, and the odor of the spirit may be detected in the expired breath. If the quantity be small the loss will be comparatively little, as the spirit will be held in solution by the water in the blood. After it has passed through the lungs, and has been driven by the left heart over the arterial circuit, it passes into what is called the minute circulation, or the structural circulation of the organism. The arteries here extend into very small vessels, which are called arterioles, and from these infinitely small vessels spring the equally minute radicals or roots of the veins which are ultimately to become the great rivers bearing the blood back to the heart. In its passage through this minute circulation the alcohol finds its way to every organ. To this brain, to these muscles, to these secreting or excreting organs, nay even into this bony structure itself, it moves with the blood. In some of these parts which are not excreting, it remains for a time diffused, and in those parts where there is a large percentage of water it remains longer than in other parts. From some organs which have an open tube for conveying fluids away, as the liver and kidneys, it is thrown out or eliminated, and in this way a portion of it is ultimately removed from the body. The rest passing round and round with the circulation, is probably decomposed and carried off in new forms of matter; but concerning this, more on a future occasion

When we know the course which the alcohol takes in its passage through the body, from the period of its absorption to that of its elimination, we are the better able to judge what physical changes it induces in the different organs and structures with which it comes in contact. It first reaches the blood, but, as a rule, the quantity of it that enters is insufficient to produce any material effect on that fluid. If, however, the dose taken be poisonous or semi-poisonous, then even the blood, rich as it is in water—and it contains seven hundred and ninety parts in a thousand—is affected. The alcohol is diffused through this water, and there it comes in contact with the other constituent parts, with the fibrine, that plastic substance which, when blood is drawn, clots and coagulates, and which is present in the proportion of from two to three parts in a thousand; with the albumen which exists in the proportion of seventy parts; with the salts which yield about ten parts; with the fatty matters; and lastly, with those minute, round bodies which float in myriads in the blood (which were discovered by the Dutch philosopher, Leuwenhock, as one of the first results of microscopical observation, about the middle of the seventeenth century), and which are called the blood globules or corpuscles. These last named bodies are, in fact, cells; their discs, when natural, have a smooth outline, they are depressed in the centre and they are red in color; the color of the blood being derived from them. We have discovered in recent years that there exist other corpuscles or cells in the blood in much smaller quantity, which

Action of Alcohol on the Blood.

are called white cells, and these different cells float in the blood-stream within the vessels. The red take the centre of the stream; the white lie externally near the sides of the vessels, moving less quickly. Our business is mainly with the red corpuscles. They perform the most important functions in the economy; they absorb, in great part, the oxygen which we inhale in breathing, and carry it to the extreme tissues of the body; they absorb, in great part, the carbonic acid gas which is produced in the combustion of the body in the extreme tissues, and bring that gas back to the lungs to be exchanged for oxygen there; in short, they are the vital instruments of the circulation.

With all these parts of the blood, with the water, fibrine, albumen, salts, fatty matter, and corpuscles, the alcohol comes in contact when it enters the blood, and, if it be in sufficient quantity, it pro duces disturbing action. I have watched this disturbance very carefully on the blood corpuscles, for in some animals we can see these floating along during life, and we can also observe them from men who are under alcohol by removing a speck of blood, and examining it with the microscope. The action of the alcohol, when it is observable, is varied. It may cause the corpuscles to run too closely together, and to adhere in rolls; it may modify their outline, making the clear-defined smooth outer edge irregular or crenate, or even starlike; it may change the round corpuscle into the oval form, or, in very extreme cases it may produce what I may call a truncated form of corpuscles, in which the change is so great that if we did not trace it through all its stages we should be puzzled to know whether the object looked at were indeed a blood-cell. All these changes are due to the action of the spirit upon the water contained in the corpuscles; upon the capacity of the spirit to extract water from them. During every stage of modification of corpuscle thus described, their function to absorb and fix gases is impaired, and when the aggregation of the cells, in masses, is great, other difficulties arise, for the cells united together pass less easily than they should through the minute vessels of the lungs and of the general circulation, and impede the current, by which local injury is produced.

A further action upon the blood instituted by alcohol in excess, is upon the fibrine or the plastic colloidal matter. On this the spirit may act in two different ways, according to the degree in which it affects the water that holds the fibrine in solution. It may fix the water with the fibrine, and thus destroy the power of coagulation; or it may extract the water so determinately as to produce coagulation. These facts bear on a new and refined subject of research with which I must not trouble you further, except to add that the inquiry explains why in acute cases of poisoning by alcohol the blood is sometimes found quite fluid, at other times firmly coagulated in the vessels.

These are the only points I have time to touch upon in respect to the physical action of alcohol upon blood. I must pass next to blood vessels, and trace out the action upon these fine ramifications of the larger vessels which we call the minute circulation. Upon these parts the spirit exerts a singular influence, from which arise a series of phenomena, characteristic of action when even a moderate quantity of spirit is taken into the body. That we may follow out this position clearly, it is essential that I should for a few minutes put alcohol out of sight altogether and describe the mechanism and governance of this minute circulating system.

If any of you ever visited the Royal College of Physicians you would find there a system of blood-vessels dissected and traced out by the immortal discoverer of the circulation of the blood himself, William Harvey; and I think it would strike you, as you looked on, that all the organs of the body, which constitute the body in its entirety, are built upon these minute vessels. It is as though Harvey had suggested the thought that the vascular system was the primary part of the animal organisation, and that upon it were planted and developed all the structures. The arteries are all beautifully shown branching out into their extreme divisions and giving the outline of the limbs, of the brain, of the visceral parts, and of the other organs. The veins are seen springing or continuing from these extreme arterial parts, as rivers may be said to spring, and to form at last trunks of large and larger size by which they bring back the blood to the centre of the circulation to be vivified there and carried on again.

From this distribution of blood in these minute vessels the structures of organs derive their constituent parts; through these vessels brain matter muscle, gland, membrane is given out from the blood by a refined process of selection of material, which, up to this time, is only so far understood as to enable us to say that it exists.

The minute and intermediate vessels are more intimately connected than any other part with the construction and with the function of the living matter of which the body is composed. Think you that this mechanism is left uncontrolled? No; the vessels, small as they are, are under distinct control. Infinitely refined in structure, they nevertheless have the power of contraction and dilatation, which power is governed by nervous action of a special kind. If we pass to the lower class of animals, we find, running along the body, in addition to its vascular system, a series of points of nervous matter, consisting of what are called ganglia. These ganglia are connected together in chain, and from them filaments of nerves emanate, which are distributed to all the active moving parts of the body. In such lower animals the nervous system thus described stands alone, and when we rise in the scale and come even to man we find still the same primitive nervous chain. But we find also now another and more highly developed nervous system, the centres of which are locked up in the brain and spinal column, from which centres nerves of special sense go into the organs of sense, nerves of sensibility or common sensation go to the skin and other sensitive surfaces, and nerves of voluntary motion go to the muscles, all combining to perform their respective functions in the animal economy.

Thus man has two nervous systems: the primary nervous chain and the added centres, with their fibres. The two systems are connected by their fibres in different parts, but they are still distinct, both anatomically and functionally. The primary nervous system is called the system of the organic vegetative or animal life; it governs all those motions which are purely involuntary, and its centres are believed by some, and I think with perfect correctness, to be the seats of those faculties which we call emotional and instinctive. The centres of the brain and spinal cord, with their parts, are the centres of the motor and volitional and of the reasoning powers; of all those faculties, that is to say, which are directly under the influence of the will.

Keep in mind, if you please, the two nervous systems, and add to the remembrance this one additional fact, that all those minute blood-vessels at the extremities of the circulation are under the control of the primary or organic nervous supply. Branches of nerves from those organic centres accompany every arterial vessel throughout the body to its termination, and without direction from our will regulate the contraction and dilation of the blood-vessels to their most refined distribution. This fact was suspected by the older anatomists, but it remained for modern research to make it a demonstration. Thus it has now been proved that if the organic nervous supply of a part of the minute circulation be cut off by division of the organic nerve feeding that part, the vessels become paralysed, as these flexor muscles of my hand, which now grasp so firmly, would be paralysed were their voluntary nervous supply divided.

It will be clear at once that an important advancement of knowledge respecting the course of the blood through the minute circulation has been gained; but our knowledge does not rest at this point. When certain simple physical impressions are made upon the organic nerves, the disturbance of their supply is indicated by distant phenomena, and the blush which mantles, and the pallor which overspreads the cheek, under the influence of mental emotion or shock, are phenomena of this order.

I can bring to your notice an experiment, showing the production of paralysis, and of all the phenomena above quoted by the mere action of cold upon the organic nervous fibre. By evaporating ether from the back of my hand quickly, I can freeze the skin, and thereby produce paralysis. I take the ether away, and now into the paralysed vessels, which are capable of offering no efficient resistance, the blood rushes, distending the vessels, remaining for a moment stagnant in them, and giving a brilliant red color or crimson blush over the part. I feel in this part the glow commonly called hot-ache; it is the blush which occurs on the cheek, and it is from the same physiological condition.

Still further in advance, and with the mention of the fact, I am brought back to the subject proper of my lecture: we have learned that certain chemical agents can so influence the organic nervous chain as to disturb its functions, after the manner of a pure physical act. When the peculiar fluid the nitrite of amyl, to which I have before called your attention, came before me for investigation, I divined, from the symptoms it produced, that it influenced the organic nervous fibre precisely after the manner of a division of that fibre. I dipped a spill of paper into the liquid, brought that near to my nose, inhaled the vapor, and immediately felt my face in a red glow, as you see it again at this moment, and felt my heart beating rapidly, as I feel it beating at the present time. I reasoned, naturally, and as events proved, correctly, that this fluid, by its action on the organic nerves, paralysed the vessels of the minute circulation, and finding this to obtain with one chemical agent I traced it in others, and found a class of chemical substances, all of which have this same property of relaxing the blood-vessels at their extreme parts. The whole series of the nitrites possess this power; ether possesses it; but the great point I want to bring forth from this description is, that the substance we are specially dealing with, alcohol, possesses the self same power. By this influence it produces all those peculiar effects which in every-day life are so frequently illustrated. It paralyses the minute blood-vessels, and allows them to become dilated with the flowing blood.

If you attend a large dinner party, you will observe after the first few courses, when the wine is beginning to circulate, a progressive change in some of those about you who have taken wine. The face begins to get flushed, the eye brightens, and the murmur of conversation becomes loud. What is the reason of that flushing of the countenance? It is the same as the flush from blushing, or from the reaction of cold, or from the nitrite of amyl. It is the dilatation of vessels following upon the reduction of nervous control, which reduction has been induced by the alcohol. In a word, the first stage, the stage of vascular excitement from alcohol, has been established.

The action of the alcohol extending so far does not stop there. With the disturbance of power in the extreme vessels, more disturbance is set up in other organs, and the first organ that shares in it is the heart. With each beat of the heart a certain degree of resistance is offered by the vessels when their nervous supply is perfect, and the stroke of the heart is moderated in respect both to tension and to time. But when the vessels are rendered relaxed, the resistance is removed, the heart begins to run quicker, like a watch from which the pallets have been removed, and the heart-stroke, losing nothing in force, is greatly increased in frequency, with a weakened recoil stroke. It is easy to account in this manner for the quickened heart and pulse which accompany the first stage of deranged action from alcohol, and you will be interested to know to what extent this increase of vascular action proceeds The information on this point is exceedingly curious and important. After I had observed the effect of alcohol on the circulation generally, I attempted to calculate the rate at which it expedited the rate of circulation by observing its effect on the beat of the heart in the pigeon. Alcohol may be administered to this bird quite painlessly, and, as the animal quickly goes to sleep under the influence, and is therefore perfectly quiet, the beatings of its heart can be calculated with precision. I traced in these observations an increase of beats of the heart amounting, in the course of two hours, to one-fourth beyond what was natural. Then I essayed to make researches on myself, but many circumstances intervened, connected with the persistent labor and anxiety of professional life, which prevented me conducting the necessary operations so correctly as I desired, and as I might perhaps at another time have done. Fortunately, the information has been far more ably supplied by the researches of Dr. Parkes, of Netley, and the late Count Wollowicz. The researches of these distinguished inquirers are so valuable I make no apology for giving them in detail. The observers conducted their inquiries on the young and healthy adult man. They counted the beats of the heart, first at regular intervals, during what were called water periods, that is to say, periods when the subject under observation drank nothing but water ; and next, taking still the same subject, they counted the beats of the heart during successive periods in which alcohol was taken in increasing quantities. Thus step by step they measured the precise action of alcohol on the heart, and thereby the precise primary influence induced by alcohol. The results are stated by themselves as follows :—

The average number of beats of the heart in 24 hours (as calculated from eight observations made in 14 hours), during the first, or water period, was 106,000; in the earlier alcoholic period it was 127,000 or about 21,000 more; and in the later period it was 131,000 or 25,000 more.

"The highest of the daily means of the pulse observed during the first or water period was 77.5; but on this day two observations are deficient. The next highest daily mean was 77 beats.

"If, instead of the mean of the eight days, or 73.57, we compare the mean of this one day, viz., 77 beats per minute, with the alcoholic days, so as to be sure not to over-estimate the action of the alcohol, we find:—

"On the 9th day, with one fluid ounce of alcohol, the heart beat 4,300 times more.

"On the 10th day, with two fluid ounces, 8,172 times more.

"On the 11th day, with four fluid ounces, 12,960 times more.

"On the 12th day, with six fluid ounces, 30,672 times more.

"On the 13th day, with eight fluid ounces, 23,904 times more.

"On the 14th day, with eight fluid ounces, 25,488 times more.

"But as there was ephemeral fever on the 12th day, it is right to make a deduction, and to estimate the number of beats in that day as midway between the 11th and 13th days, or 18,432. Adopting this, the mean daily excess of beats during the alcoholic days was 14,492, or an increase of rather more than 13 per cent.

"The first day of alcohol gave an excess of 4

per cent., and the last of 23 per cent.; and the mean of these two gives almost the same percentage of excess as the mean of the six days.

"Admitting that each beat of the heart was as strong during the alcoholic period as in the water period (and it was really more powerful), the heart on the last two days of alcohol was doing one-fifth more work.

"Adopting the lowest estimate which has been given of the daily work of the heart, viz., as equal to 122 tons lifted one foot, the heart during the alcoholic period did daily work in excess equal to lifting 15.8 tons one foot, and in the last two days did extra work to the amount of 24 tons lifted as far.

"The period of rest for the heart was shortened, though, perhaps, not to such an extent as would be inferred from the number of beats, for each contraction was sooner over. The heart, on the fifth and sixth days after alcohol was left off, and apparently at the time when the last traces of alcohol were eliminated, showed in the sphygmographic tracings signs of unusual feebleness; and, perhaps, in consequence of this, when the brandy quickened the heart again, the tracings showed a more rapid contraction of the ventricles, but less power than in the alcoholic period. The brandy acted, in fact, on a heart whose nutrition had not been perfectly restored."

It will seem at first sight, almost incredible that such an excess of work could be put upon the heart, but it is perfectly credible when all the facts are known. The heart of an adult man makes, as we see above, 73.57 strokes per minute. This number multiplied by sixty for the hour, and again by twenty-four hours for the entire day, would give nearly 106,000 as the number of strokes per day. There is, however, a reduction of stroke produced by assuming the recumbent position and by sleep, so that for simplicity's sake we may take off the 6,000 strokes, and speaking generally may put the average at 100,000 in the entire day. With each of these strokes the two ventricles of the heart, as they contract, lift up into their respective vessels three ounces of blood each, that is to say, six ounces with the combined stroke, or 600,000 in the twenty-four hours. The equivalent of work rendered by this simpler calculation would be 116 foot tons; and if we estimate the increase of work induced by alcohol we shall find that four ounces of spirit increase it one-eighth part; six ounces, one-sixth part; and eight ounces, one-fourth part.

The stage of primary excitement of the circulation thus induced lasts for a considerable time, but at length the heart flags from its over action, and requires the stimulus of more spirit to carry it on in its work. Let us take what we may call a moderate amount of alcohol, say two ounces by volume, in form of wine, or beer, or spirits. What is called strong sherry or port may contain as much as twenty-five per cent. by volume. Brandy over fifty; gin, thirty-eight; rum, forty-eight; whisky, forty-three; vin ordinaire, eight; strong ale, fourteen; champagne, ten to eleven; it matters not which, if the quantity of alcohol be regulated by the amount present in the liquor imbibed. When we reach the two ounces, a distinct physiological effect follows, leading on to that first stage of excitement with which we are now conversant. The reception of the spirit arrested at this point, there need be no important mischief done to the organism; but if the quantity imbibed be increased, further changes quickly occur. We have seen that all the organs of the body are built upon the vascular structures, and therefore it follows that a prolonged paralysis of the minute circulation must of necessity lead to disturbance in other organs than the heart.

By common observation the flush seen on the cheek during the first stage of alcoholic excitation is presumed to extend merely to the parts actually exposed to view. It cannot, however, be too forcibly impressed that the condition is universal in the body. If the lungs could be seen, they too would be found with their vessels injected; if the brain and spinal cord could be laid open to view, they would be discovered in the same condition; if the stomach, the liver, the spleen, the kidneys, or any other vascular organs or parts could be exposed, the vascular engorgement would be equally manifest. In the lower animals I have been able to witness this extreme vascular condition in the lungs, and there are here presented to you two drawings from nature, showing, one the lungs in a natural state of an animal killed by a sudden blow, the other the lungs of an animal killed equally suddenly, but at a time when it was under the influence of alcohol. You will see, as if you were looking at the structures themselves, how different they are in respect to the blood which they contained, how intensely charged with blood is the lung in which the vessels had been paralysed by the alcoholic spirit.

I once had the unusual, though unhappy, opportunity of observing the same phenomenon in the brain structure of a man who, in a paroxysm of alcoholic excitement, decapitated himself under the wheel of a railway carriage, and whose brain was instantaneously evolved from the skull by the crash. The brain itself, entire, was before me within three minutes after the death. It exhaled the odor of spirit most distinctly, and its membranes and minute structures were vascular in the extreme. It looked as if it had been recently injected with vermilion. The white matter of the cerebrum, studded with red points, could scarcely be distinguished, when it was incised, by its natural whiteness; and the pia-mater, or internal vascular membrane covering the brain, resembled a delicate web of coagulated red blood, so tensely were its fine vessels engorged.

I should add that this condition extended through both the larger and the smaller brain, the cerebrum and cerebellum, but was not so marked in the medulla or commencing portion of the spinal cord.

The action of alcohol continued beyond the first stage, the function of the spinal cord is influenced. Through this part of the nervous system we are accustomed, in health, to perform automatic acts of a mechanical kind, which proceed systematically even when we are thinking or speaking on other subjects. Thus a skilled workman will continue his mechanical work perfectly, while his mind is bent on some other subject; and thus we all perform various acts in a purely automatic way, without calling in the aid of the higher centres, except something more than ordinary occurs to demand their service, upon which we think before we perform. Under alcohol, as the spinal centres become influenced, these pure automatic acts cease to be correctly carried on. That the hand may reach any object, or the foot be correctly planted, the higher intellectual centre must be invoked to make the proceeding secure. There follows quickly upon this a deficient power of co-ordination of muscular movement. The nervous control of certain of the muscles is lost, and the nervous stimulus is more or less enfeebled. The muscles of the lower lip in the human subject usually fail first of all, then the muscles of the lower limbs, and it is worthy of remark that the extensor muscles give way earlier than the flexors. The muscles themselves by this time are also failing in power; they respond more feebly than is natural to the nervous stimulus; they, too, are coming under the depressing influence of the paralysing agent, their structure is temporarily deranged, and their contractile power reduced.

This modification of the animal functions under alcohol marks the second degree of its action. In young subjects there is now, usually, vomiting with faintness, followed by gradual relief from the burden of the poison.

The alcoholic spirit carried yet a further degree,

the cerebral or brain centres become influenced; they are reduced in power, and the controlling influences of will and of judgment are lost. As these centres are unbalanced and thrown into chaos, the rational part of the nature of the man gives way before the emotional, passional, or organic part. The reason is now off duty, or is fooling with duty, and all the mere animal instincts and sentiments are laid atrociously bare. The coward shows up more craven, the braggart more boastful, the cruel more merciless, the untruthful more false, the carnal more degraded. "*In vino veritas*" expresses, even indeed to physiological accuracy, the true condition. The reason, the emotions, the instincts, are all in a state of carnival, and in chaotic feebleness.

Finally, the action of the alcohol still extending, the superior brain centres are overpowered; the senses are beclouded, the voluntary muscular prostration is perfected, sensibility is lost, and the body lies a mere log, dead by all but one-fourth, on which alone its life hangs. The heart still remains true to its duty, and while it just lives it feeds the breathing power. And so the circulation and the respiration, in the otherwise inert mass, keeps the mass within the bare domain of life until the poison begins to pass away and the nervous centres to revive again. It is happy for the inebriate that, as a rule, the brain fails so long before the heart that he has neither the power nor the sense to continue his process of destruction up to the act of death of his circulation. Therefore he lives to die another day.

Thus there are four stages of alcoholic action in

the primary form:—(*a*) A stage of vascular excitement and exhaustion; (*b*) a stage of excitement and exhaustion of the spinal cord, with muscular perturbation; (*c*) a stage of unbalanced reasoning power and of volition; (*d*) a stage of complete collapse of nervous function.

Such is an outline of the primary action of alcohol on those who may be said to be unaccustomed to it, or who have not yet fallen into a fixed habit of taking it. For a long time the organism will bear these perversions of its functions without apparent injury, but if the experiment be repeated too often and too long, if it be continued after the term of life when the body is fully developed, when the elasticity of the membranes and of the blood vessels is lessened, and when the tone of the muscular fibre is reduced, then organic series of structural changes, so characteristic of the persistent effects of spirit, become prominent and permanent. Then the external surface becomes darkened and congested, its vessels, in parts, visibly large; the skin becomes blotched, the proverbial red nose is defined, and those other striking vascular changes which disfigure many who may probably be called moderate alcoholics, are developed. These changes, belonging as they do to external surfaces, come under direct observation; they are accompanied with certain other changes in the internal organs, which we shall discover in a future lecture to be more destructive still.

LECTURE IV.

THE POSITION OF ALCOHOL AS A FOOD. EFFECTS OF ALCOHOL ON THE ANIMAL TEMPERATURE. HYGIENIC LESSONS.

THE question that lies before us for discussion in this lecture is short and definite. It is included in the three words: Is alcohol food?

We have studied in the previous lecture the purely physical action of alcohol on the animal body, that which stands apart from the action of food, and we have learned from the study that over the nervous system and over the vascular supply this spirit exerts a specific influence. We now inquire whether the influence ends there, or whether there may be, in addition, either a sustaining, and constructing, or a heat-giving power—that is to say, a force-giving quality in it. If there be, then the simple physical effects are perchance tolerable, or at all events are not sufficient to militate against the advantages which lie on the food side of the question.

It may be well to rest for a moment to consider the position of men and animals upon the earth in relation to the means given to them for their support as living, moving, and, in the higher animals, thinking structures. This position is well-defined. The theory that man was made originally out of the dust of the earth is, after all, the most scientific theory that has ever been advanced as to his primeval origin, if the word *dust* be only extended so as to include the actual compound substance of the earth. For in the earth are to be found not only all the elements out of which he is constructed, but even certain of the elements in the same kind of combination as we find them in him. In the earth water, salts, and organic matter are found; in man the same are found. The man is in many respects of motion a reflex of the motion of the earth, presenting periodicities of movements, and of movements in a circle in like mode. As if to complete the analogy, this remains true, that the earth yields spontaneously to man, either from herself directly or from the vegetable kingdom which lies between her and man, all the requirements for his existence. Whatever, therefore, man invents, though it may seem to be a great necessity, is not a necessity except to those who, being trained to its use, have been led artificially to believe it essential. Thus nature has produced water and milk for man to drink, and they are, in truth, all the fluids that are essential. This lesson, which nature teaches by her rule of provision for the necessities of animal life, is supplemented by many other facts, each equally authoritative. There is ever before us the great experiment that all classes of living beings beneath man require as drink none other fluids except those I have named. We see the most useful of these animals performing laborious tasks, undergoing extremes of fatigue, bearing vicissitudes of heat and of cold, and enduring **work, fatigue, and vicissitude for long series of** years, sustained by their solid food, with no other fluid than simple water. We see again whole nations and races of men who labor hard, endure fatigue and exposure, and who live to the end of a long and healthy life, taking with their solid sustenance water only as a beverage.

When we turn to the physiological construction either of man or of a lower animal, we discover nothing that can lead us to conceive the necessity for any other fluid than that which nature has supplied. The mass of the blood is composed of water, the mass of the nervous system is composed of water, the mass of all the active vital organs is made up of the same fluid: the secretions are watery fluids, and if in any of these parts any other agent than water should replace it, the result is an instant disturbance of function that is injurious in proportion to the displacement.

When we turn therefore to the use of such a fluid as alcohol under any of its disguises—as spirit, as wine, as beer, as cider, as perry, as liqueur,— we are driven *à priori* to look upon it as something superadded to the necessities of life; to look upon it, in a word, as a luxury. In such sense it has always been received amongst those nations which have most indulged in it. It is something added to the ordinary life; something unnecessary, but agreeable. Wine, added to the meal, transforms the meal into a feast; it is supposed to make glad the heart, but it is never supposed that if the wine were not possessed the life would be shortened. When now we offer wine, it is, by the effect of **habit and education, an offering of a thing that is** super-necessitous, and in such wise a compliment, an indication of desire or of willingness to be exceedingly hospitable.

All the evidence of a general kind which can be gathered from these observations points to the uselessness, for man, of such an artificial agent as alcohol. But, after all, an assumption so derived may be false. We have already seen that when alcoholic spirit is taken into the animal body it produces in it exceedingly marked effects; it may therefore, by accident, I might almost say, play in some manner the part of a food and supplement water. Indeed, it is a form of water in which a compound of carbon and hydrogen has replaced hydrogen. Let us, then, ask the question: Can alcohol be in any sense accepted as performing any other part in the body save that physical part which we have considered? Can it have happened that man, by his invention, has added, to nature, a food? And let us answer the question as candidly as the facts of experiment and experience will permit.

CONSTRUCTIVE MATERIALS OF THE BODY.

The living animal body is constructed out of a few simple forms of matter which possess, during life, the power of motion. It is, in its living state, a noun and a verb. Whatever helps to maintain it in perfect order of construction, whatever enables it to move of its own mere will and motion, may be considered as a food. The one gives matter and mass, the other gives force or spirit to the mass. With the progress of organic chemistry after the discovery of the art of organic analysis, it soon became evident that what are called foods are divisible into two great classes; those which supply material or tissue, and those which supply heat or other variety of force. Gradually it was detected that the building foods all contain the element nitrogen as an essential part, and that the force-supplying foods are free of nitrogen and are hydro-carbons, substances that will undergo combustion by oxidation, and liberate force for the motive uses of the economy. So, foods have for a long time been sharply classified as nitrogenous or tissue-feeding, and as respiratory or heat-producing. At the present moment this long accepted view is undergoing some modification. It is being elicited that the nitrogenous foods are to a certain degree heat-producing; but I need not at this stage enter on the nice question involved. I may safely, for the practical purpose we have in view, let the division of the classes of foods remain as described above.

The nitrogenous foods exist in the animal body in the form of what is called colloidal matter, the word *colloidal* being a term signifying a jelly-like substance. The purest form of this matter is found in the blood in the white, elastic, plastic matter, called fibrine. By repeated washings of a portion of this substance, I have prepared here, from the blood of the ox, a beautiful specimen of this colloid of the blood. Of a similar colloidal substance the moving muscles are formed. In a fluid state, and permanently fluid at the temperature of the living body, the colloid called albumen forms part of organic structure. Under the names of gelatine and chondrine, a nitrogenous colloidal substance forms the organic matter of the skeleton, of the cartilages, of the sheaths of muscles, of the tendons. The eye-ball is constructed out of a series of colloidal tissues. All the membranes which envelope the visceral organs, and which possess elasticity, are colloidal. The outer covering or skin is colloidal, the nails are the same. Even in the brain and nervous matter there is distributed a colloid. Thus, if we sum up the various parts of the body we may say that all the active masses of structure are nitrogenous and colloidal.

In combination with this active matter there are, however, two other material ingredients, viz., water and saline substance. Upon its combination with water the activity of the colloid depends. Upon the saline rests the various kinds of combination of the colloid with the water. In bone the gelatine is combined with a salt, called phosphate of lime, with carbonate of lime, and other salts, in much larger proportion than itself. In fibrine the colloidal substance is nearly divested of saline; but in all parts these three material compounds make up the animal structures.

Lying outside these structures in the natural state, but really as an adventitious formation, is one other animal product, viz., fat; a substance detrimental to the motion of the active parts when present in excess, but at the same time capable of combustion, and of yielding heat by the process.

We have now before us the constructive or building parts of the animal body. Excepting the water, the salts, and the fat, they all contain nitrogen, and they take their specific quality from that specific fact. We know that the source of them is the vegetable kingdom, that they are formed by nature in that kingdom, are transferred from the vegetable to the animal, are not made by any natural process within the animal, have not yet been made by any artificial process known to the chemist, and can therefore only be supplied from the one natural supply.

Alcohol contains no nitrogen, it has none of the qualities of these structure-building foods; it is incapable of being transformed into any of them; it is therefore not a food in the sense of its being a constructive agent in the building up of the body.

In respect to this view there is, I believe, now no difference of opinion amongst those who have most carefully observed the action of alcohol. There is, however, a difference in relation to its action as a fat-forming food. It appears to be on evidence that men and animals beginning, while in a perfect state of health, to take in excess certain fluids containing alcohol become fattened. Notoriously, ale and beer fatten; and in some parts of the country certain animals—calves, for instance—are rapidly fattened by the process of feeding them with a mixture of barley flour and gin. But through all these apparent evidences there may run an error. The fattening may not be due to the alcohol itself, but to the sugar or the starchy material that is taken with it. As a matter of general experience on which I have tried to arrive at the truth with as much accuracy as can be obtained, I am led to the conclusion that pure spirit drinkers among men, I mean those who do not mix sugar with the spirit, and who dislike spirit which is artificially sweetened, are not fattened by the spirit they take. This tallies also with the observations on the action of absolute alcohol on inferior animals, for they certainly, under that influence, if they are allowed liberty to move freely, do not fatten.

The question of the effect of alcohol in fattening presents still another difficulty. Alcohol, when it is largely taken, unless the will of the imbiber be very powerful, is wont to induce desire for undue sleep, or at least desire for physical repose. Under such conditions there is an interference with the ordinary nutritive processes. The wasted products of nutrition are imperfectly eliminated, the respiration becomes slower and less effective, and there is set up a series of changes leading, independently of the alcohol as a direct producer of fat, to development and to deposit of fatty tissue in the body. All these circumstances militate against the hypothesis of the origin of fatty material direct from alcohol, nor is there any obvious chemical fact that supports the hypothesis. We understand chemically the transformation of starchy matter into one form of sugar, and we infer that in the animal body sugar is transmutable into fat. We know also that we can transmute sugar into alcohol, but as yet we see no way back from alcohol into sugar; if we did, the difficulty of tracing alcohol into fat would probably be over.

Physiological argument nevertheless lends some countenance to the view that alcohol may, by an unknown process, be transferable into fat. It is true that some confirmed alcoholics who do not wax fat in the ordinary sense of the term, that is to say, who do not fill out with fat, from the separation of fatty matter in their cellular tissue outside the vital organs, do, in certain instances, undergo a process of fatty change within their organic structures. Their muscles, including the heart, become the centres of the degeneration called "fatty," and by the interposition of cells of fat in the minute muscular elements, the activity of the fabric is destroyed, sometimes to a fatal destruction. The same degenerative change may extend also to other organs, to the brain and to such active glands as the liver and the kidney.

At first view it occurs to the mind that here is evidence of effect upon cause. At the same time it is not so clear that the effect is direct from alcohol; for when we proceed to examine into all the data that lie before us, we discover such an absence of uniformity in differing examples of the fatty change that we lose alcohol as the clue to discovery. Some alcoholics truly present the fatty modification of tissue, other alcoholics do not present it, so that alcohol may be in active operation and may neither be promoting the production of fat from other material nor yielding it. Lastly, the fatty change of tissue may progress, in the absence of alcohol, in the tissues of those who altogether abstain.

In conclusion, therefore, on this one point of alcohol, its use as a builder of the substantial parts of the animal organism, I fear I must give up all hope of affirmative proof. It does not certainly help to build up the active nitrogenous structures. It probably does not produce fatty matter, except by an indirect and injurious interference with the natural processes.

If alcohol be not a substance out of which the animal tissues are formed, may it not be a source of energy of actual motion ; may it not supply the power of doing work? Alcohol, we see, contains two elements that will burn in the presence of oxygen, viz., carbon and hydrogen, and although by their combination already with oxygen in the alcohol a certain measure of their potential energy is lost, they are still capable of combining with more oxygen. This is proved by various experiments. When alcohol is burned, that is to say when its combustible elements combine with free oxygen, there results from the chemical combination a certain degree of heat. The heat produced does not approach that obtained by an equal weight of hydrogen, it is not so great as that produced by an equal weight of carbon, but it is greater than that caused by the combustion of phosphorus, and very much greater than that caused by the combustion of sulphur.

The combustion thus spoken of is that active combustion which is excited when a light is brought into contact with alcohol so that its vapor may burn. But it is not actually necessary that such instant active combustion should be set up. If we distribute alcohol over a wide surface in the presence of some chemical substances it will then by its combination with oxygen liberate a greater or lesser degree of heat. If we saturate a portion of paper with alcohol, and on that paper pour a little of the finely-divided powder called platinum black, we at once get evidence of heat which may be so active that perfect combustion may ensue. In this instance the alcohol is transformed, as in burning, in great part, nay it may be altogether, into carbonic acid and water, which means the completed combustion. If in place of absolute alcohol, in this experiment, we were to use alcohol diluted with water, then instead of obtaining the active combination and combustion we should get a slower oxidation with the production of substances to which attention has already been directed, viz., aldehyde, acetic acid, and volatile acetic ether.

DISPOSAL OF ALCOHOL IN THE ORGANISM.

We are brought now to one of the most important parts of our study. We see that, under favoring conditions, alcohol will oxidise in the presence of the air. We see that it will oxidise in two ways—actively, with the production of much heat and with the formation of carbonic acid and water; passively, with the production of aldehyde and acetic acid.

In the human body do any similar changes take place? Throughout the whole of the vast sheet of the minute circulation there is ever in progress, during life, a process of slow oxidation of carbon and hydrogen, by which heat is produced, and carbonic acid and water are produced. The heat is proved by the animal warmth which is ever present in our bodies while we live; the carbonic acid and water, as products, are proved by their continued presence in the secretions from the lungs, skin, and other organs.

Alcohol, we have seen, is carried by the blood into this minute circulation. Is it possible it can pass through that ordeal and undergo no chemical change? If it does undergo any change, what is its nature? These questions have occupied the attention of many gifted minds; but they are not yet solved. Let me endeavor to put the position in which they stand plainly before you.

The earlier physiologists of this century came, naturally enough, to the conclusion that the alcohol taken into the body is consumed there with the evolution of heat. A certain development of heat in the superficies of the body, and a certain sensation of glow which follows upon the imbibition of spirit lent countenance to this suspicion. But in course of time, independently of any knowledge of the effect produced by alcohol in the minute circulation of the blood, it began to be doubted whether alcohol was disposed of in the organism by its combustion. Some observers had noticed, in conducting the examination of the body after death from excess of alcohol, that the odor of the substance was present in the tissues, especially in the nervous tissue, and it was doubted whether the alcohol might not under some circumstances remain in the organism without undergoing any change at all. In 1860 two eminent Frenchmen—Lallemand and Perrin, assisted by Duroy, published a prize essay on alcohol, in which this view was maintained, or, as the authors would probably say, was originated; for in truth they were the first to state the view on direct scientific evidence. From the result of many experiments, they came to the conclusion that alcohol taken into the living body accumulates in the tissues, especially in the liver and in the brain, and that it is eliminated by the fluid secretions, notably by the renal secretion, as alcohol. They sought in the different tissues for evidence of the secondary products of the oxidation of alcohol, for aldehyde, acetal, acetic acid, and they found none of those products, except some acetic acid in the stomach, which acid they concluded was formed from the alcohol received directly into the stomach, and from the action exerted upon it there by the gastric juice. The experiments carried on by these inquirers were so numerous and careful, and the results they arrived at were so definitely stated, that their labors were for a season accepted as conclusive by many men of science, and by the majority of the public. It was ascertained by other experimentalists that alcohol is eliminated by the system in the direct way, as alcohol, and the question of elimination rested as if it had been solved.

The interval of credence in these assertions was not very prolonged. An English physician soon commenced to cross a lance with his learned French peers, and to point out certain distinct errors in their results. I have no doubt many of you know, before I mention his name, that he to whom I refer was the physician who last year lost his life from the performance of his professional duties--the late Dr. Anstie. Respecting this observer, whose friendship I owned for many years, it is meet for me to pay this public tribute of respect; that no man I ever knew combined with vigor of mind, more incomparable industry and courage, or a more honorable regard for scientific truth and honesty. The subject we are now considering has lost no investigator more ably learned for the work that still remains to be done.

From Dr. Anstie came the earliest expressions of doubt relative to this hypothesis of what is called the direct elimination of alcohol by the secretions, and from him have come the latest objections. His arguments have been sustained abroad by Schulinus, and, in this country, by Drs. Thudichum and Dupré, whose work on wine will, even in another century, be more highly prized, if that be possible, than it is now. The sum and substance of the labors of these observers is stated in a few words. They prove that while it is true that, under certain circumstances, alcohol taken into the body will pass off in the secretions unchanged, the quantity so eliminated is the merest fraction of what has been injected, and that there must be some other means by which the spirit is disposed of in the organism. In a lecture I delivered on this subject in the year 1869, I ventured to suggest, in commenting upon a series of Dr. Thudichum's remarkable researches, that perhaps one element of research was wanting to prove conclusively the fallacy of the direct elimination hypothesis. I thought that sufficient time had not been allowed between the administration of the spirit and the final determination made for it in the excreted fluids. It was not, I argued, shown how much spirit the tissues would hold unchanged. The objection was sound, but it has been removed by more recent experiment.

In the last research conducted by Anstie, in which he was assisted by Dupré, the results of the experiments were unmistakable in their bearing on the points now under our consideration. The history of these labors is recorded in full in the last paper written by Dr. Anstie, and published in the journal called the *Practitioner*, for July, 1874.

The test that had been commonly employed for determining the presence of alcohol in the fluid suspected of containing it, was the color test. A solution is made consisting of bichromate of potassa, with diluted sulphuric acid. When to this solution alcohol is added, there is a change of color from the brownish red to green; owing to the reduction of the chromic acid to the green oxide of the base chromium. By marking the difference of color produced a scale can be adopted which will show the extent of the reduction, and thereby the amount of the spirit that has caused the change. This process was improved by Dr. Dupré. He distilled the fluid in which alcohol was believed to be present, and then, after treating the distillate with the bichromate and sulphuric acid solution, he tested with a standard solution of soda for the amount of acetic acid which would be produced by the oxidation of alcohol were that fluid present.

This modification of test was and is a very considerable advance, since it enabled the observers to extend their determinations with greater accuracy of detail. In the research they conducted with it two facts of singular interest were elicited. The first fact was discovered by Dr. Dupré. It is that from the secretions of persons who do not drink alcohol at all a fluid can be distilled which affects the chromic test as if alcohol were actually present in the secreted fluids, and that this hitherto unsuspected product is oxidised into an acid so like acetic acid it cannot be distinguished from it, and is apparently identical with it. To be plain, Dr. Dupré's discovery suggests that no man can be, in strict scientific sense, a non-alcoholic, inasmuch as, "will he nill he," he brews in his own economy a "wee drap." It is an innocent brew certainly, but it is brewed, and the most ardent abstainer must excuse it. "Argal, he that is not guilty of his own death shorteneth not his own life." The fault, if it be one, rests with nature, who, according to our poor estimates, is no more faultless than the rest of her sex.

The second fact, which came chiefly from the labors of Dr. Anstie, is that from animals under alcohol, not one of the secretions, not all the secretions combined, yield any more than a fractional amount of the alcohol that has been administered. The experiments were by necessity made on the inferior animals, but they supplied none the less conclusively the fact stated. It was proved that an animal, a terrier dog, weighing ten pounds, could take with comparative impunity nearly 2000 grains of absolute alcohol in ten days, and that on the last day of this regimen he only eliminated by all the channels of elimination 1.13 grains of alcohol. This fact was of itself sufficiently remarkable, but another still more important remains to be told. In completion of his research, when an animal had been treated with alcohol, as above described, Anstie killed it, instantly and painlessly, two hours after it had received the last quantity—95 grains—of spirit. Then the whole body, including every fragment of tissue with all the fluid and solid contents, was subjected to analysis, with the result of discovering only 23.66 grains of spirit.

We are driven by the evidence now before us to the certain conclusion that in the animal body alcohol is decomposed; that is to say, a certain portion of it (and if a certain portion why not the whole?) is transmutable into new compounds. The inference that might be drawn is fair enough that the alcohol is lost by being burned in the body. It is lost in the body, and out of the body it will burn. If it will burn in the organism it will supply force, for it enters as the bearer of so much potential energy. In combining with oxygen is there then a development of force or heat to the extent that would be developed in the combustion of the same quantity in the lamp, or from the distribution of it over the platinum black? At the same time, and in corroboration, is the product of its combustion, carbonic acid, to be discovered in the excretions? If there be heat, and if there be product of carbon consumed in oxygen, then alcohol must rank as a heat-forming food.

DOES ALCOHOL CAUSE INCREASE OF ANIMAL HEAT?

In putting before you this inquiry, I am prepared to answer it by direct knowledge gained from individual experiment. In the course of some researches I had to make for reports rendered to the British Association for the Advancement of Science, it became part of my duty to ascertain what effect certain chemical agents exert over the animal temperature. Amongst these agents was alcohol.

At the time when my researches commenced— viz., in the year 1864, there was nothing definitely known on the subject. The thermometer was not then in such general use as it is now, and it had not been applied, as far as I know, to this particular determination. Generally, however, it had been assumed by the majority of persons that alcohol warms the body, and to "take just a drop to keep out the cold" had been the practice which the experience of ages seemed to justify. It is fair, at the same time, to say that Dr. Lees, and some other far-seeing observers, had for many years held and asserted a different view. They had not entered into minuteness of experimental detail, but they had observed from the effects of alcohol on those who had been exposed to cold in the extreme North and in other regions of ice and snow, that the drinkers did not live on like other men. Thus, in so far as I had what is called experience to guide me, I found conflict of opinion. It was not my business, however, to accept guidance of this kind, but to appeal to the only safe guide, the direct interrogation of nature by experiment.

It were impossible for me to recount the details of the long research,—extending, with intervals of rest, over three years,—which was conducted in my laboratory, to determine the influence of alcohol on the animal temperature. The effects were observed on warm-blooded animals of different kinds, including birds; on the human subject in health, and on the same subject under alcoholic disease. Similar experiments were made in different external temperatures of the air, ranging from summer heat to ten degrees below freezing point. The whole were carried on from experiment to experiment, without regard either to comparison or result until the general character of result began to proclaim that a rule existed which could rarely be considered exceptional. The facts obtained I may epitomise as follows:

The progressive stages of change of animal function from alcohol are four in number. The first is a stage of excitement when there exists that relaxation and injection of the blood-vessels of the minute circulation with which we have become conversant. The second is the stage of excitement with some muscular inability and deficient automatic control. The third is a stage of rambling, incoherent, emotional excitement, with loss of voluntary muscular power, and ending in helpless unconsciousness. The fourth and final stage is that in which the heart itself begins to fail, and in which death, in extreme instances of intoxication, closes the scene. These stages are developed in all the warm-blooded animals, and the changes of temperature throughout the whole are relatively the same.

In the first stage the external temperature of the body is raised. In birds—pigeons—the rise may amount to a full degree, on Fahrenheit's scale; in mammals it rarely exceeds half a degree. In man it may rise to half a degree, and in the confirmed inebriate, in whom the cutaneous vessels are readily engorged, I have seen it run up to a degree and a half. In this stage the effect on the extremities of the nerves is that of a warm glow, like what is experienced during the reaction from cold.

The heat felt in this stage might be considered as due to the combustion of the alcohol: it is not so; it is in truth a process of cooling. It is from the unfolding of the larger sheet of the warm blood and from the quicker radiation of heat from that larger surface. During this stage, which is comparatively brief, the internal temperature is declining; the expired air from the lungs is indicating, not an increase, but the first period of reduction in the amount of carbonic acid, and the reddened surface of the body is so reduced in tonicity that cold applied to it increases the suffusion. It is this most deceptive stage that led the older observers into the error that alcohol warms the body

In the second stage, the temperature first comes down to its natural standard, and then declines below what is natural. The fall is not considerable. In birds it reaches from one and a half to two degrees. In other animals, dogs and guinea pigs, it rarely exceeds one degree; in man it is confined to three-fourths of a degree. In a room heated to 65° or 70° the decrease of animal temperature may not actually be perceived; but it is quickly detected if the person in whom it is present pass into a colder atmosphere, and it lasts, even when the further supply of alcohol is cut off, for a long period—viz., from two and a half to three hours. It is much prolonged by absence of food.

During the third degree the fall of temperature rapidly increases, and as the fourth stage is approached it reaches a decline that becomes actually dangerous. In birds the reduction may be five degrees and a half, and in the other animals three. In man it is often from two and a half to three degrees. There is always during this stage a profound sleep or coma, and while this lasts the temperature continues reduced.

It is here worthy of incidental notice that, as a rule, the sleep of apoplexy and the sleep of drunkenness may be distinguished by a marked difference in the animal temperature. In apoplexy the temperature of the body is above, in drunkenness below, the natural standard of 98° of Fahrenheit's scale.

Under favorable circumstances a long period is required before the body recovers its natural warmth after such reduction of heat as follows the extreme stage of alcoholic intoxication. With the first conscious movements of recovery there is a faint rise, but such is the depression that these very movements exhaust and lead to a further reduction. I have known as long a period as three days required, in man, to bring back a steady natural return of the full animal warmth.

Through every stage, then, of the action of alcohol—barring that first stage of excitement—I found a reduction of animal heat to be the special action of the poison. To make the research more perfectly reliable, I combined the action of alcohol with that of cold. A warm-blooded animal, insensibly asleep in the third stage of alcoholic narcotism, was placed in a chamber, the air of which was reduced in temperature to ten degrees below freezing point, together with another similar animal which had received no alcohol. I found that both sleep under these circumstances, but the alcoholic sleeps to die; the other sleeps more deeply than is natural, and lives so long as the store of food it is charged with continues to support life. Within this bound it awakes, in a warmer air, uninjured, though the degree of cold be carried even lower, and be continued for a much longer time.

One more portion of evidence completes the research on the influence of alcohol on the animal temperature. As there is a decrease of temperature from alcohol, so there is proportionately a decrease in the amount of the natural products of the combustion of the body. The quantity of carbonic acid exhaled by the breath is proportionately diminished with the decline of the animal heat. In the extreme stage of alcoholic insensibility,— short of the actually dangerous,— the amount of carbonic acid exhaled by the animal and given off into the chamber I constructed for the purposes of observation was reduced to one-third below the natural standard. On the human subject in this stage of insensibility the quantity of carbonic acid exhaled has not been measured, but in the earlier stage of alcoholic derangement of function the exhaled gas was measured with much care by a very earnest worker, whose recent death we have also to deplore— Dr. Edward Smith. In these early stages Dr. Smith found that the amount of carbonic acid was reduced in man, as I have found it in the lower animals, so that the fact of the general reduction may be considered as established beyond disputation.

We are landed then at last on this basis of knowledge. An agent that will burn and give forth heat and product of combustion outside the body, and which is obviously decomposed within the body, reduces the animal temperature, and prevents the yield of so much product of combustion as is actually natural to the organic life.

What is the inference? The inference is that the alcohol is not burned after the manner of a food which supports animal combustion; but that it is decomposed into secondary products, by oxidation, at the expense of the oxygen which ought to be applied for the natural heating of the body.

For some time to come the physiological world

will be studiously intent on the discovery of the mode by which alcohol is removed from the organism. It is a subject on which I shall one day be able to speak, I hope, with some degree of experimental certainty, but on which at this moment I am not prepared to offer more than an indication of the probable course of research. I may venture to add, in advance, two or three suggestions to which my researches, as far as they go, point.

Firstly, I believe there is a certain determinable degree of saturation of the blood with alcohol, within which degree all the alcohol is disposed of by its decomposition. Beyond that degree the oxidation is arrested, and then there is an accumulation of alcohol, with voidance of it, in the unchanged state, in the secretions.

Secondly, the change or decomposition of the alcohol in its course through the minute circulation, in which it is transformed, is not into carbonic acid and water, as though it were burned, but into a new soluble, chemical substance, probably aldehyde, which returns by the veins into the great channels of the circulation.

Thirdly, I think I have made out that there is an outlet for the alcohol, or for the fluid product of its decomposition, into the alimentary canal, through the secretion of the liver. Thrown into the canal, it is, I believe, subjected there to further oxidation, is in fact oxidised by a process of fermentation attended with the active development of gaseous substances. From this surface the oxidised product is in turn re-absorbed in great part and carried into the circulation, and is disposed of by combination with bases or by further oxidation.

Here, however, I leave the theoretical point to revert to the practical, and the practical is this; that alcohol cannot by any ingenuity of excuse for it, be classified amongst the foods of man. It neither supplies matter for construction nor heat. On the contrary, it injures construction and it reduces temperature.

EFFECT OF MUSCULAR POWER.

Behind the question of the effect of alcohol upon the animal temperature was another subject for inquiry. It was fair to ask whether, if heat were not produced by the spirit, some additional stimulus might be communicated by it to the muscular fibre. There is nothing in what we see relating to the action of alcohol in man that would lead us to suppose it capable of giving an increased muscular power, and it is certain that animals subjected even for short periods of time to its influence lose their power for work in a marked degree. Indeed, if we were to treat our domestic animals with this agent in the same manner that we treat ourselves, we should soon have none that were tamable, none that were workable, and none that were edible. I thought it, nevertheless, worth the inquiry whether at any stage of the alcoholic excitement living muscle could be induced to show an extra amount of power. I therefore submitted muscle to this test. I gently weighted the hinder limb of a frog until the power of contraction was just overcome then by a measured electrical current I stimulated the muscle to extra contraction, and determined the increase of weight that could thus be lifted. This decided upon in the healthy animal, the trial was repeated some days later on the same animal after it had received alcohol in sufficient quantities to induce the various stages of alcoholic modification of function. The result was that through every stage the response to the electrical current was enfeebled, and so soon as narcotism was developed by the spirit, it was so enfeebled that less than half the weight that could be lifted in the previous trial, by the natural effort of the animal, could not now be raised even under the electrical excitation.

In man and in animals, during the period between the first and third stages of alcoholic disturbance, there is often muscular excitement, which passes for increased muscular power. The muscles are then truly more rapidly stimulated into motion by the nervous tumult, but the muscular power is actually enfeebled.

HYGIENIC LESSONS.

The facts I have endeavored to bring forward in this as well as in the last lecture will suggest to the mind many thoughts bearing upon the health of individuals and communities, in so far as health is affected by the potent agent, alcohol. I need hardly, indeed, presume to offer any suggestions, but one or two of a specially practical and everyday character may be ventured.

I am bound to intimate that the popular plan of administering alcohol for the purpose of sustaining the animal warmth is an entire and dangerous error, and that when it is brought into practice during extremely cold weather it is calculated to lead even to fatal consequences, from the readiness with which it permits the blood to become congested in the vital organs. I cannot too forcibly impress the fact that cold and alcohol act, physiologically, in the same manner, and that, combined in action, every danger resulting from either agent is doubled.

Whenever we see a person disposed to meet the effects of cold by strong drink it is our duty to endeavor to check that effort, and whenever we see an unfortunate person under the influence of alcohol it is our duty to suggest warmth as the best means for his recovery. These facts prompt many other useful ideas of detail, in our common life. If, for instance, our police were taught the simple art of taking the animal temperature of persons they have removed from the streets in a state of insensibility, the results would be most beneficial. The operation is one that hundreds of nurses now carry out daily, and applied by our police-officers, at their stations, it would enable them not only to suspect the difference between a man in an apoplectic fit and a man intoxicated, but would suggest naturally the instant abolition of the practice of thrusting the really intoxicated into a cold and damp cell, which to such a one is actually an anteroom to the grave.*

---

* Since the delivery of this lecture I am informed that in the London Metropolitan District the cells in which the intoxicated

Once more: I would earnestly impress that the systematic administration of alcohol for the purpose of giving and sustaining strength is an entire delusion. I am not going to say that occasions do not arise when an enfeebled or fainting heart is temporarily relieved by the relaxation of the vessels which alcohol, on its diffusion through the blood, induces; but that this spirit gives any persistent increase of power by which men are enabled to perform more sustained work is a mistake as serious as it is universal.

Again, the belief that alcohol may be used with advantage to fatten the body is, when it is acted upon, fraught with danger. For if we could successfully fatten the body we should but destroy it the more swiftly and surely; and as the fattening which follows the use of alcohol is not confined to the external development of fat but extends to a degeneration through the minute structures of the vital organs, including the heart itself, the danger is painfully apparent.

In conclusion, whatever good can come from alcohol, or whatever evil, is all included in that primary physiological and luxurious action of the agent upon the nervous supply of the circulation to which I have endeavored so earnestly to direct your attention. If it be really a luxury for the heart to be lifted up by alcohol; for the blood to course more swiftly through the brain; for the thoughts to flow more vehemently; for words to

---

are received are not open to the objections named. I am g'ad to be able to make this correction.

come more fluently; for emotions to rise ecstatically, and for life to rush on beyond the pace set by nature; then those who enjoy the luxury must enjoy it,—with the consequences.

LECTURE V.

THE SECONDARY ACTION OF ALCOHOL ON THE ANIMAL FUNCTIONS, AND ON THE PHYSICAL DETERIORATIONS OF STRUCTURE INCIDENT TO ITS EXCESSIVE USE.

It is my business in this course of lectures to treat upon the specific action of absolute alcohol. I have therefore specially avoided all reference to the spirituous drinks of which it forms a part. As a rule in every form of strong drink the source of the action of it, for good or for evil, is the spirit it contains, and the influence of the drink is potent according to the amount of that spirit present in it. To put the matter simply, if all the liquors sold under various names—wine, brandy, gin, rum, whisky, ale, stout, perry, cider,—were divested of their alcoholic spirit, they would contain comparatively little of anything that would affect those who partook of them.

DELETERIOUS ADDITIONS TO ALCOHOLIC DRINKS.

As I am, however, about to speak of the deleterious action of alcohol, it is fair I should admit that some bad effects do spring from so-called wine and kindred drinks independently of the pure spirit they contain. Something less of evil than now obtains would be secured if none but natural wines and ales were taken by the people. To return to the times before brantwein was distilled and to have no intoxicating beverages save pure wine and sound ale, were doubtless an improvement on the state of things which now exists; for, in truth, at the present time the characters of pure ethylic wine are hardly known. A *bonâ-fide* wine derived from the fermentation of the grape purely, cannot contain more than seventeen per cent. of alcohol, yet our staple wines, by an artificial process of fortifying and brandying, which means the adding of spirit, are brought up in sherries to twenty, and in ports to even twenty-five per cent. Some wines and spirits are believed to be charged with amylic alcohol. Other wines are charged with foreign volatile substances to impart what is called bouquet, and still other so-called wines—I allude specially to the effervescing liquids sold under that name—are actually often undergoing the fermenting process at the time they are imbibed, and thus are invited to complete their fermentation in that sensitive bottle, the human stomach.

If the subject were specially looked into, a very important chapter of facts might be collected bearing upon the injurious effects of these additions to ales, wines, and spirits. I have noticed the evils that follow upon the administration of an alcoholic drink that has been adulterated with amylic alcohol, and have shown that they are exceedingly serious. The disturbances excited by the other faults, when they do not arise from excess of absolute alcohol, are shown in symptoms of indigestion and in the promotion of an acid condition of tne secretions of the body, beyond what is natural.

Presuming therefore it be actually determined by any one that he will take some alcoholic fluid, he will do nearest to that which is most wise if he takes wines or other spirituous drinks in which the quantity of alcohol is simply confined to the natural amount, in which the process of fermentation has ceased, and in which no foreign substance has been introduced to add either bouquet, body, piquancy, narcotising influence, or other artificial quality.

ABSINTHE.

The admitted addition of some actively poisonous substances to alcohol, in order to produce a new luxury, is the evil most disastrous. The drink sold under the name of *absinthe* is peculiarly formidable. In this liquor five drachms of the essence of absinthium, or wormwood, are added to one hundred quarts of alcohol. Thus the liquor is not only very strong as a mere alcoholic drink, but it is charged with another agent which has been discovered to exert the most powerful and dangerous action upon the nervous functions. The essence of absinthium in doses of from thirty to fifty grains produces in dogs and rabbits signs of extreme terror and trembling, followed by stupor and insensibility. In larger doses it causes epileptiform convulsions, foaming at the mouth, and stertor of the breathing. Its effects, as they occur from the taking of it in the form of absinthe in man, have been most ably described to me by one who indulged in it until it induced in him the peculiar epileptiform seizure. He described the effects as resembling those produced by *haschish*, the narcotic of the East which has been known for ages as the *nepenthes* of Homer, and which owes its properties to extract of Indian hemp or *Cannabis indica*. The partial insensibility caused by the absinthe is attended with the ideal existence of long intervals of time, in which the events of a whole life are arrayed and appreciated, to be succeeded by terrific hallucinations and intellectual weakness, ending in unconscious struggling as if for life. In time, if the use of the absinthe be continued, these phenomena become permanently established and the result is inevitably fatal.

The doubly poisonous absinthe is made the more seductive to its victims by the fact that it excites a morbid craving for food which is never felt except when it is tempted by the destroying agent. Indeed such are the terrible consequences incident to this agent, that I agree with Dr. Decaisne in maintaining that it ought, by legal provision, to be forbidden as an article for human consumption in all civilized communities. Even in small quantities taken daily, say one or two wineglassfuls, it causes quickly a permanent dyspepsia, and, what is of still more consequence, it tempts its victims on and on, so that they cannot take food until absinthe has prompted the desire for it, by which time they are too often hopelessly and mortally in its power.

Until recently absinthe has not been publicly offered for sale in this country on a large scale.

But now, unhappily, the poison is openly announced even here, and the consumption is on the increase; I am doing therefore a public duty in denouncing its use solemnly from this platform, whence so much that is beneficial to society has for a century past been spoken.

ADDITION OF OTHER AGENTS.

The intentional additions of poisonous agents to the alcohol of ales, wines, and spirits pale when absinthe appears in sight, but they are not to be ignored. It is true that we very often hear accounts of the effects for evil of bad wine, when, in fact, the evil is due to the excess of ordinary alcohol that has been taken by the complainant. At the same time it is not to be denied that there exists in our midst a system of mixing, compounding, blending, and reducing wines and spirits, which, carried even to artistic perfection, is additionally prejudicial to the business of selling the various alcoholic beverages.

To be just to our own age, this artistic performance is not an invention of it. The adulteration of wine is indeed one of the oldest devices, extending from the Greeks and Romans onwards to this day. In the Middle Ages many prohibitory acts were passed against it by various governments. As late as the close of the seventeenth century an act was passed by Duke Everhard Louis of Würtemberg making it an offence punishable with death and confiscation of property to adulterate wine with bismuth, sulphur, or the salt of lead called litharge, now known as the yellow protoxide of lead. In the year 1705-6, John Jacob Ernhi, of Eslingen, was actually beheaded for carrying out adulteration with the forbidden poisonous lead compound.

Into our modern civilization a different system of treating strong drinks, in order to rectify bad qualities or to impart new, is, as a rule, followed. The plan of using gypsum or sulphate of lime to remove the acidity of wine, a practice that was followed both by the Greeks and Romans, is, however, still resorted to; so also is the practice of using lime for the same purpose, and for which Jack Falstaff so severely criticises the landlord of the "Boar's Head":

"You rogue, here's lime in this sack: There is nothing but roguery to be found in villanous man: yet a coward is worse than a cup of sack with lime in it; a villanous coward."

But, on the whole, the new day has brought new plans and new intentions, having reference to the different forms of drinks, namely, ales, wines, and spirits, which pass from the hands of the vendor to the consumer.

ALES.

The practice of adulteration the least hurtful is carried on in ales; that at all events is my experience of the ales sold in London, and I speak from a practical knowledge of the facts. A few years ago a well-known statist asked me to undertake for him a research on the ales sold in London, with a view to the detection of the adulterations in them. For many weeks this gentleman himself collected beers and ales from different retail houses in the most diverse parts of this metropolis, and neither trouble nor expense was spared in the examination of these samples, in order to arrive at correct results as to the composition of the fluids thus retailed. I may state at once that I did not in any one instance find a truly dangerous adulteration. I found that to many samples common salt had been added, and to some sugar; but the grand adulteration was water, by which the consumer was, if I may so express it, fraudulently benefited and the government proportionately defrauded. If this aqueous adulteration were not carried on, our registrars of deaths and collectors of revenues would both show heavier totals.

There is a prevailing notion that to malt liquor, bitter substances, such as strychnine, or narcotic substances, such as *cocculus indicus*, are added. Neumann says that in his time, that is just one hundred years ago, *clary*, *cocculus indicus*, and *Bohemian rosemary* were added to malt liquors in order to increase their intoxicating powers, and he states that the last-named substance, Bohemian rosemary, produced a raving intoxication. I know it is also urged, in this day, that there is no known application for the quantity of *cocculus indicus* that is sold except it be for the adulteration of malt liquors. I will not dispute the matter, but I content myself with stating that I have never detected any foreign body of the kind, and that in the whole of my experience of the effect of malt liquors on man, I have never known a symptom produced indicative of the effects of such substances.

The stronger ales and stouts are injurious mainly from the alcohol they contain. Those which have not ceased fermenting, and from which gas is escaping, produce a persistent dyspepsia in persons who indulge in them, a dyspepsia attended with flatulency, painful distension of the stomach, and with loss of proper muscular power of the stomach, by which deficiency the trituration of food is impeded and rendered imperfect. At the same time the action of the gastric fluids upon the food is made less effective. There is at the present day in the market a substance used as an addition to ales, which is called *saccharina*. It is sold in the form of the ordinary sugar-loaf. It is made by the action of diluted sulphuric acid upon starchy matter, and is, in fact, a grape sugar. It gives to the ale body and sweetness. It is in itself a fattening food, and as it is the same as that form of sugar which is found in those who suffer from the disease called diabetes, and which produces the symptoms of that disease, it cannot be taken in quantity without some indirect risk of danger.

WINES.

The evils arising from wines, apart from those which are due to the natural ethylic alcohol they should contain, are derived from several sources. The wine that has not ceased to ferment, and when uncorked is found to be charged with gas, is often as injurious as beer in which the fermentation has not ended. It produces a fermenting process within the body, and gives rise to those phenomena of dyspepsia to which allusion has already been made. Wine that has once been acid and has been treated with lime in order that the acidity may be neutralised, is open to the objection of an excess of salts of lime. It has been urged against wines treated in this manner that they lead to calculous disease when they are taken in quantity for long periods. I must answer to this suggestion that I have not had experience of the slightest evidence that would support it, nor do I think there is sufficient of such wine consumed to warrant any conclusion of the kind. Wine if adulterated with amylic alcohol is unquestionably dangerous, owing to those physiological effects produced by the adulterant to which I specially directed attention in the second lecture of this course. Wines that are beaded are injurious, owing to the foreign mixture for beading that has been added to them, and which I shall presently describe.

Some substances that form in natural wines exert an effect on the animal body when they are taken into it. These substances are principally aldehyde and acetic acid. Aldehyde when it is present in wine communicates to it a natural bouquet. You will find on the table a pure specimen of aldehyde, and you will also find specimens of natural wines, kindly lent to me by Mr. Denman, in which this change of alcohol by oxidation has taken place. In the year 1848 the late Sir James Simpson, of Edinburgh, discovered that aldehyde would produce anæsthetic sleep when its vapor was inhaled, and I have since submitted it to experiment with a view of testing its action on the living body. I find it is a rapidly intoxicating agent, sharp to the nerves of sense, and acting with greater rapidity than alcohol, and with a less prolonged effect, for it is soluble in water, and is so volatile that it boils at 72° Fahr. It is therefore quickly diffused and quickly eliminated from the body. The action of aldehyde upon the living body has been as yet insufficiently studied. It has a close relation to the narcotic action of alcohol, and the symptoms it produces are so similar I am inclined to believe that the narcotism which follows the administration of alcoholic spirit is partly due to its production.

The presence of acetic acid in wines is on the whole not injurious, if the wine in other respects be free of adulteration. The tendency of this acid itself is to promote the digestion of albuminous foods, and I have sometimes observed in persons whose digestive power is feeble, signs of improvement under its use. In saying this I do not however wish to convey that therefore a rough acid wine should be taken for indigestion, for the acid in such instances may be administered without the wine and perhaps with greater advantage. I only wish to record that acidity of wine, in which fermentation has ceased, is not a source of additional injury. The astringent acid—called tannic—of some wines has been advanced as useful in the cases of certain persons who suffer from laxity of body, and who require astringent remedies. It would be wrong to dispute that there may be in wine a virtue of this kind, but it is not peculiar to wine. It can be secured when it is wanted without wine at all, and in a more certain way,

This remark holds equally good in respect to what may be favorably spoken of as the saline substances which some wines naturally present. I mean to say that the saline constituents can be administered with more certain and therefore with better effect, independently of wine.

SPIRITS.

Into the different spirits commonly sold, several substances are introduced which exert more or less of baneful influence on the body that receives them. The addition of amylic alcohol has been already condemned and need not again be mentioned, and I omit intentionally, for the sake of brevity, a great number of other added substances which do not seem to me to be active for evil, though they were possibly better left out of the animal organism. After these are withdrawn there remain many other agents which cannot fairly be omitted from our consideration. There is oil of juniper, oil of bitter almonds, potassa, alum, nitric acid, oil of vitriol, or sulphuric acid, and butyric acid. In even small quantities every one of these agents is injurious to the body if it be taken for any long continued period of time. The oil of juniper is an active diuretic, and thereby is injurious to the excreting power of one of the most important of the vital organs. The oil of bitter almonds contains, unless it be specially purified, hydrocyanic or prussic acid, and exerts then in small and often-repeated quantities a prejudicial influence on the nervous functions. Potassa causes a dry and caustic action upon the mucous membrane of the mouth, throat, and stomach, for the production of which action it is actually added systematically, that it may give the peculiar sharpness called "biting the palate."

Alum is a powerful astringent, producing constipation, and sustaining a persistent dyspepsia so long as it is being swallowed. Nitric acid is an astringent, exerting also a physiological action on the liver. Sulphuric acid is an astringent; and butyric acid, as I found in an original research which I once conducted with it, causes a congested or inflammatory condition of the whole track of the mucous membrane.

Thus each one of these agents added to the alcoholic drinks increases the evils that are likely to arise from the alcohol itself. Let us admit that the added evils are small, nay, I had nearly said, infinitesimal, when considered by the measurement of one administration. But who can measure by that standard? When once the taste for any of these unnatural substances is acquired it grows by what it feeds on, and that which was infinitesimal at the beginning becomes after long continuance a serious charge for the body to bear daily.

The spirit in common use that is most subject to the chemicals I have named is gin. Gin has to be made cordial, to be sweetened, to be rendered creamy and smooth, to be flavored, to be made biting to the palate, to be beaded, and what not else. To be made "cordial" it must be charged with oil of juniper, with essence of angelica, with oil of bitter almonds, with oil of coriander, and with oil of carraway. To sweeten it, it must be treated with oil of vitriol, oil of almonds, oil of juniper, spirits of wine and loaf sugar; to "force down" the same it must be further treated with a solution of alum and carbonate of potassa. To be rendered creamy and smooth, it must be sweetened with sugar, and lightly charged with a small quantity of garlic, Canadian balsam, or Strasburg turpentine. To give it piquancy, it must have had digested in it shreds of horse-radish. To be made biting to the palate, it must receive that touch of caustic potash of which I have spoken.

As you see the habituated gin-drinker partaking of his favorite drink you observe, often, that he enjoys it the more if it be what he calls "pearly," or "beaded." He holds up the precious liquid in his glass, and as he sees the oily fluid roll down the side, as beads, leaving each a creamy train behind it, he rejoices in his treasure. It is *crême de la crême* of gin. Those wicked, pearly drops are, to his flushed eyes, the proofs of the purity and excellence of what he would probably tell you was, without mistake, the genuine article. The genuineness consists in the fact that our enthusiastic friend's gin has been beaded by the addition of the following artistic mixture:—An ounce of oil of sweet almonds has been added to an ounce of oil of vitriol. These have been rubbed together in a mortar with two ounces of loaf sugar until a paste has been formed. The paste has next been dissolved in spirit of wine until a thin liquid has been produced; and this, added to one hundred gallons of gin, has given the fine pearly bead that is so much admired.

Redding, in his history and description of modern wines, narrated in his day the many receipts that were openly published in the then existing publicans' guides and licensed victuallers' directories for the artificial manufacturing of wines, and for modifying spirituous liquors. I have gone for my information to a similar work of the present day, "The New Mixing and Reducing Book," which is, I understand, one of the handbooks of the retailer, the same to him as the pharmacopœia is to the druggist, and to be followed in all the varied arts as implicitly. I cannot leave this book without reading from it a quotation that bears directly on the health of the poorer classes, who indulge in gin.

"Gin, it may be observed, is of all the spirits ordinarily kept by a publican the one which, when cleverly managed, yields him the greatest and securest profit. The reason of this is that there is hardly any definite selling strength for gin, especially if it be sweetened. Within very wide limits no complaint is made by customers on the score of weakness, provided only the gin is creamy, palatable, and sharp tasted. But the slightest taint, or the slightest fault of color, or a sensible difference in the usual flavor, will lead to dissatisfaction and loss of custom. Strong or unsweetened gin is in comparatively little request, and then with few exceptions only amongst the respectable or monied classes. At least three-fourths of the spirits sold over the counter of a public house consists of a sweetened or made-up gin; and as the sugar greatly alters the character of the liquor and deadens the original strength, it is possible for the retailer to consult his own interests by a liberal addition of water without in any degree exciting the disapprobation, or injuring the health of those who patronise his establishment.

"As a tolerably safe general rule there will be no occasion to fear dissatisfaction when sweetened gin is not brought below 35 or even 40 per cent. U. P. It is then nearly five times as strong as old ale. Much more is thought of a pleasant warming aromatic taste or smack than of simple alcoholic strength. But as the most careful man may sometimes overshoot the mark in reducing, it is advisable to know how to restore the requisite degree of pungency and sharpness, without having recourse to the use of so expensive an agent as spirit of wine. Supposing, then, that by accident the strength of a parcel of gin has been lowered rather too far, a good and cheap remedy is the following: —For 100 gallons, 1 ounce of cassia, ½ ounce of chilies. Steep for a week in a pint of spirit of wine; then mix well with the gin."

The other spirituous liquors, rum, whisky, and brandy, are less falsified than gin. Rum is occasionally adulterated with an essential oil like butyrin and with butyric acid, these two substances being present in some natural rum, to which they give a special flavor. Whisky is modified by blending, so as to communicate qualities of smoothness and softness. The yellowish color given to whisky is produced by pouring the spirit into sherry casks.

or by stirring it up with the lees of wine. These refined whiskies are prepared for the rich and sumptuous; the poor, it is recommended, should be treated with the spirit they understand best; a sharp and potent drink, that will bring the tears into the eyes, and make the throat smart as it goes down.

Brandy, except when treated with fusel oil, is not, I believe, adulterated with any injurious compound. But it carries with it naturally a peculiar ether, which gives to it a special odor. This ether is very heavy when compared with ethylic ether. Its specific gravity is 862, taking water at 1,000, and its boiling point is 479° on Fahrenheit's scale. It is all but insoluble in water, to which, however, it communicates its peculiar odor. It exerts on the body an injurious influence; it causes nausea, thirst, and pain in the stomach. It seems also to arrest the due secretion of bile.

SECONDARY PHYSIOLOGICAL ACTION OF SIMPLE ALCOHOL.

I leave now the consideration of the evils arising from the action of the different extraneous substances that are present in alcoholic drinks to resume the study of the action of ethylic alcohol itself when it is free of any such combinations. I have to consider under this head the effect of the consumption of alcohol in its slow and progressive course, in what may be called its secondary manifestations of effect upon those who for long periods of their lives submit themselves to its influence.

I have shown that in the course of acute intoxication from this spirit there are four degrees or stages, each degree marked by different series of phenomena. In the secondary, or, technically speaking, chronic intoxication, from the same agent, there are in like manner four distinct degrees, each presenting distinct phenomena. A minority of persons who habitually take alcohol escape with impunity from injury. Some of these escape because they only subject themselves to it on a scale so moderate they can scarcely be said to be under its spell. If they take it regularly they never exceed an ounce to an ounce and a half of the pure spirit in the day; and if they indulge in a little more than this, it is only at recreative seasons, after which they atone for what they have done by a temporary total abstinence. Others take more freely than the above, but escape because they are physiologically constituted in such manner that they can rapidly eliminate the fluid from their bodies. These, if they are moderately prudent, may even go so far as to indulge in alcohol and yet suffer no material harm. But they are a limited few, if the term may be applied to them, who are thus privileged. The large majority of those who drink alcohol in any of its disguises are injured by it. As a cause of disease it gives origin to great populations of afflicted persons, many of whom suffer even to death without suspecting from what they suffer, and unsuspected. Some of these live just short of the first stage of natural old age; others to ripe middle age; others only to ripe adolescence.

DETERIORATION OF THE BODY UNDER THE FIRST DEGREE.

The first degree of the secondary action of alcohol is evidenced in those who by constant habit imbibe an alcoholic stimulant to the simple extent of producing arterial relaxation, and of setting the heart at liberty to perform an increased series of motive contractions. They do not, as a rule, receive what is commonly called an excess of any alcoholic drink, but they become trained to a sensation of want for it and to an appetite which, while all seems to go well, they have no desire to resist, though they may keep it within what they conceive are its due limits. Such persons confine their libations to four or six ounces of alcohol per day, a couple of glasses of sherry or of ale at luncheon, three or four glasses of wine at dinner, one or two at dessert, and a mixture of spirit and water before going to bed. Such is a common and a "temperate day," but reckoned up it means at least from four to six ounces of alcohol. The primary effect of such a quantity we know. Continued daily it induces a new physiological and altogether unnatural condition, in which the sense of acquired necessity enforces desire, until at last the spirit is made to became a positive requirement of the organic and the mental life. Every extra effort must be preceded by the resort to the stimulant. Every prolonged weariness must be relieved by the same measure; but when the effect of the stimulant has speedily subsided, there is left a greater exhaustion than before. Another resource to the artificia' aid completes the exhaustion, and makes it pass into dulness and drowsiness without natural and sound sleep, and with an unbearable sense of after prostration.

For many years, in the young and adolescent, this alcoholic life may be carried on without any evidence being rendered of the progress of physical deterioration. In the young the processes of assimilation, of secretion, and of excretion, are in their full activity, and the poisonous agent with which the blood and tissues are saturated is disposed of so readily and promptly, it does not stay long enough in contact with these parts to vitiate them. This is a very homely way of putting the fact, but it is scientifically true. The young, therefore, seem to escape, and I believe that up to the close of the first term of the natural life, that is to say, to the close of that period of full growth and development which extends to thirty years, they sometimes escape so successfully that if they could but stop in their course at that point they might go through the remaining terms of existence without any further important modification of function.

Unfortunately, it is the rarest of events that a person artificially stimulated by alcohol, to the period named, gives up the practice. The majority are utterly ignorant of the dangers that are ahead, and the sense of support to which they have been educated by the practice leads them on to pursue it with even a greater reliance upon it than before, and with a feeling of more urgent demand. In a word, the sensation that they cannot do without it, the sensation of lowness and depression when it is by any accident withheld, and the contrast of lightness and activity when it is regained, are so powerful, in their influences upon the mind, there is no resisting the belief of the absolute necessity.

But when the body is fully developed; when the extra vital capacity which attended youth is expended in growth and development; when all the organs have assumed their full size and activity; when the balance of secretion is so nicely set in all parts that not one secretion can be disturbed without a disturbance of the whole; when the spring of the elastic tissues is reduced; when the lungs cannot fail ever so little in their function of throwing off the gaseous products of combustion without a vicarious extrusion of gases into the alimentary canal; when the completed organic moving parts become encumbered with fatty matter interposed between them, or laid out around them; then the effect of alcoholic spirits begins to be realised. The fluid is now retained longer in the living house; is decomposed less quickly; is thrown out by primary or secondary elimination less speedily.

The action of alcohol under these new conditions, so favorable in every sense to the series of changes it is capable of effecting, is twofold. The action in the first place is purely mechanical. We are aware that it leads to temporary paralysis of the vessels of the minute circulation, and that upon this the heart responds with a quicker propelling stroke. Thus the vessels throughout the whole of the body are dilated, and are held in a state of unnatural relaxation and unnatural tension. Under this persistent pressure their diameters change in course of time, and the whole of the marvellous webwork of blood, upon which the organs of the body are constructed, is deranged, in its mechanical distribution, over its extended surface. During this time, too, the function of the heart becomes perverted. The heart is truly an automatic organ, but it is still an organ which feels none the less severely the effect of the stimulus. If it make to-day an unnatural number of one hundred and twenty-five thousand strokes, it cannot to-morrow sink back, from absence of its stimulus, to the normal one hundred thousand without evidencing some disturbance of action, some feebleness, some hesitation, or some palpitation. In fact, as it is an organ which by its own stroke feeds its own structure with blood, it is the first to suffer from irregular supplies of blood. Thus, under alcohol, the nutrition of the heart is mechanically modified. Whipped into undue work, it becomes like the muscles of the blacksmith's arm or the opera-dancer's leg, of undue size and power; and in proportion as this evil increases, the necessity for the stimulus it calls for grows more urgent.

In turn this extreme power and force of the heart tells upon the vessels that are fed by its impulsive stroke, and so all the organs that are constructed upon those vessels appreciate with abnormal sensitiveness the whip of the stimulus, and the languor when the whip is withheld.

Of itself this extreme sensitiveness of the heart is sufficiently momentous, but the ultimate results upon the body at large are perhaps more important than the pure local change that is instituted in that perfect and elaborate pulsating mechanism. The heart not only becomes enlarged, but its various valvular and other mechanical parts, subjected to prolonged strain, are thrown out of proportion. The orifices in it, through which the great floods of blood issue in their courses, are dilated. The exquisite valves become stretched, and prevented from assuming their refined adaptations. The minute filamentous cords which hold the valves in due position and tension are elongated, and the walls of the ventricles or forcing-chambers are thickened, or as we say, technically, are hypertrophied. Throughout the whole of its structures the central throbbing organ is modified both in its mechanism and in its action.

But such central modification cannot possibly go on long without the institution of other changes at the opposite extremity or circumference of the circuit of the blood. At one moment the vital organs feel the pressure of the too powerful stroke of blood; at another moment they are suddenly aware of an enfeebled stroke. The brain is, for the instant, conscious of a flicker of power: it is like the faintest flicker of gas, which is observed when, by an accident, the pressure is disturbed at the main, but it is there, and the person who experiences it is cognisant of its central origin. So matters progress often for months, or for years, without further evidence of subjective or objective sign of increasing evil. The worst evidence that exists is, probably, the necessity for a more frequent repetition of the stimulus under additional stress of work or excitement.

While these changes in the simple mechanism of the circulation are in course of advancement, there are also in development certain other changes which are much more delicate and minute, yet not less important. These consist of direct deteriorations of structure of the organic tissues themselves. We are, at the present time, only on the border-land of a new knowledge on this subject, and I myself am, in this matter, a mere outpost wandering wonderingly, and trying to observe what is going on, but as yet, though thus advanced, unprepared to speak with so much precision and fulness of detail as I would desire. The following explanation, simply spoken, illustrates the degenerative changes of organic structure from the continued use of alcohol.

Alcohol produces physical deterioration by destroying the integrity of the colloidal matter of which the tissues are composed. I have explained that all the organic parts are constructed out of colloidal substance; that every such part, including the blood-vessels, to their minutest ramifications, is composed of this colloid material arranged in different forms and plans to suit the design of the part, whether it be a tube, like an artery, a bundle of cross-cut fibres like a muscle, or a refracting globe like the crystalline lens of the eyeball. That these parts should be kept in their integrity, in the midst of their diversity, the ultimate structure of which they are composed must be held in proper measure of construction with water. Disturb the relationship that should exist between the colloid and its combining water, and the character of the colloid is at once changed. Take, for example, some colloidal albumen in the fluid state. Pour a little of it on to a glass plate as a thin watery film. Then spread over it a little finely powdered caustic soda, by which to remove and fix some of the water which previously held it as a liquid. The thin liquid is transformed into a transparent membrane which possesses elasticity. Into a porcelain cup pour a small quantity of the same solution, and then drop into the solution a bead of soda; soon you can lift the solution from the cup in a solid mass, shaped like a concavo-convex transparent lens. I could multiply these facts indefinitely, but I am anxious to indicate only one particular fact, viz., that alcohol and its derivative aldehyde possess also, by their affinity for water, the property of destroying the integrity of the colloidal form of matter. Thus they solidify, or render pectous the colloidal structures. Take a solution of albumen and add to it alcohol. The albumen is rendered thick or pectous. Take a solution of caseine; add to it aldehyde; the caseine is rendered thick or pectous.

Animal tissues subjected to alcohol can be perverted to any degree, and in the most diverse and apparently contradictory ways. I can hold blood permanently fluid with alcohol; I can solidify it with the same agent. I can reduce the size and modify the shape of the blood corpuscles, and I can so modify those fine and delicate animal membranes which dialyse or allow to pass through them the saline matter of the blood and secretions, that the process of dialysis shall be impeded, and that which should pass through shall be left in combination with the membrane. I can destroy the elasticity of the blood-vessels in the same way, for that depends upon the presence in them of a gelatinous colloid elasticity also called elasticin.

When, therefore, alcohol holds long-continued contact with the perfectly developed colloidal tissues, its action upon them to produce physical deterioration is simply inevitable, and from this cause arise those fatal lesions of local organs which mark the different phases and stages of alcoholic disease. The commencement of the change sometimes shows itself visibly on the surface of the body. The vessels of the face become permanently enlarged and suffused with blood. In cold weather, the blood circulating imperfectly through these vessels, and, not fully aërated, gives to the skin that dull leaden hue which is so characteristically significant of prolonged indulgence. In hot weather, the blood circulating more freely and purely, gives to the skin a red hue and often a deep red blotch, which is hardly less demonstrative.

In this stage of alcoholic disease eruptions upon the skin occur to declare the injurious action of the spirit upon the colloidal gelatinous textures. The epidermis or scarf-skin is imperfectly thrown off; it dies upon the surface, but owing to deficient vascular and nervous tone beneath, it is not replaced so quickly as is natural. Thus the dead *débris*, in form of scale and sometimes with fluid beneath, accumulates; the superficial nervous surface which should be protected by the newly formed epidermis is exposed, and irritation and pain follow as a consequence.

The evils, in the slighter stages of alcoholic disease, are often connected with others, which are perhaps passing, but which give rise to very unpleasant phenomena. There is what is called a dyspepsia or indigestion, to relieve which the sufferer too frequently resorts to the actual cause of it as the cure for it. There is thirst, there is uneasiness of the stomach, flatulency, and a set of so-called nervous phenomena, which keep the mind irritable, and make trifling cares and anxieties assume an exaggerated and unnatural character. From the earliest period in the history of the drinking of alcohol these phenomena have been observed. "Who," says Solomon, referring to this action, "Who hath woe? Who hath contentions? Who hath babbling? Who hath wounds without cause? Who hath redness of the eyes?"

What modern physiologist could define better the steady and progressive effect of alcohol upon those who, even under the guise of temperate men, trust to it as a support? And yet these evils are minor compared with certain I have to bring forward in the next and concluding lecture.

LECTURE VI.

PHYSICAL DETERIORATIONS FROM ALCOHOL (*continued*).—INFLUENCE OF ALCOHOL ON THE VITAL ORGANS.—MENTAL PHENOMENA INDUCED BY ITS USE.—SUMMARY.

Towards the close of my last lecture I touched on the effects of the continued action of alcohol upon the colloidal structures of the body, indicating that it is impossible for these structures to escape deterioration. I must dwell for a few moments longer on this subject.

The parts which first suffer most from alcohol are those expansions in the animal body which the anatomists call the membranes. The membranes are colloidal structures, and every organ is enveloped in them. The skin is a membranous envelope. Through the whole of the alimentary surface, from the lips downwards, and through the bronchial passages to their minutest ramifications, extends the mucous membrane. The lungs, the heart, the liver, the kidneys are folded in delicate membranes which can be stripped easily from these parts. If you take a portion of bone, you will find it easy to strip off from it a membranous sheath or covering; if you open and examine a joint you will find both the head and the socket lined with membrane.

The whole of the intestines are enveloped in fine membrane called *peritoneum*. All the muscles are enveloped in membranes, and the fasciculi or bundles and fibres of muscles have their membranous sheathing. The brain and spinal cord are enveloped in three membranes; one nearest to themselves, a pure vascular structure, a net-work of blood-vessels; another, a thin serous structure; a third, a strong fibrous structure. The eyeball is a structure of colloidal humors and membranes, and of nothing else. To complete the description, the minute structures of the vital organs are enrolled in membranous matter.

It was held by the old anatomists that this membranous arrangement of the body is mainly mechanical. The parts and organs, according to their view, are supported and held in position by these membranous sheaths and pouches and coverings. Doubtless this is a portion of their usefulness, for in fact they do hold all the structures together in the most perfect order. But this is only a small part of their duties. The membranes are the filters of the body. In their absence there could be no building of structure, no solidification of tissue, no organic mechanism. Passive themselves, they nevertheless separate all structures into their respective positions and adaptations.

The animal receives from the vegetable world and from the earth the food and drink it requires for its sustenance and motion. It receives colloidal food for its muscles; combustible food for its motion; water for the solution of its various parts; salt for constructive and other physical purposes.

These have all to be arranged in the body; and they are arranged by means of the membranous envelopes. Through these membranes nothing can pass that is not for the time in a state of aqueous solution like water or soluble salts. Water passes freely through them, salts pass freely through them, but the constructive matter of the active parts that is colloidal does not pass; it is retained in them until it is chemically decomposed into the soluble type of matter. When we take for our food a portion of animal flesh, it is first resolved, in digestion, into a soluble fluid before it can be absorbed; in the blood it is resolved into the fluid colloidal condition; in the solids it is laid down within the membranes into new structure, and when it has played its part it is digested again, if I may so say, into a crystalloidal soluble substance ready to be carried away and replaced by addition of new matter, then it is dialysed or passed through the membranes into the blood, and is disposed of in the excretions.

See then what an all-important part these membranous structures play in the animal life. Upon their integrity all the silent work of the building up of the body depends. If these membranes are rendered too porous, and let out the colloidal fluids of the blood—the albumen for example—the body so circumstanced dies; dies as if it were slowly bled to death. If, on the contrary, they become condensed or thickened, or loaded with foreign material, then they fail to allow the natural fluids to pass through them. They fail to dialyse, and the result is, either an accumulation of the fluid in a closed cavity, or contraction of the substance enclosed within the membrane, or dryness of membrane in surfaces that ought to be freely lubricated and kept apart. In old age we see the effects of modification of membrane naturally induced; we see the fixed joint, the shrunken and feeble muscle, the dimmed eye, the deaf ear, the enfeebled nervous function.

It may possibly seem at first sight that I am leading immediately away from the subject of the secondary action of alcohol. It is not so. I am leading directly to it. Upon all these membranous structures alcohol exerts a direct perversion of action. It produces in them a thickening, a shrinking, and an inactivity that reduces their functional power. That they may work rapidly and equally they require to be at all times charged with water to saturation. If into contact with them any agent is brought that deprives them of water, then is their work interfered with; they cease to separate the saline constituents properly, and, if the evil that is thus started be allowed to continue, they contract upon their contained matter in whatever organ it may be situated, and condense it.

In brief, under the prolonged influence of alcohol those changes which take place from it in the blood corpuscles, and which have already been described, extend to the other organic parts, involving them in structural deteriorations, which are always dangerous, and are often ultimately fatal.

PRIMARY EFFECTS ON VITAL FUNCTIONS.

I remarked in my last lecture that the slow or

chronic effect of alcoholic drink upon the body was to induce a series of stages analogous in all respects, except in period of duration, to the process of acute poisoning by the same agent. In the first prolonged stage there occur phenomena of disease which are as characteristic of the agency, when it is known, as they are deceptive when the agency is not known.

The ultimate changes that follow the use of alcohol by those who indulge in it, in what is too often considered a temperate degree, are actual local changes within one or other of the vital organs. But before such actual deterioration obtains there are usually other phenomena transitory in character yet unequivocal. I pointed out certain of these in the last lecture, but I did not specify them all.

In addition to that irritation of mind and suffering "of wounds without cause," to which I then drew attention, an extreme emotional derangement is often produced. The afflicted man—and I fear I must say woman also, for women are sometimes afflicted—the afflicted man under this primary prolonged influence of alcohol becomes nervous and excitable, ready at any moment to cry or to laugh, without valid reasons for either act. The emotional centres are alternately raised and depressed in function by the poison, but after a time the depression overcomes the exhilaration, and the impulse is to a maudlin sentimentality extending even to tears. The slightest anxieties are then exaggerated, and there is experienced at the same time an indecision and deficiency of self-confidence which is doubly perplexing. When an act is done when a letter, for instance, or other piece of business has been finished and despatched, an uneasy feeling of distrust is felt that perhaps some mistake has been made, which distrust passes rapidly into a sentiment that the thing cannot be helped; it is bad luck, but it must take its chance. In various other directions this distrust shows itself, and the worst of all is, that the very doubt prompts the desire for another application for relief to the evil that is the cause of the burthen. A small dram more of the stimulant, not an overpowering draught that will cause quick and sure insensibility, but just a mouthful, that is the assumed remedy, and that is the certain promoter of the sorrow.

We know now, as surely as if we could see within the body, what is the condition of the organs of the person afflicted in the manner thus defined. We are conscious that the vessels of the brain, of the lungs, of the liver, of the kidneys, of the stomach are paralysed, and are injected to full distention with blood. Some of these parts have actually been seen under this state, and the fact of the red injected condition directly demonstrated.

Alcoholic Dyspepsia.

Of all the systems of organs that suffer under this sustained excitement and paralysis, two are injured most determinately, viz., the digestive and the nervous. The stomach, unable to produce in proper quantity the natural digestive fluid, and also unable to absorb the food which it may imperfectly digest, is in constant anxiety and irritation. It is oppressed with the sense of nausea; it is oppressed with the sense of emptiness and prostration; it is oppressed with a sense of distention; it is oppressed with a loathing for food, and it is teased with a craving for more drink. Thus there is engendered a permanent disorder which, for politeness' sake, is called dyspepsia, and for which different remedies are often sought but never found. Antibilious pills—whatever they may mean—Seidlitz powders, effervescing waters, and all that pharmacopœia of aids to further indigestion, in which the afflicted who nurse their own diseases so liberally and innocently indulge, are tried in vain. I do not strain a syllable when I state that the worst forms of confirmed indigestion originate in the practice that is here explained. By this practice all the functions are vitiated, the skin at one moment is flushed and perspiring, at the next is pale, cold, and clammy, and every other secreting structure is equally disarranged.

Nervous Derangements.

The nervous structures follow, or it may be precede, the stomach in the order of derangement. We have not yet traced out with sufficient care the conditions of the centres of the organic chain of nerves, but we know that they are reduced in power; and, in regard to those higher and reasoning centres, the brain and its subsidiary parts, the spinal cord and voluntary nerves, we are aware that they are supplied with blood through vessels weakened, and in a condition either of undue tension or undue relaxation. Moreover, the delicate membranes which envelope and immediately sur-round the nervous cords are acted upon more readily by the alcohol than the coarser membranous textures of other parts, and thus a combined arrangement of evils affects the nervous matter. The perverted condition of the nervous centres gives rise to many striking phenomena, extending from them to the nervous cords and to the organs of sense. The irregular supply of blood to the retina causes temporary disturbances of vision, with appearances before the eyes of those specks and small rounded semi-transparent discs, which are called by the learned *muscæ volitantes*. From the imperfect tension of the arteries, the blood which rushes through them causes their dilatation, and in the bony canals of the skull an impingement is made upon the bony structure. Vibrations which extend to the neighboring organs of hearing are thus produced, giving rise to sounds of a murmuring, ringing, or humming character, according to the modification of the arterial tension.

The perverted condition of the membranous covering of the nerves gives rise to pressure within the sheath of the nerve, and to pain as a consequence. To the pain thus excited the term neuralgia is commonly applied, or tic; or if the large nerve running down the thigh be the seat of the pain, "sciatica." Sometimes this pain is developed as a tooth-ache. It is pain commencing in nearly every instance at some point where a nerve is enclosed in a bony cavity, or where pressure is easily excited, as at the lower jawbone near the centre of the chin, or at the opening in front of the lower part of the ear, or at the opening over the eyeball in the frontal bone.

Alcoholic Insomnia or Sleeplessness.

Lastly on this head, the perverted state of the vessels of the brain itself, the unnatural tension to which they are subjected from the stroke of the heart they are now so incompetent to resist, sets up in the end one telling, and of all I have yet named, most serious phenomenon; I mean *insomnia*—inability to partake of natural sleep. There is a theory held by some physiologists that sleep is induced by the natural contraction of the minute vessels of the brain, and by the extrusion, through that contraction, of the blood from the brain. I am myself inclined, for reasons I need not wait to specify now, to consider this theory incorrect; but it is nevertheless true that during natural sleep the brain is receiving a reduced supply of blood; that when the vessels are filled with blood without extreme distention, the brain remains awake, and that when the vessels are engorged and over-distended, there is induced an insensibility which is not natural sleep, but which partakes of the nature of apoplexy. This sleep is attended with long and embarrassed breathing, blowing expirations, deep snoring inspirations, and uneasy movements of the body, even with convulsive motions. From such sleep the apparent sleeper awakes unrefreshed and unready for the labors of the day. The effect of alcohol then on the brain is to maintain the relaxation of vessels, to keep the brain charged with blood, and so to hold back the natural repose. Under this form of divergence from the natural life, the sleepless man lies struggling with unruly and unconnected trains of thought. He tries to force sleep by suppressing with a great effort all thought, but in an instant wakes again. At last the more he tries the less he succeeds, until the morning dawns. By that long time the spirit that kept his cerebral vessels disabled and his heart in wild unrest having become eliminated, he is set free, and the coveted sleep follows. Or perhaps, wearied of waiting for the normal results, he rises, and with an additional dose of the great disturber, or with some other tempting narcotic drug of kindred nature, such as chloral, he so intensifies the vascular paralysis as to plunge himself into the oblivion of congestion, with those attendant apoplectic phenomena, which he himself hears not, but which, to those who do hear, are alarming in what they forebode, when their full meaning is appreciated. Connected with this sleep there is engendered in some persons a form of true epilepsy, which all the skill of physic is hopeless to cure, until the cause is revealed and removed.

And now I think I have said everything that I have time to say respecting the general phenomena incident to this primary stage of slow alcoholic intoxication in those who, in the world's eye, as well as in their own, are temperate individuals—individuals who enjoy the choice things of this life heartily; who understand a glass of wine, and who can take a good many glasses—or a good many little "goes" of spirit if that be all

—but who are never known by friend or foe to be worse for anything they take; who grow mellow as an apple under the mellowing cheer, but never fall, nor lose their power of taking less guarded companions safely home.

ORGANIC DETERIORATIONS.

The continuance of the effects of alcohol into a more advanced stage leads to direct disorganisation of vital structures. When once this stage has been reached not one organ of the body escapes the ravage. According to the build or the hereditary construction of the individual, however, or according sometimes to what may be considered as a local accident, some particular organ undergoes a change which gives a specific character to the whole of the phenomena that are afterwards presented. We then say of the person in whom such change occurs that he is afflicted with such a particular disease, letting the general sink into the local manifestation. Many purely local modifications of structures and parts are in this manner induced in the blood, in the minute structure of the moving organs—the muscles, in the fixed vital organs, such as the brain, the lungs, the liver, the heart, the kidneys. In the blood the influence is exerted upon the plastic fibrine and upon the corpuscles; in the brain, on the membranes at first, and afterwards on the nervous matter they enclose; in the lungs, on the elastic, spongy, connective tissue, which is, strictly speaking, also membranous; in the heart, on its muscular elements and membranes; in the liver, primarily on its membranes;

in the kidneys, on their connective tissues and membranes.

SPECIAL STRUCTURAL DETERIORATIONS.

The organ of the body that perhaps the most frequently undergoes structural changes from alcohol is the *liver*. The capacity of this organ for holding active substances in its cellular parts is one of its marked physiological distinctions. In instances of poisoning by arsenic, antimony, strychnine, and other poisonous compounds, we turn to the liver, in conducting our analyses, as if it were the central depôt of the foreign matter. It is, practically, the same in respect of alcohol. The liver of the confirmed alcoholic is probably never free from the influence of the poison; it is too often saturated with it.

The effect of the alcohol upon the liver is upon the minute membranous or capsular structure of the organ, upon which it acts to prevent the proper dialysis and free secretion. The organ at first becomes large from the distention of its vessels, the surcharge of fluid matter and the thickening of tissue. After a time there follow contraction of membrane, and slow shrinking of the whole mass of the organ in its cellular parts. Then the shrunken, hardened, roughened mass is said to be "hobnailed," a common but expressive term. By the time this change occurs, the body of him in whom it is developed is usually dropsical in its lower parts, owing to the obstruction offered to the returning blood by the veins, and his fate is sealed.

Now and then, in the progress to this extreme

change and deterioration of tissue, there are intermediate changes. From the blood, rendered preternaturally fluid by the alcohol, there may transude, through the investing membrane, plastic matter which may remain, interfering with natural function, if not creating active mischief. Again, under an increase of fatty substance in the body, the structure of the liver may be charged with fatty cells, and undergo what is technically designated fatty degeneration. I touch with the lightest hand upon these deteriorations, and I omit many others. My object is gained if I but impress you with the serious nature of the changes that, in this one organ alone, follow an excessive use of alcohol.

In the course of the early stages of deterioration of function of the liver from organic change of structure, another phenomenon, leading speedily to a fatal termination, is sometimes induced. This new malady is called diabetes, and consists in the formation in enormous quantity within the body of glucose or grape sugar, which substance has to be eliminated by dialysis, through the kidneys—often a fatal elimination. The injury causing this disease through the action of alcohol may possibly be traced back to an influence upon the nervous matter; but the appearance of the phenomenon is coincident with the derangement of the liver, and I therefore refer to it in this place.

The *kidney*, in like manner with the liver, suffers deterioration of structure from the continued influence of alcoholic spirit. Its minute structure undergoes fatty modifications; its vessels lose their due elasticity and power of contraction; or its membranes permit to pass through them that colloidal part of the blood which is known as albumen. This last condition reached, the body loses power as if it were being gradually drained even of its blood. For this colloidal albumen is the primitively dissolved fluid out of which all the other tissues are, by dialytical processes, to be elaborated. In its natural destination it has to pass into and constitute every colloidal part.

The *lungs* do not escape the evil influence that follows the persistent use of alcohol. They, indeed, probably suffer more than we at present know from the acute evils imposed by this agent. The vessels of the lungs are easily relaxed by alcohol; and as they, of all parts, are most exposed to vicissitudes of heat and cold, they are readily congested when, paralysed by the spirit, they are subjected to the effects of a sudden fall of atmospheric temperature. Thus, the suddenly fatal congestions of lungs which so easily befall the confirmed alcoholic during severe winter seasons.

Alcoholic Phthisis; or, The Consumption of Drunkards.

There are yet other and more prolonged, and more certainly fatal mischiefs induced in the lungs by the persistent resort to alcohol; and to one of these I would direct special attention. It is that deterioration of lung tissue to which, in the year 1864, I gave originally the name of *alcoholic phthisis*, or the *consumption of drunkards*. The facts were elicited at first in this manner. In a public hospital to which I acted as physician, I had brought before me, in the course of many years, two thou-

Alcoholic Phthisis. 163

sand persons who were stricken with consumption. I gathered the history of the lives of these, and of the reasons why they had passed into the all but hopeless malady from which they suffered. In my analysis of these histories I found that the leading causes of the malady were, in the great majority of instances, predisposition from hereditary taint; exposure to impure air; want; or certain other allied causes. But the analysis being conducted rigidly, I discovered that, when every individual instance had been classified as due to the causes stated above, there remained thirty-six persons, or nearly two per cent., who were excluded from them, who appeared to suffer purely from the effects of alcohol, and in whom the consumption had been brought into existence by the use of alcohol.

The added observations of eleven years, since the above named fact was recorded in the *Social Science Review*, as a new fact in the history of the disease, have only served to prove, in the minds of other men as well as my own, the truth of the record.

The persons who succumb to this deterioration of structure induced by alcohol are not the exceedingly young, neither are they the old. They are usually over twenty-eight and under fifty-five. The average age may be taken as forty-eight. They are persons of whom it is never expected that their death will be from consumption; and they are generally males. They are probably considered very healthy;—men who can endure anything, sit up late at night, run the extreme of amusements, and yet get through a large amount of business. They sleep well, eat pretty well, and drink very well. They are often men of excellent build of body, and of active minds and habits. They are not a class of drinkers of strong drinks who sleep long, take little exercise, and grow heavy, waxy, pale—

"Sleek-headed men and such as sleep o' nights."

On the contrary, they take moderate rest, and see as much as they can. Neither in the ordinary sense are they drunkards: they may never have been intoxicated in the whole course of their lives; but they partake freely of any and every alcoholic drink that comes in their way, and they bear alcohol with a tolerance that is remarkable to observers. They are hard drinkers as distinguished from sots. Beer is to them as water, wine is weak; the only thing that upsets them is stiff grog in relays, or a mixture of spirituous drinks carried to the extent of what they call, in grim joke—in which death surely joins—"piling the agony."

As a rule these cannot live in what they consider to be comfort without a daily excess of alcohol, which excess must needs be renewed on emergencies, if there be greater amount of work to be done, less sleep to be secured, or more life to be lived.

As specimens of animal build these persons are often models of organic symmetry and power. In fact they resist the enemy they court for so long a time because of the perfection of their organisation. More than half of those whom I have seen stricken down with alcoholic phthisis have said that they had never had a day's illness in their lives before; but questioned closely it was found that none of them had actually been quite well. Some of them had suffered from gout; others from rheumatism or neuralgia. They had felt severely any depression such as that which arises from a cold, and if they had been subjected suddenly to causes of excitement or exhaustion, they had detected, without actually realising its full meaning, that their balance of power against weakness was reduced, that the end of the beam called strength was rising, and that an extra quantity of alcohol was required to bring back equilibrium. As a rule men of this class are thoughtless of their own health and their own prospects, for they have an abundant original store of energy. They are designated as "happy-go-lucky" men, or as men who "always fall on their feet," which truly they do, but not without injury.

The countenance of the alcoholic consumptive differs from that which is usually considered the countenance of the consumptive person, and equally from that which all the world adjudges as belonging to the man who indulges freely in strong drink. Who does not remember the wan, pale, sunken cheek of the youth on whom ordinary consumption has set its mark? And who, again, does not recall the *facies alcoholica*—the blotched skin, the purple-red nose, the dull, protruding eye, the vacant stare of the confirmed sot? The alcoholic consumptive has none of these characteristics. His face is the best part of him in all his history. When his muscles have lost their power, and his clothes hang loosely on his shrunken limbs, he is still of fair proportion in the face; he has little pallor, and he is expressive in feature, so that his friends are apt to be deceived and to believe that there must be hope for his recovery, even when he is beyond every hope. I remember being actually taken aback on one occasion on finding, in a man who seemed, from his face, to be in perfect health, complete destruction of his lungs from the encroachments of disease; and I cannot be surprised, therefore, that others, less informed, should share in such an imperception of danger when it is close at hand. Nobody, in a word, "pities the looks" of these sufferers, and good eyes are necessary to learn that pity is called for.

The phenomena are not always developed at a time when the sufferer from them is indulging most freely in alcohol. On the contrary, it is by no means uncommon that the habit of excessive indulgence has been stopped for some time previously to their development. The reasons assigned by the patients for abstinence vary. One man may have been strongly advised by his friends to desist, or may himself have undergone a certain measure of reform; another has been led by the reading or hearing of arguments on temperance; a third, by want of means to obtain the indulgence; but by far the larger number tell you that a time came when the desire for so much drink did not occur to them. They will state that they tried the round of the various spirits, but found that none agreed with them as before, so that at last they were driven to rely on beer as the only drink they cared for. We read all this off clearly enough from a physiological point of view. We see that, in fact, the body has been resisting the alcohol; that it could not do away with it as it did when all the excreting organs were in their full prime; and that those drinks only can be borne in which the amount of alcohol is least. But the sufferer does not comprehend the fact, and therefore he not unfrequently concludes that his increasing languor and debility are due to the necessary withdrawal of the stimulus on which he seems to have been actually feeding during the greater part of his life.

The signs which first indicate failure of health are usually those of acute pleurisy. There is pain in the side, quick, sharp, starting. The term "stitch" in the side is commonly applied to this pain, and is expressive enough. After a time the pain becomes continuous, and when it subsides, suppressed breathing, or difficulty of filling the chest, is at once felt and recognised. This difficulty is due to the circumstance that a portion of lung has become adherent to the inner surface of the chest. The next sign indicating that the disease (consumption) is present, is, usually, vomiting of blood. In two-thirds of the examples to which my attention has been directed this has been the sign that has first caused serious alarm, and it is commonly on such event that the physician is called in, who examines the chest with the stethoscope, and finds too often a condition that is hopeless. From the appearance of that sign all is—down, down, down towards the grave.

There is no form of consumption so fatal as that

from alcohol. Medicines affect the disease very little, the most judicious diet fails, and change of air accomplishes but slight real good. The sick man with this consumption may linger longer on the highway to dissolution than does his younger companion, but there is this difference between them, that the younger companion may possibly find a by-path to comparative health, while the other never leaves it, but struggles on straight to the fatal end. In plain terms, there is no remedy whatever for alcoholic phthisis. It may be delayed in its course, but it is never cured, and not unfrequently instead of being delayed it runs on to a final termination more rapidly than is common in any other type of the disorder.

The origin of this series of changes from alcohol is again from the membranes. The course of it is through the membranous tissues. The vessels give way after a severe congestive condition, and blood is exuded, or extravasated into the lung. These conditions lead to the destruction of the substance of the pulmonary organs, upon which, and upon the organic changes that follow such destruction, the acute symptoms of the malady under consideration, become quickly and fatally pronounced.

Alcoholic Disease of the Heart.

The heart, not less than the rest of the vital parts, is subjected to deterioration of structure from alcohol. We need not wonder at this when we recall the strain to which it is subjected by the agent, the excess of work it is made to perform. I touched on the mechanical evils that befall the heart from these circumstances in my last lecture, and the structural evils which I have now to specify are not less grave. The membranous structures which envelope and line the organ are changed in quality, are thickened, rendered cartilaginous, and even calcareous or bony. Then the valves, which are made up of folds of membrane, lose their suppleness, and what is called valvular disease is permanently established. The coats of the great blood-vessel leading from the heart, the aorta, share, not unfrequently, in the same changes of structure, so that the vessel loses its elasticity and its power to feed the heart by the recoil from its distention, after the heart, by its stroke, has filled it with blood.

Again, the muscular structure of the heart fails, owing to degenerative changes in its tissue. The elements of the muscular fibre are replaced by fatty cells; or if not so replaced are themselves transferred into a modified muscular texture in which the power of contraction is greatly reduced.

Those who suffer from these organic deteriorations of the central and governing organ of the circulation of the blood learn the fact so insidiously, it hardly breaks upon them until the mischief is far advanced. They are, for years, conscious of a central failure of power from slight causes, such as over-exertion, trouble, broken rest, or too long abstinence from food. They feel what they call a "sinking," but they know that wine or some other stimulant will at once relieve the sensation. Thus they seek to relieve it until at last they discover that the remedy fails. The jaded, over-worked, faithful heart will bear no more; it has run its course, and, the governor of the blood stream broken, the current either overflows into the tissues, gradually damming up the courses, or under some slight shock or excess of motion ceases at the centre.

Other Organic Changes.

In the eyeball certain colloidal changes take place from the influence of alcohol, the extent of which have as yet been hardly thought of, certainly not in any degree studied, as in future they will be. We have learned of late years that the crystalline lens, the great refracting medium of the eyeball, may, like other colloids, be rendered dense and opaque, by processes which disturb the relationship of the colloidal substance and its water. By this means even the lens of the living eye can be rendered opaque, and the disease called cataract can be artificially produced. Sugar and many salts in excess, in the blood, will lead to this perversion of structure, and after a long time alcohol acting in the manner of salt is capable, in excess, of causing the same modification of the eyeball. Moreover, alcohol injures the delicate nervous expanse upon which the image of all objects we look at is first impressed. It interferes with the vascular supply of this surface, and it leads to changes of structure which are indirectly destructive to the perfect sense of sight.

In yet another mode alcohol perverts the animal

mechanism. By some as yet obscurely definable interference with the natural transmutation of the colloidal substances into saline or crystalloidal, it gives rise to the production of an excess of some salines which appear in the fluid renal secretion. These saline matters accumulated in the blood from inability of the excreting organs to dispose of them, are directly injurious, and exist as possible causes for the promotion of cataractous changes in the crystalline lens and of varied changes in other of the colloidal tissues and membranes. They are also the cause of a disease local in character produced by the aggregation of the saline products, particle by particle, into a compact mass like a stone, or to what is technically called *calculus*. In writing the history of one of the districts of England in which this disease is very prevalent, I expressed many years ago the view that alcoholic indulgence was one of the most telling agencies in the production of the malady. I have seen nothing since that would lead me to alter that statement.

Organic Nervous Lesions from Alcohol.

Lastly, the brain and spinal cord, and all the nervous matter become, under the influence of alcohol, subject, like other parts, to organic deterioration. The membranes enveloping the nervous substance undergo thickening; the blood-vessels are subjected to change of structure, by which their resistance and resiliency is impaired; and the true nervous matter is sometimes modified, by softening or shrinking of its texture, by degeneration of its cellular structure, or by interposition of fatty particles.

These deteriorations of cerebral and spinal matter give rise to a series of derangements, which show themselves in the worst forms of nervous disease—epilepsy; paralysis, local or general; insanity.

But not a single serious nervous lesion from alcohol appears without its warning. As a man who, when drinking at the table, is warned, by certain unmistakable indications, that the wine is beginning to take decisive effect on his power of expression and motion, so the slow alcoholic is duly apprised that he is in danger of a more permanent derangement. He is occasionally conscious of a failing power of speech; in writing or speaking he loses common words. He is aware that after fatigue his limbs are unnaturally weary and heavy, and he is specially conscious that a sudden fall of temperature lowers too readily his vital energies. The worst sign of impending nervous change is muscular instability, irrespective of the will; that is to say, an involuntary muscular movement whenever the will is off guard. This is occasionally evidenced by sudden muscular starts which pass almost like electrical shocks through the whole of the body; but it is more frequently and determinately shown in persistent muscular movements and starts at the time of going to sleep. The volition then is resigned to the overpowering slumber, and naturally all muscular movement, except the movement of the heart and of the breathing, should rest with the will. But now this beautiful order is disturbed. In the motor centres of the nervous organisation the foreign agent is creating disturbance of function. The fact is communicated to the muscles by the nervous fibres, and the active involuntary start of the lower limbs rouses the sleeper in alarm. Ignorant of the import of these messages of danger, the habituated alcoholic continues too frequently his way, until he finds the agitated limbs unsteady, wanting in power of co-ordinated movement—paralysed.

Deeply interesting as these phenomena from alcohol are, I must leave them here, omitting many others equally significant and equally plain, when they are once pointed out, even to the unprofessional mind. Let it be understood that in each description I have recorded only what alcohol can physically do to the animal economy. It is not always the cause of all or any of these phenomena. They may be induced by other influences and other agents, but it is an agency capable of effecting them, and it is actively employed in the work.

ON SOME OF THE MENTAL PHENOMENA INDUCED BY ALCOHOL.

The purely physical action of alcohol has been so far treated upon in the preceding pages. To that must now be added a few sentences on the influence this agent exerts over the mental functions. Of course such influence is actually manifested by and through physical means, but as yet these are not sufficiently clear to enable us to trace out the mental aberration through the physical process that has led to it. It is better therefore and simpler to treat the present subject in the mere abstract, passing from the agent to its results, without reference to the intermediate line of connection between cause and effect. These mental phenomena in the chronic phase, correspond to the phenomena which belong to the second and third stages of acute alcoholic intoxication.

Loss of Memory or Speech.

One of the first effects of alcohol upon the nervous system in the way of alienation from the natural mental state, is shown in loss of memory.

This extends even to forgetfulness of the commonest of things; to names of familiar persons, to dates, to duties of daily life. Strangely too, this failure, like that which indicates, in the aged, the era of second childishness and mere oblivion, does not extend to the things of the past, but is confined to events that are passing. On old memories the mind retains its power; on new ones it requires constant prompting and sustainment.

If this failure of mental power progress, it is followed usually with loss of volitional power. The muscles remain ready to act, but the mind is incapable of stirring them into action. The speech fails at first, not because the mechanism of speech is deficient, but because the cerebral power is insufficient to call it forth to action. The man is reduced to the condition of the dumb animal. Aristotle says, grandly, animals have a voice; man speaks. In this case the voice remains, the speech is lost; the man sinks to the lower spheres of the living creation, over which he was born to rule.

The failure of speech indicates the descent still deeper to that condition of general paralysis in which all the higher faculties of mind and will are powerless, and in which nothing remains to show the continuance of life except the parts that remain under the dominion of the chain of organic or vegetable nervous matter. Our asylums for the insane are charged with these helpless specimens of humanity. The membranes of the nervous centres of thought and volition have lost, in these, the dialysing function. In some instances, though less frequently than might be supposed, the nervous matter itself is modified, visibly, in texture. The result is the complete wreck of the nervous mechanism, the utter helplessness of will, the absolute dependence upon other hands for the very food that has to be borne to the mouth. The picture is one of breathing death; of final and perpetual **dead intoxication.**

Dipsomania.

A second effect of alcohol on the mental organisation is the production of that craving for its incessant supply to which we give the name of dipsomania. In those who are affected with this form of alcoholic disease, a mixed madness and insanity is established, in which the cunning of the mind alone lives actively, with the vices that ally themselves to it. The arrest of nervous function is partial, and does not extend to the motor centres so determinately as to those of the higher reasoning faculties. But the end, though it may be slow, is certain, and the end is, as a rule, that general paralysis which I have just described. The dipsomaniac is, however, capable of recovery, within certain limits, on one and only one condition, that the cause of his disease be totally withheld.

Mania a Potu.

The effect of alcohol on the mental functions is shown in yet another picture of modern humanity writhing under its use. I mean in the form of what may be called intermittent indulgence to dangerous excess. This form of disease has been named the *mania a potu*, and it is one of the most desperate of the alcoholic evils. The victims of this class are not habitual drunkards or topers, but at sudden intervals they madden themselves with the spirit; they repent; reform; get a new lease of life; relapse. In intervals of repentance they are worn with remorse and regret; in the intervals of madness they are the terrible members of the community. In their furious excitement they spread around their circle the darkness of desolation, fear, and despair. Their very footsteps carry dread to those who, most helpless and innocent, are under their fearful control. They strike their dearest friends; they strike themselves. Retaining sufficient nervous power to wield their limbs, yet not sufficient to guide their reason, they become the dangerous alcoholic criminals whom our legislators, fearing to touch the cause of their malady, would fain try to cure by scourge and chain.

To us physiologists these "maniacs a potu" are men under the experiment of alcohol, with certain of their brain centres (which I could fairly define if the present occasion were befitting) paralysed, and with a broken balance, therefore, of brain power, which we, with infinite labor and much exactitude, have learned to understand. Our remedy for such aberration of nervous function, if we were legislators, would be simple enough. We should not whip the maniac back again to the drink; we should try to break up the evil by taking the drink from the maniac. But then we are only physiologists. We have nothing to do with that £117,000,000 of invested capital, and we are not practical in reference to it.

TRANSMITTED DISEASE.

The most solemn fact of all bearing upon these mental aberrations produced by alcohol, and upon the physical not less than the mental, is, that the mischief inflicted on man by his own act and deed cannot fail to be transferred to those who descend from him, and who are thus irresponsibly afflicted. Amongst the many inscrutable designs of nature none is more manifest than this, that physical vice, like physical feature and physical virtue, descends in line. It is, I say, a solemn reflection for every man and every woman, that whatever we do to ourselves so as to modify our own physical conformation and mental type, for good or for evil, is transmitted to generations that have yet to be.

Not one of the transmitted wrongs, physical or mental, is more certainly passed on to those yet unborn than the wrongs which are inflicted by alcohol. We, therefore, who live to reform the present age in this respect, are stretching forth our powers to the next; to purify it, to beautify it, and to lead it toward that millennial happiness and blessedness, which, in the fulness of time, shall visit even the earth, making it, under an increasing light of knowledge, a garden of human delight, a Paradise regained.

SUMMARY.

In summary of what has past, I may be briefness itself.

This chemical substance, alcohol, an artificial product devised by man for his purposes, and in many things that lie outside his organism a useful substance, is neither a food nor a drink suitable for his natural demands. Its application as an agent that shall enter the living organization is properly limited by the learning and skill possessed by the physician—a learning that itself admits of being recast and revised in many important details, and perhaps in principles.

If this agent do really for the moment cheer the weary and impart a flush of transient pleasure to the unwearied who crave for mirth, its influence (doubtful even in these modest and moderate degrees) is an infinitesimal advantage, by the side of an infinity of evil for which there is no compensation, and no human cure.

APPENDIX.

I. REFERENCES TO TABLES.

TABLE I.

NAMES OF ANCIENT ROMAN WINES.

1	4	6
Falernum	Vetus	Cnidum
Massicum	Novum	Adrium
Setinum	Recens	
Surrentinum	Hornum	7
	Trimum	
2	Molle	Mustum
Chium	Lene	Protropum
Lesbium	Vetustate edentulum	Mulsum
Leucadium	Asperum	Sapa
Naxium	Calenum	Defrutum
Mamertinum	Cœcubum	Carenum
Thasium	Albanum	
Mœnium	Merum	8
Mareoticum	Fortius	Passum
		Passum creticum
3	5	
Album	Coum	9
Nigrum	Rhodium	
Rubrum	Myndian	Murrhina
	Halicarnassum	

TABLE II.

WINES OF ITALY.

Vesuvius.

Vino Greco
Mangiaguerra
Verracia
Vino Vergine

Tuscany.

Florence (white and red)
Monte Pulciano
Montalneo
Porte Hercole

Lombardy.

Modenese
Montserrat
Marcemino
Brescian
Veronese
Placentine
Lumelline
Pucine

Naples.

Campania or Pausilippo
Muscatel
Surentine
Salernitan
Chiarello
Carcassone
Lachryma Christi
Aibano
Montefiascone

Nomentan
Monteran
Velitrin
Prœnetic
Il Romanesca
D'Orvieto

Sicilian, Sardinian, and Corsican.

Catanean
Panormitan
Messinian
Syracusan

Genoa.

Vino di Monte Vernaccia
Vino Tinto
Madeira

WINES OF MADEIRA AND CANARIES ISLANDS.

Madeira Sec
Canary or Palm Sec

WINES OF FRANCE AND SWITZERLAND.

Languedoc
Picardy
Champagne
Burgundy
Vino Amabile, or **Vino di Cinque Terre**
Vino Razzese
Muscadine

TABLE II.—*Continued.*

Rosatz
Vino Piccante

WINES OF GERMANY.

Tyrolese Tramin
Etsch
Wine of Worms
Edinghof
Ambach
Rhenish
Mayne
Moselle
Neckar
Elsass
Hock
Bohemian
Silesian
Thuringian
Misnian
Naumberg
Brandenburg

WINES OF AUSTRIA AND HUNGARY.

Klosterneuberg
Brosenberg

Edenburg
Tokay

WINES OF SPAIN AND PORTUGAL.

Aland
Alicant
Sherry (or Xeres)
Spanish Malmsey
Tarragan
Salamanca
Malaga
Cordova
Galicia
Andalusia
Vino de Toro
Spanish
Vin de Beaune (or Partridge eye)
Cote Roti
St. Laurence
Frontiniac
Muscat de Lion
Cahors
Hermitage
Grave
Vin d'Haye

Neufchatel
Velteline
Lacote
Reiff

TABLE III.

TABLE OF THE CONTENTS OF DIFFERENT WINES IN A QUART OF EACH.

	Highly Rectified Spirit.			Thick, Unctuous Resinous Matter.			Gummy and Tartareous Matter.			Water.			
	oz.	dr.	gr.	oz.	dr.	gr.	oz.	dr.	gr.	lbs.	oz.	dr.	gr.
Aland	1	6	0	3	2	0	1	5	0	2	5	3	0
Alicant	3	6	0	6	0	20	0	1	40	2	2	6	0
Burgundy . . .	2	2	0	0	4	0	0	1	40	2	9	0	20
Carcassone . . .	2	6	0	0	4	10	0	1	20	2	8	4	30
Champagne . .	2	5	20	0	6	40	0	1	0	2	8	3	0
French	3	0	0	0	6	40	0	1	0	2	8	0	20
Frontignac . . .	3	0	0	3	4	0	0	5	20	2	4	6	30
Vin Grave . . .	2	0	0	0	6	0	0	2	0	2	9	0	0
Hermitage . . .	2	7	0	1	2	0	0	1	40	2	7	5	20
Madeira	2	3	0	3	2	0	2	0	0	2	4	3	0
Malmsey . . .	4	0	0	4	3	0	2	3	0	2	1	2	0
Vino di Monte Pulciano . .	2	6	0	0	3	0	0	2	40	2	3	0	20
Moselle	2	2	0	0	4	20	0	1	30	2	9	0	10
Muscadine . . .	3	0	0	2	4	0	1	0	0	2	5	4	0
Neufchatel . . .	3	2	0	4	0	0	1	7	0	2	2	7	0
Palm Sec . . .	2	3	0	2	4	0	4	4	0	2	2	5	0
Pontack	2	0	0	0	5	20	0	2	20	2	9	0	40
Old Rhenish . .	2	0	0	1	0	0	0	2	20	2	8	5	40
Rhenish	2	2	0	0	3	20	0	1	34	2	9	1	6
Salamanca . . .	3	0	0	3	4	0	2	0	0	2	3	4	0
Sherry	3	0	0	6	0	0	2	2	0	2	0	6	0
Spanish	1	2	0	2	4	0	9	4	0	2	10	5	0
Vino Tinto . . .	3	0	0	6	4	0	1	6	0	2	0	6	0
Tokay	2	2	0	4	3	0	5	0	0	2	0	3	0
Tyrol Red Wine .	1	4	0	1	2	0	0	4	0	2	8	6	0
Red Wine . . .	1	6	0	0	4	40	0	2	0	2	9	3	20
White	2	0	0	0	7	0	0	3	0	2	7	0	0

TABLE IV.

LIST OF SUBSTANCES THAT WILL PRODUCE ANÆSTHETIC SLEEP.

Nitrous oxide gas
Carbonic oxide gas
Carbonic acid gas
Bisulphide of carbon
Light carburetted hydrogen (hydride of methyl or marsh gas)
Methylic alcohol
Methylic ether gas
Chloride of methyl gas
Bichloride of methylene
Terchloride of formyl, or chloroform
Tetra-chloride of carbon
Heavy carburetted hydrogen gas (olefiant gas or ethylene)
Ethylic or absolute ether
Chloride of ethyl
Bichloride of ethylene (Dutch liquid)
Bromide of ethyl, or hydrobromic ether
Hydride of amyl
Amylene
Benzol
Turpentine spirit

TABLE V.

ALCOHOLS.

	Elementary Composition.
Methylic or Protylic (wood spirit)	C H_3 HO
Ethylic or Deutylic (common alcohol)	C_2 H_6 HO
Propylic or Trilylic	C_3 H_7 HO
Butylic or Tetrylic	C_4 H_9 HO
Amylic or Pentylic (potato spirit, fusel oil)	C_5 H_{11} HO
Hexylic	C_6 H_{13} HO
Heptylic or Œnanthic	C_7 H_{15} HO
Octylic	C_8 H_{17} HO
Decatylic	C_{10} H_{21} HO
Cetylic	C_{16} H_{33} HO
Melylic	C_{30} H_{61} HO

TABLE VI.

RADICALS OF ALCOHOLS.

Composition.	Old name.	New name.
$C\ H_3$	Methyl	Protylen.
$C_2\ H_5$	Ethyl	Deutylen.
$C_3\ H_7$	Propyl	Tritylen.
$C_4\ H_9$	Butyl	Tetrylen.
$C_5\ H_{11}$	Amyl	Pentylen.
$C_6\ H_{13}$	Hexyl	Hexylen.
$C_7\ H_{15}$	Heptyl	Heptylen.
$C_8\ H_{17}$	Octyl	Octylen.
$C_{10}\ H_{21}$	Decatyl	—
$C_{16}\ H_{33}$	Cetyl	—
$C_{30}\ H_{61}$	Melyl	—

TABLE VII.

ALCOHOLS.

Name.		Chemical composition.	Vapor density. $H_2=1$.	Specific gravity. Water 1000.	Boiling point.	
Old.	New.				Cen.	Fah.
Methylic	Protylic	$C\ H_4\ O$	16	814 at 0″ C	60	140
Ethylic	Deutylic	$C_2\ H_6\ O$	23	792 "	78	172
Butylic	Tetrylic	$C_4\ H_{10}\ O$	37	803 "	110	230
Amylic	Pentylic	$C_5\ H_{12}\ O$	44	811 "	132	270

TABLE VIII.

Alcohols.	Aldehydes.	Acids.
Mythylic $C\ H_4\ O$	Formaldehyde . $C\ H_2\ O$	Formic . $C\ H_2\ O_2$
Ethylic . $C_2\ H_6\ O$	Aldehyde . . . $C_2\ H_4\ O$	Acetic . $C_2\ H_4\ O_2$
Propylic $C_3\ H_8\ O$	Propionaldehyde $C_3\ H_6\ O$	Proponic $C_3\ H_6\ O_2$
Butylic . $C_4\ H_{10}\ O$	Butylaldehyde . $C_4\ H_8\ O$	Butyric . $C_4\ H_8\ O_2$
Amylic . $C_5\ H_{12}\ O$	Valeraldehyde . $C_5\ H_{10}O$	Valerianic $C_5\ H_{10}O_2$

TABLE IX.

ETHERS.

Name.	Composition.	Form.	Boiling point.
Methyl Ether	$C_2\ H_6\ O$	Gas	..
Ethyl "	$C_4\ H_{10}\ O$	Fluid	94° Fah.
Propyl "	$C_6\ H_{14}\ O$	"	153° Fah.
Butyl "	$C_8\ H_{18}\ O$	"	219° Fah.
Amyl "	$C_{10}\ H_{22}\ O$	"	348° Fah.

TABLE X.

CHLORIDES.

Name.		Chemical composition.	Vapor density. $H_2 = 1.$	Specific gravity. Water 1000.	Boiling point.	
Old.	New.				Cen.	Fah.
Methyl .	Protyl .	$C\ H_3\ Cl$	25	Gas	..	..
Ethyl .	Deutyl .	$C_2\ H_5\ Cl$	32	921 at 0" C.	11	52
Butyl .	Tetryl .	$C_4\ H_9\ Cl$	46	880 "	70	158
Amyl .	Pentyl .	$C_5\ H_{11}\ Cl$	53	..	102	216

TABLE XI.

IODIDES.

Name.		Chemical composition.	Vapor density.	Specific gravity.	Boiling point.		Per cent of Iodine.
Old.	New.		$H_2 = 1.$	Water 1000.	Cen.	Fah.	
Methyl	Protyl	$C\ H_3\ I$	71	2240	42	108	89.4
Ethyl	Deutyl	$C_2\ H_5\ I$	78	1946	72	162	81.4
Butyl	Tetryl	$C_4\ H_9\ I$	92	1604	120	248	69.0
Amyl	Pentyl	$C_5\ H_{11}\ I$	99	1511	146	295	64.1

TABLE XII.

NITRITES.

Name.		Chemical composition.	Vapor density.	Specific gravity.	Boiling point.	
Old.	New.		$H_2 = 1.$	Water 1000.	Cen.	Fah.
Methyl.	Protyl.	$C\ H_3\ N\ O_2$	30	..	..	..
Ethyl.	Deutyl.	$C_2\ H_5\ N\ O_2$	37	0.917	18	64
Butyl.	Tetryl.	$C_4\ H_9\ N\ O_2$	51	..	64	147
Amyl.	Pentyl.	$C_5\ H_{11}\ N\ O_2$	58	0.877	96	205

II. REFERENCES TO WORDS AND DERIVATIONS.

While the delivery of these Lectures was in progress, I received from John F Stanford, Esq., M.A., F.R.S., a philological scholar, whose dictionary of Anglicised foreign words and phrases will, it is to be hoped, soon appear—many very useful and interesting notes relating to derivations of words and terms respecting alcohol. By his kind permission I add a few of his notes in this place.

Alcohol.—The best Arabic scholars write the word Al-Kool, though there is no word in Arabic which corresponds to the meaning assigned to it in the English language.

Aqua Vitæ.—This word, Mr. Stanford reminds me, is used by Shakspeare.

(*Nurse.*) "Give me some aqua vitæ."—*Romeo and Juliet*, Act. iii. sc. 2.

"I would as soon trust an Irishman with my aqua vitæ bottle."—*Merry Wives of Windsor.*

Aqua vitæ was, Mr. Stanford believes, made before any other spirit, viz., about 1260 A.D., by the monks of Ireland, who got the secret from Spain, the Spaniards having got it from the Moors, and the Moors (Arabs) from the Chinese. Whisky, he thinks, was possibly the oldest term applied to aqua vitæ. The etymon is usige-biatha, which in Erse means aqua vitæ, corrupted afterwards to usquebaugh. This compound term shared the fate of many other words, and was abbreviated to *usige*, whence whisky.

Arrac.—Hindustane for an alcohol, distilled from palm-tree juice and several other juices: it is the aqua vitæ of the East. The word is corrupted to Raki in Russia, Turkey, and Germany, or sometimes to Râkk. The intoxicating liquor made from the juice of the palm-tree is called in India and Ceylon Toddee, whence the Scotch term "Toddy." There is a coarse Arrac called Pariah Arrac, very generally consumed throughout India, which is rendered narcotic by addition of extract of Indian hemp. The importation of Arrac or Rack was regulated by 11 Geo. I. c. 30. It was imported to make punch, so called Rack punch.

Gin.—This term Mr. Stanford traces from French

ginévre, abbreviated from the Italian *ginepro*, Latin *juniperus*, English *juniper*, the berries of the juniper being used in the distillation of the spirit as a flavoring substance.

Gin-sing.—This is the term used by the Chinese for the famous Mandrake narcotic reputed to be worth its weight in gold for medicinal purposes, and at the head of their pharmacopœia.

Metheglin.—Was the name of a fermented honey-drink of Cornwall, an intoxicating narcotic beverage.

Potheen or Poteen—Irish, Poitin.—A small pot or still, the name of the liquor being derived from the still in which it was made. Poitin is probably from the Latin *potio*, a drink.

Rum.—Mr. Stanford believes the word "rum" to be an abbreviation, by aphæresis, of sacca-rum, not an original native name.

Normal School.

THE
ACTION OF ALCOHOL
ON
THE BODY.

THE ACTION OF ALCOHOL

ON

THE BODY.*

BY BENJAMIN W. RICHARDSON, M.D., F.R.S.

SUPPOSE it were possible for every one in this large assemblage to say with all truthfulness, while recasting the experiences of life: "I know of one particular agent or thing which has directly killed one person whom I knew. The human being thus slain had the slaying agent under his own absolute control. He need not have touched it unless he had willed so to do, and he would never have felt any want for it if he had not been trained to feel the want!"

Suppose this audience, as an English audience merely, were enlarged until it included all who might fairly form an audience capable, by experience and years and capacity of mind, to make a correct statement on what they had clearly and definitely seen. Suppose every one of them could say: "I, too, know that the same agent has killed one person who lived in my circle of acquaintance, so that taking us all in combination in the span of our lives, which may fairly be included in thirty years, the fatal effects of the said agent have been witnessed by ten millions of observers!"

Suppose we could listen to a foreign voice speak-

---

* An Address delivered in the Sheldonian Theatre, at Oxford, at the request of the CHURCH OF ENGLAND TEMPERANCE ASSOCIATION.

ing to us from across the Atlantic, and could hear it declare on the authority of an official census return: "For the last ten years this one agent has imposed upon the nation (the United States) a direct expense of $600,000,000; an indirect expense of $600,000,000; has destroyed 300,000 lives; has sent 100,000 children to the poorhouses; has committed at least 150,000 people into prisons and workhouses; has made at least 1,000 insane; has determined at least 2,000 suicides; has caused the loss by fire or violence of $10,000,000 worth of property; has made 200,000 widows and 1,000,000 orphans!"

Suppose, returning to our own country, we were to discover that among those unhappy persons who fill our asylums for the insane, two out of three were brought there owing to the direct or indirect effects of this destroyer. That amongst the paralyzed who sit or lie there day after day, until inevitable death takes them away—all of them already in the shroud of a living death, toneless, speechless, helpless, existing only by their mere vegetative part—that nine-tenths of these are brought to the condition in which we see them by the direct or indirect effects of this one destroyer.

Suppose we entered the cells of our prisons, and amongst those we met wearing out their lives in solitude, shame, and misery, so that the noblest of all that is human, *work*, sank the victims into a sense of deeper degradation; and suppose as we stood that we heard the voice of the most scientific scholar who ever graced the judicial bench of England since the days of the illustrious Chancellor Bacon, saying, as the voice of Mr. Justice Grove lately said, that the most potent influence for securing these incarcerations, and for placing the miserables before us in such terrible position, was this same agent.

Suppose we could at the present moment see before us, passing in sad panoramic display, some of the broken-heartedness of this still unhappy country. Tortured women, undergoing torture, or listening with palpitating hearts, and with their children scared and hidden away, waiting for the dreaded footsteps of him whose faintest sound ought to be the joy of their expectant lives. Could we see all the weeping mothers and fathers hoping against hope for the reformation of their children; mourning a loss that the grave even will relieve—loss to truth, honor, self-respect, affection, duty, honesty, every virtue on which parents find new life in their offspring. Suppose, seeing these things in their unutterable vastness, we could say they are the work of the one and the same destroyer!

Suppose we could, day by day, keep under our observation for one year the thousand depots in which this agent is stored up, and from which it is dispensed in million potions a day to smite and to slay young and middle-aged and old, rich and poor, deluder and deluded, polluted and polluting. Could we watch the inroads of death into each of those centers of distributing death,' and discover that out of them the marauder tore 138 to 100 of his other victims elsewhere, and seeing this fact could recognize that death, more than just, acted on the sellers through the things sold!

Suppose we took into our consideration the reckoning that the capital which is invested in this destroyer represents in the British Islands alone the sum of £117,000,000 sterling. That the duties paid in one year amount at least to £30,000,000 of money; that each tax-payer who has an income of £500 a year is assessed £31 toward this imposition, whether he avail himself or not of the means to injure himself by the cause of the imposition!

Suppose we knew of two classes of people who were seeking, in forestallment of calamity to their families, to insure their lives, and that the distinction into classes lay simply in one matter:—That a certain Class (B) habitually subjected itself, and a certain Class (C) did never subject itself, to this particular substance. Suppose it were found in respect to these applicants that Class B showed a mortality of 7 per cent. below the calculated average of life, and Class C a mortality of 26 per cent. below that average; that from bonuses, or returns from amount of premium paid, Class B received 34 per cent., Class C 53 per cent.; that dealers in the particular agent under review were hardly admissible even into Class B, and that their vocation added a mortality of two out of three compared with the vocations of Class C!

Suppose, in passing through our hospitals for the cure of the sick, the physician in attendance were to name all the forms of disease there, and were to say, as he might most honestly, these names, very different in kind, and seeming to denote very different maladies—gout, paralysis, albuminuria, apoplexy, delirium tremens, enfeebled heart, eczema, epilepsy, consumption (in one phase of that disease at least), liver disease or cirrhosis, dropsy—to say nothing of other maladies under dispute as to their origin; these names do truly but indicate various forms of disease originating in one agency to which these afflicted have been directly or indirectly subjected!

Suppose it were possible, after this general survey, to be able to cast up the sum of misery represented in such varying disguises, and to prove that they are all the work of one common enemy of mankind, should we not hesitate, almost in fear, fear which familiarity itself would not utterly conquer, as we ask ourselves: Is it really true? Is there such an enemy, such a power, such a *bona fide* devil in our midst?

The facts must stand for themselves in all their terrible reality. There is such a devil, though he is not in polite language called so. He assumes various names. The learned—owing to his infinite subtlety, a subtlety as refined as the impalpable powder with which ancient ladies of the East dressed their hair—call him *alcohol*. The unlearned call him *beer*. The savages call him *fire-water*. The rollicking scholars call him *wine*. The slangsters call him *B. and S.*, or *cocktail*, or *gin-sling*. Gentler lips, that ought to know less of him and more of botany, sometimes call him *cherries*. We will call him to-day, because of his subtlety, and because, after all, the term defines him best for our purpose, *alcohol*.

In this audience it is unnecessary to go over again, with proofs in hand, the details of the charges I have made against this subtile agent.

He has been arraigned for them over and over again; he has been proved guilty of them all over and over again. Yet hath he always escaped scot-free, and continued his marauding, kept together his retinue, and defied his enemies. He has paid his servants in their own coin and his own, making them obey, killing them as they obeyed, and, stretching out his empire over their graves, has imprinted his brand on the offspring they have raised, whether the offspring approved or loathed the badge of his service.

WHY THE ENEMY EXISTS.

The startling question hereupon faces us—Why is this subtile enemy thus allowed to go free? He is not recently discovered as a new enemy. Not at all! Solomon detected him, and the good race of preachers who take their lead from that wise man have continued his denunciation. The Esculapians from the first have detected him, and, with a few fluctuating periods of complacency or dalliance, have run him down. The law-makers have denounced him in all ages.

And yet he lives!

There are two reasons why this enemy survives and flourishes, which reasons are personal to man. I mean by this that they belong to man individually, according to his likings and beliefs. These are primary or direct reasons because personal. There are other reasons which have sprung out of the personal, and have slipped into the rule of what is called political necessity. These are indirect reasons, and they rest exclusively on the direct.

They hold, therefore, notwithstanding their immense practical importance, a second place. They would speedily be set aside so soon as the first came under the control of the majority of the nation. They may even now be brought under correction with a view to the removal of the errors they sustain.

I am aware that many of those who are most earnest in the cause of Temperance, look to the removal of the primary reasons, by which alcohol retains its place, as the grand remedy; and certain it is that until those primary reasons are removed, the greatest reform in legislative action can be but of slight and temporary service. It seems, however, to me, that sufficient has already been done in the way of influencing the education of the people toward the truth, to enable the Legislature, backed by the large and increasing constituency which holds to Temperance, to begin to invent some practical measure which shall put suppression of the common enemy under certain forms of legal recognition, so that the moral reformer may have a clear course, instead of being impeded, as he is at this time, by the protection which the law systematically extends to the evil he would root up.

I will return to this topic again, at a later stage of my discourse. Let me recur now to the two primary reasons by which the use of alcohol, with all its attendant calamities, is sustained.

AN INBRED ENEMY.

There is an old proverb which says that "What is bred in the bone will never come out of the flesh." The proverb is not quite correct anatomically. It should have said, "What is bred in the brain will never come out of the flesh." Even then it would be imperfect, physiologically, and should read, "What is bred in the brain will never come out of the flesh in one generation." The proverb, with all its faults, is impressive and expressive. It tells correctly enough that those sins which are engrafted into men are not readily eradicated. In this question of alcohol and the errors of life and taste depending upon it, the saying is signally correct. In communities which take wine as a general custom, there exists a system of breeding the custom, which is not dispelled in one, nor completely in two, generations. This is a peculiarity of the action of alcohol on the nervous organization, or on that essence of nervous organization subtler than the mere nerve-matter into which the impressions are instilled, that the impression it makes remains, and is transmitted, like feature, and taste, and disease, from the parent to the child. Of the nature of the inscrutable design, by which attributes and faculties, evil as good and good as evil, pass from the born to the unborn, I pretend to know nothing beyond the fact. But to me it always seems, as I think it must to you, one of the most solemn passages of human knowledge. To know that even in this world we none of us ever die. That our acts, our virtues, our failures, our physical conditions, appetites, passions, pass on to other generations. That the forms we mould ourselves to by acts original to ourselves, pass on to other generations. That habits and passions we subdue in ourselves are subdued, as far as we are concerned, in other generations that spring from us.

Therefore, in relation to the influence of this destroying agent, alcohol, one of the primary reasons for its continued use is that the desire, or appetite, or passion, for it has been transmitted to us by our predecessors. If there were no such foundation of appetite and passion for it, any one of the arguments against it to which I have adverted were sufficient to destroy its potency. With such foundation all the arguments, and as many more equally cogent, were of no direct avail with the masses that are influenced.

Happily, the virtues are transmitted not less readily than the errors of mankind; and so in considering this primary cause of the continued power of the destroyer we are not driven as men without hope to doubt our efforts for the destruction of the power. Our efforts, in every instance where they succeed in the present, are multiplied so many times into the future, that a generation or two will plant a new order, and make what is to us the most difficult portion of our labor the easiest part of the future emancipation.

In every effort it is always best to look the gravest difficulty first in the face; and I put this difficulty in view at once, that all may see and detect for themselves the mode of removing it. Detect that its removal is certain, and some day rapid, if the course of reformation be steadfastly pursued: detect also that patience is necessary, and that time spent is not time lost, but is time employed, in the most useful way, for securing the harvest of good results, the success that will assuredly follow.

FALSE BELIEFS.

The second primary cause for the continued power of alcohol in the world is falseness of belief as to the effect of the agent upon the body and the bodily powers. From the hilarity produced by wine, and which was originally conceived to be its only virtue, to "make glad the heart," there has crept into the habits of men the desire to be made hilarious at every meal. From this desire has come the practice of introducing wine or other spirituous drinks at certain meals regularly; and from this, again, by association of wine and its allies with food, has come the idea that the hilarity-provoking stimulant is also a food.

To this view Science herself, in opposition to common-sense experience, gave, some years ago, her sanction. It was a sanction slowly rendered, and never perfectly rendered. It was a sanction founded on the analogy of physical action of alcohol outside the body, its property of preserving from putrefaction, and its burning, rather than on any correct observation as to its true physiological action on living animal organisms. But there is no denying that the sanction was given, and that it has inflicted, for a time, an incomparable wrong. It has given a reason for the habitual use of alcohol which is, I repeat, a primary reason. It suggests not only that alcohol is a food, but that it is a necessary food. A food man can not do without. A sustaining food, which in this overworked day is more requisite than ever.

A few persons, whose eyes are opened to the

fallacy of this reasoning, use it notwithstanding, because in their hearts they are infatuated with the liking for alcohol, and are glad to find any excuse that shall minister to their own inclinations. The majority of persons whose eyes are not opened to the truth, believe in this reasoning absolutely, and act upon it with implicit honesty. These often tell you with perfect candor they regret as much as can be regretted the evils they can not fail to recognize; but, say they, of what use is it deploring evils that spring from a necessity? I have never yet met with a legislator who declined to legislate against alcohol who did not express as the reason for his action this theory of necessity. I have never yet conversed with a member of my own learned profession, who was in favor of alcohol, who did not assign the self-same argument. I have never yet spoken with a clergyman on that side of the question who did not follow the politician and the doctor, and adduce not only their reason, but their authority.

It is the duty of us who have seen the true light on the question of temperance to deal plainly and faithfully with the reasoning on this point of necessity. That false doctrine eradicated, the power of alcohol for all its evil is undermined. That left in doubt, the power of alcohol to continue all its evils remains practically untouched. I believe, therefore, that from the position I now, by your favor, occupy, I can not do better than tackle this reasoning again on scientific evidence: and on the ground that—

"Truth can never be confirmed enough,
Though doubt should ever sleep,"—

venture in a few sentences to repeat what I have spoken on many public occasions on this vital matter.

ORIGINAL RESEARCHES ON THE ACTION OF ALCOHOL.

In so speaking, I can not, I think, do better or simpler than narrate the individual method of inquiry by which, in an independent way, I was brought, without being able to avoid the result, to the conclusion I submit to you, viz., that the popular prevailing idea that alcohol, as a food, is a necessity for man has no basis whatever from a scientific point of view.

Let me say, that at the commencement of the labors which brought me to the conclusion above stated, I had no basis in favor of or preconceived opinion respecting alcohol.

Like many other men of science, I had been too careless or too oblivious of those magnificent labors which the advocates of temperance for its own sake had, for many previous years, through good report and evil report, so nobly and truthfully carried out. But for what may be called one of the accidents of a scientific career, I might indeed, to the end of my days, have continued negative on this question.

The circumstance that led me to the special study of alcohol is simply told. In the year 1863 I directed the attention of the British Association for the Advancement of Science, during its meeting at Newcastle, to the action of a chemical substance called nitrite of amyl, the physiological properties of which I had for some months previously been subjecting to investigation. My researches attracted so much attention, that I was desired by the physiological section of the Association, over which Professor Rolleston most ably presided, to continue them, and, in the end, I was enabled to place in the hands of the physician one of the most useful and remarkable medicinal agents that has ever been supplied by the chemist for the relief of human suffering. The success of this research led the Association to entrust me with further labors, and in the course of pursuing them, other chemical substances, nearly allied to that from which I started, came under observation. Amongst these was the well-known chemical product which the Arabian chemist, Albucasis, is said first to have distilled from wine, which on account of its subtlety was called alcohol, which is now called ethylic alcohol, and which forms the stimulating part of all wines, spirits, beers, and other ordinary intoxicating drinks.

In my hands this common alcohol, and other bodies of the same group, viz., methylic, propylic, butylic, and amylic alcohols, were tested purely from the physiological point of view. They were tested exclusively as chemical substances apart from any question as to their general use and employment, and free from all bias, for or against their influence on mankind for good or for evil.

The method of research that was pursued was the same that had been followed in respect to nitrite of amyl, chloroform, ether, amylene, and other chemical bodies, and it was in the following order: First, the mode in which living bodies would take up or absorb the substance was considered This settled, the quantity necessary to produce a decided physiological change was ascertained, and was estimated in relation to the weight of the living body on which the observation was made. After these facts were ascertained the special action of the agent was investigated on the blood, on the motion of the heart, on the respiration, on the minute circulation of the blood, on the digestive organs, on the secreting and excreting organs, on the nervous system and brain, on the animal temperature, and on the muscular activity. By these processes of inquiry, each specially carried out, I was enabled to test fairly the action of the different chemical agents that came before me.

In the case of alcohol, tried by these tests, I found then a definite order of facts, the principal of which I may narrate. It was discovered that alcohol, being a substance very soluble in water, would enter the body by every absorbing surface: by the skin, by the stomach, by the blood, and by the inhalation of its vapor in the lungs. But so greedy is it for water that it must first be diluted before it can be freely absorbed. If it be not so diluted it will seize the water from the tissues to which it is applied, and will harden and coagulate them. In this way it may even be made to coagulate the blood itself, and in some instances of rapid poisoning by it, the death has occurred from the coagulation of blood within the vessels, or in the heart.

The quantity required for absorption in order to produce distinct effects is from twenty to thirty grains of the fluid to the pound weight of the animal body, in those who have not become habituated to the influence of it. In quantities that can be tolerated it affects the blood, making that fluid unduly thin or coagulating it, according to the amount of it that is carried into the circulating system. It acts on the blood-corpuscles, causing them to undergo modifications of shape and size, and reducing their power of absorbing oxygen from the air. It changes the natural action of the heart, causing the heart to beat with undue rapidity and increasing the action, in extreme instances, to such a degree that the organ in an adult man is driven to the performance of an excess of work equal to the labor of lifting over twenty-four tons weight one foot in twenty-four hours. In some instances the number of extra strokes of the heart produced by alcohol has reached 25,000 in the twenty-four hours. The effect on the respiration follows that on the heart, and is correspondingly deranged.

On the minute blood-vessels, those vessels which form the terminals of the arteries and in which the vital acts of nutrition and production of animal heat and force are carried on, alcohol produces a paralyzing effect in the same manner as does the nitrite of amyl. Hence the flush of the face and hands which we observe in those who have partaken freely of wine. This flush extends to all parts, to the brain, to the lungs, to the digestive organs. Carried to its full extent it becomes a congestion, and in those who are long habituated to excess of alcohol the permanency of the congestion is seen in the discolored, blotched skin, and, too often, in the disorganization which is planted in the vital organs, the lungs, the liver, the kidney, the brain.

On the digestive system alcohol acts differently according to the degree in which it is used. In small quantities it excites the mucous membrane of the stomach so as to increase the secretion of gastric juice, and from that circumstance some think it assists digestion. In larger quantities it impairs the secretion and weakens digestion, producing flatulency and distension of the stomach. On the liver, if the action of the spirit be at all excessive, the influence is bad. Organic change of the structure of the liver is very easily induced. The same is true in respect to the action of the agent on the kidney.

On the nervous system alcohol exerts a double action. There are two nervous systems in man and in the higher animals, viz., the vegetative or mere animal nervous system, and the cerebral and spinal nervous system which receives the pictures of the external universe, and is the seat of the functions of reason and of the supremer mental faculties. On both these systems, vegetative and reasoning, alcohol produces diverse actions, all of which are perverse to the natural. At first it paralyzes those nervous fibers of the organic or vegetative system which control the minute vessels of the circulation. By this means a larger supply of blood is driven by the heart into the nervous centers, and nervous action from them is first excited, afterward blunted; the brain is in a glow, and that stage of mental exhilaration which is considered the cheering and exciting stage of wine-drinking is experienced. After a time, if the action progresses, the opposite condition obtains; the function of the higher mental centers is depressed, the mere animal centers remain uncontrolled masters of the intellectual man, and the man sinks into the lower animal in everything but shape of material body. In the lower animals a state of actual madness accompanies this stage, and in man, sometimes, the same terrible condition is also witnessed.

Not only are the brain and nervous centers thus paralyzed, the other vital organs of the body which have their fine, minute vascular structures governed by the nervous current, the lungs, the brain, the liver, the kidney, the lining or mucous surface of the digestive system, the various serous surfaces of the body, are also through their weakened vessels surcharged with blood. They are congested as the skin is when the body of the drinker is flushed with wine; or, to use another *simile*, as the surface of the body is after the vessels, long stricken by cold, are relaxing and glowing red under the application of heat.

In this manner, by the course of experiment, I learned, step by step, that the true action of alcohol, in a physiological point of view, is to create paralysis of nervous power. It acts precisely as I had seen nitrite of amyl and some other chemical bodies act.

Previously to the performance of these researches, some distinguished physiologists had shown that mechanical division of the nervous cords which govern the vascular supply of special parts of the body leads to flushing those parts with blood. I traced, a little later, that the local paralyzing action of extreme cold was practically the same process, and was therefore followed by the same effects. And now in these inquiries into the influence of chemical agents, I discovered an exact analogy, nay, I may say, in all but the method, an identity of principle. If we could temporarily divide with the knife all the nervous supplies of the vascular structures of the body, we should temporarily produce the same conditions as are produced by such diffusive escaping agencies as nitrite of amyl or alcohol. We should set the heart at liberty to work against reduced resistance; we should see the vessels of the skin and other parts intensely injected with blood; and, if we repeated the process many times, we should witness structural changes of parts, organic disease, structural diseases; such changes as are produced in those who suffer from excess of alcohol during long periods of time.

In brief, my experimental inquiries led me to discern, without original intention of such discernment, that the power for which alcohol is esteemed, its power as an agent to liberate the heart, to excite the nervous centers and influence the passions, to afterward congest the centers and dull the passions, to make men violent and mad, then imbecile and palsied, is, all through, one power in various stages of development and degree: a power not exercised for the elevation, but for the reduction of all the functions of life.

Pursuing still the plan I had set forth for the general method of investigating the action of chemi cal substances on animal bodies, I was led to study the influence of alcohol on the animal temperature. The prevailing view on this subject had been that alcohol increases and maintains the animal temperature. This view, it is true, had been challenged. Dr. Aitken had challenged it many years ago in the first volume of the Literary and Philosophical Society of Manchester. The illustrious Beddoes had challenged it. The late Dr. Cheyne, of Dublin, had challenged it. Dr. Carpenter, Dr. Lees, and some others whose prescience had been far more acute than mine, had challenged it. In perfect candor, the inference had been drawn by many observers that alcohol reduces the animal temperature; that those who are exposed to extremes of cold are best fortified against cold when they abstain from alcohol and depend on warm unintoxicating drinks; and that the popular idea on the subject was wrong. At the same time, it is certain that the impressions of these eminent scientists were not so confirmed by direct and absolute experimental research as to satisfy the world in general of their correctness. For my own part, I was ignorant, and that is why I sought for certain knowledge. To the research I devoted three years, from 1863 to 1866, modifying experiments in every conceivable way, taking advantage of seasons and varying temperatures of season, extending observation from one class of animal to another, and making comparative researches with other bodies of the alcohol series than the ethylic or common alcohol.

The results, I confess, were as surprising to me as to any one else. They were surprising from their definitiveness and their uniformi y. They were most surprising from the complete contradiction they gave to the popular idea that alcohol is a supporter and sustainer of the animal temperature.

It will be borne in mind that I have described a flush from alcohol as the first effect of it in its first stage, when into the paralyzed vessels the larger volume of blood is poured. In that stage, that is to say in the earlier part of it, I found an increase of temperature. This increase, however, was soon discovered to be nothing more than radiation from an enlarged surface of blood; a process, in fact, of rapid cooling, followed quickly by direct evidence of cooling. After this I found that through every subsequent stage of the alcoholic process, the stage of excitement, of temporary partial paralysis of muscle, of narcotism and deep intoxication, the temperature was reduced in the most marked degree. I placed alcohol and cold side by side in experiment, and found that they ran together equally in fatal effect, and I determined that in death from alcohol the great reduction of animal temperature is one of the most pressing causes of death. I showed that this effect of alcohol in reducing the animal temperature extends through all the members of the alcohol group of chemical substances, and that with increase of the specific weight of the spirit the reducing effect is intensified.

Thus, by particular and varied experiment, it was placed beyond the range of controversy that alcohol, instead of being a producer of heat in those who consume it, and therefore a food in that sense, is a depressor, and therefore not a food in that sense. The earliest scientists were confirmed in their peculiar views to the letter. I honor them for their originality and truth as heartily as I appreciate the privilege of having been the first to apply the modern and more accurate system of thermometric inquiry to tést, and, as it turned out, to confirm and establish their observations and practices.

From the study of the action of alcohol on the temperature of animal bodies, I proceeded next to test it in respect to its effects as a sustainer of the muscular power. Here I had the experience of the trainers of athletes to guide me, an experience which was strongly against the use of alcohol as a supporter of muscular power and endurance. I preferred, however, to test again minutely the direct effect of alcohol on muscular contraction, the result being the determination that, with the exception of a very brief period during the earliest stage of alcoholic flushing, the muscular force, like the temperature, fails under its influence. In a word, I found that the helplessness of muscle under which the inebriated man sinks beneath the table, and under which the paralyzed inebriate sinks into the grave, is a cumulative process, beginning so soon as the physiological effect of alcohol is pronounced, and continuing until the triumph of the agent over the muscular power is completed.

SUMMARY OF RESEARCH.

What I may call the preliminary and physiological part of my research was now concluded. I had learned, purely by experimental observation, that in its action on the living body, this chemical substance, alcohol, deranges the constitution of the blood; unduly excites the heart and respiration; paralyzes the minute blood-vessels; increases and decreases, according to the degree of its application, the functions of the digestive organs, of the liver, and of the kidneys; disturbs the regularity of nervous action; lowers the animal temperature; and lessens the muscular power.

Such, independently of any prejudice of party or influence of sentiment, are the unanswerable teachings of the sternest of all evidences, the evidences of experiment, of natural fact revealed to man by experimental testing of natural phenomena. If alcohol had never been heard of, as nitrite of amyl and many other chemical substances I have tested had never been heard of by the masses of mankind, this is the evidence respecting alcohol which I should have collected, and these are the facts I should have recorded from the evidence.

This record of simple experimental investigation and result respecting the action of alcohol on the body were incomplete without two other observations, which come in as a natural supplement. It will be asked: Was there no evidence of any useful service rendered by the agent in the midst of so much obvious evidence of bad service? I answer to that question that there was no such evidence whatever, and there is none. It has been urged, as a last kind of resource and excuse, that alcohol aids digestion, and so far is useful. I support, in reply, the statement of the late Dr. Cheyne, that nothing more effectively hinders digestion than alcohol. That "many hours, and even a whole night, after a debauch in wine, it is common enough to reject a part or the whole of a dinner undigested." I hold that those who abstain from alcohol have the best digestions; and that more instances of indigestion, of flatulency, of acidity, and of depression of mind and body, are produced by alcohol than by any other single cause.

This excuse removed, there remains none other for alcohol that is reasonably assignable except that temporary excitement of mind which, in spite of the assumption of its jollity and happiness, is one of the surest ultimate introductions to pain and sorrow. But if there be no excuse favored by scientific research on behalf of alcohol, there is sufficient of appalling reasons against it superadded when the pathological results of its use are surveyed upon the physiological. The mere question of the destructive effect of alcohol on the membranes of the body alone would be a sufficient study for an address on the mischiefs of it. I can not define it better, indeed, than to say that it is an agent as potent for evil as it is helpless for good. It begins by destroying, it ends by destruction, and it implants organic changes which progress independently of its presence even in those who are not born.

EXPULSION OF THE ENEMY.

I would venture now for a few minutes to pass from narrative of fact to invite attention to the question of the means that are before us for expelling from our homes, from our nation, from the world, an enemy that is so subtile and destructive.

The time has come when that expulsion is the duty of every man who is bold enough to fee that he is his brother's keeper, not less than the keeper of his own selfish interests and desires. The period of silence on this subject has passed; the period of ridicule has passed; the period of fear has passed. The period for united common work amongst all classes of society against the common foe has come.

As I touch this question, I ask myself—What has influenced me to take part in this cause? I answer—The facts I have observed in regard to the action of alcohol on the animal body; the facts of its utter uselessness; the facts of its deadly evil. I argue thereupon that if I, who had no bias against this agent, who was taught indeed in schools of science and from lips I reverenced, that the thing was a necessity of life; if I, thus trained, can be brought by new light to see the actual truth, and to be moved by it, so can all, except those who are so enslaved that their fetters have become an inseparable part of their existence.

I argue further on this, that the primary duty of all who would join in the war of expulsion of the common enemy is to teach, proclaim, demonstrate the same facts as I have to-day, with other such persuasions as may be adapted to the mind, and, I may say, to the heart, of him who is being taught. Specially would I urge that the young should be thus impressed. That in every Board school of England there should be a class beyond the three R's—a class where the claims of temperance should be impressed on the scholar with all the force of scientific instruction. If from the present

POWER OF EXAMPLE.

The next advance toward the great reformation we have in view is to place side by side with the propagation of truth the example of truth. I have done something in this crusade by my work as a teacher; but the work would be badly supported indeed if it were not seconded by the practice of that which I have taught. To say to a man who is wavering, who believes the teaching of abstinence to be right, and who yet fears to try it, I, the teacher, can do without the agent you trust in, can work better without it, can live better without it, can live much happier without it, can feel that what I once thought to be a necessity would now be an incumbrance; to say this is to be strung up to the very heart, is to feel the argument strung up to the height of tension, and every word an arrow going straight home. To be able to do less than this is to act "doubtingly," and to experience what the Lord Protector so truly defined—" whatsoever is so is not of faith; and whatsoever is not of faith is sin to him that doth it."

THE MODERATION FALLACY.

This thought leads me to add a word on what is called the practice of moderation in the use of alcohol. I believe the Church of England Temperance Association is divided by two lines, one of which marks off total abstainers, the other moderate indulgers. I am one of those who have once been bitten by the plea of moderate indulgence. Mr. Worldly Wiseman, with his usual industry, tapped me on the shoulder, as he does every man, and held a long and plausible palaver on this very subject. If I had not been a physician he might have converted me. But side by side with his wisdom there came fortunately the knowledge, which I could not, dare not, ignore, that the mere moderate man is never safe, neither in the counsel he gives to others, nor in the practice he follows for himself. Furthermore, I observed, as a physiological, or, perhaps, psychological, fact, that the attraction of alcohol for itself is cumulative. That so long as it is present in a human body, even in small quantities, the longing for it, the sense of requirement for it, is present, and that as the amount of it insidiously increases, so does the desire.

On the other hand, I learned that the entire freedom from the agent controls entirely the desire. That he who is actually emancipated is free. But that he who has a single link of the tyrant on his sleeve is still a slave, on whom more links are attached with an ease that gives no indication until the limbs are bound.

LEGISLATION AND THE PERMISSIVE BILL.

A man of science trusts, naturally, to the development of truth and to progress out of natural growth of scientific labor. He feels but secondary sympathies with the mere legislator who so often, in the present grossly empirical phase of his labor, legislates in darkness and in backward movement toward ages darker than his own. My mind, therefore, has been more directed to the educational part of the alcohol question than to the legislative. Yet I could not close this address without recurring a moment to what I have already said, viz., that the time has come when the Parliament of this country must in earnest legislate for the suppression, at least in part, of that national folly and disgrace—the raising of national funds from national degradation. It can not surely be long now that a free government will extract its resources from the graves of its people!

It is impossible to ignore these truths, and so, as legislation is forced on the attention, we who are in the forward ranks as teachers must guide the uninformed to that legislation which we consider wisest for the moment, most practicable, and most possible. For my part, at the present moment, while keeping up perfect freedom to accept any other measure that may be suggested or may occur to one's self, I see nothing better in the way of proposed legislation than the Permissive Bill. Were I in the House of Commons, I should, in the absence of a better and more comprehensive measure, give it my most earnest support. It would, as the law of the land, do more to remove temptation than anything else I can conceive possible; and what this means let all who are influenced by temptation declare. Those who are not influenced need not vote: they will do no harm.

CONCLUSION.

In summary:—The grand effort for us all to make is to stand firm, in precept and example, by what is right, and to proclaim the right without dismay or fear.

Once, while the thunder of a great conqueror was playing on a doomed city, there stood in that city, in calm repose, a poor scholar speaking to a few earnest students words which, far mightier than the cannon of the conqueror, penetrated his nation, lifted it up, and helped to make it what it now is, the conqueror of the conqueror. Let every son of temperance plant these words in his mind and heart, and he, too, shall conquer the conqueror.

"To this am I called! to bear witness to the truth. My life, my fortunes, are of little moment. The results of my life are of infinite moment. I am a priest of Truth. I am in her pay. I have bound myself to do all things, to venture all things, to suffer all things for her. If I should be persecuted for her sake; if I should even meet death in her service; what great thing shall I have done? What but that which I clearly ought to do?"

THE
ACTION OF ALCOHOL
ON
THE MIND.

THE ACTION OF ALCOHOL ON THE MIND.*

I AM tired of hearing the sound of my own voice on this all-absorbing topic—the action of alcohol on the living body; and when I recall the fact that every day, as certainly as it comes, brings to me a new invitation to hear myself and to be heard again, I feel what an indulgent auditory the British public must needs be. At the same time, I can not conceal, and no friend of true temperance could wish to conceal, an inward and deep satisfaction in the fact that so many persons are asking for new light and more light on this great subject. Neither, when the extent of the subject comes under review, is there any cause for wonder that so much repetition of statement, from those who are the foremost advocates of temperance, should be called for.

The advocates are few, they may be counted by their fifties. The inquirers are numerous, they may be counted by their millions.

Personal considerations, therefore, put aside, I

---

* An Address delivered at a meeting of the Cambridge Church Temperance Association, and the Cambridge University Temperance Union.

rejoice in the call even for repetition of statement, because the demand indicates an awakening feeling which is of the happiest omen. When millions of people had to be converted to temperance in the face of opposition on all sides, the labor looked dismal enough. Now that the opposition is melting away, and the millions are earnestly seeking for the knowledge which leads to conversion, the labor, heavy and severe still, is edged with brightness.

Therefore, on the whole, I am glad to have occasion to speak again. I am specially glad to speak in this place, and, considering where I speak from, I will try to repeat myself as little as possible. With this intent, it will be well for me to endeavor to present to you a side of the alcohol question which has not, as yet, been dwelt on in so special a manner as it deserves.

MEMS. ON PHYSICAL ACTION OF ALCOHOL.

In my address delivered last year in the Sheldonian Theatre, at Oxford, I spoke almost exclusively on the facts connected with the action of alcohol on the body. It seems to me befitting if on the present occasion I touch more particularly on the facts connected with *the action of alcohol on the mind*. Before, however, I pass to this particular topic, it may be advisable to epitomize the matter of the Oxford essay, so that those, and they must be many here, who have not read that essay, may follow the present argument dealing with mental phenomena, from the argument which was based on the study of physical phenomena.

In that essay I endeavored to show, from the ex

perimental evidence I had previously collected, that alcohol, when it finds its way into the living body, interferes with the oxidation of the blood; that it interferes with the natural motion of the heart; that it produces a paralyzing effect on the minute circulation of the blood at the point of the circulation where the quantity of blood admissible into the tissues ought to be duly regulated; that habitually used in what some—indeed, the majority of those who indulge in alcoholic drinks—consider a moderate quantity, it impedes the digestive power; that it induces organic changes ending in organic disease of vital organs, such as the liver and kidney; that it leads to similar changes in the great nervous centers, and to destruction of nervous function, ending in paralysis.

I further indicated, in the address to which I refer, that alcohol has no claim whatever to be considered a supporter of the animal temperature, and no claim whatever to be thought a supporter of muscular power. On the contrary, that, from the moment a physiological effect is produced in the body by alcohol and onwards, so long as the effect is kept up by the addition of the agent to the body, the animal heat, the nervous control over the muscles, and the independent power resident in the muscles themselves, begin and continue to decline, until at last the body, cold and senseless, falls to the ground, checked only by its own utter helplessness, and, as it were, living death, from imbibing the last drops that would make the death absolute. From all these facts I reasoned that alcohol could not, in any sense whatever, be, scientifically, set down as a food for man or any other animal; that it could not be set down as a necessity for man or any other animal; that, useless as a food, it is mischievous as a luxury; and that, indulged in as a luxury, it is far too dangerous a destroyer to be entrusted to the general management of mankind, or to the hands of those who, because of its luxurious temptations, fall under its power.

At the present time very few persons are inclined to contend against these propositions. There are some who are strongly inclined to qualify them, and who, under the desire to please the multitude by supplying it with excuses for retaining an old-established luxury, are ready to find, or rather to invent, excuses for it. The falsity of the excuses is pretty generally felt, even if it is not avowed, and it is a pretension which none who know the weakness of human nature are surprised to see advanced.

EXTRA-NEEDS ARGUMENTS FOR ALCOHOL.

The whole defense of alcohol rests indeed now on what is called the extra needs of man as a thinking and reasoning being, as a something more than a mere animal. The arguments that are adduced on this score run somewhat in the following order:

1. Alcohol, it is admitted, may not truly be a food in the gross and economical meaning of the term. It may not supply any structure-forming material; it may not yield any force for the movements of the body; but it is nevertheless a stimulus, and, in so far, a food for the mind. The lower animals do not want it—are, in fact, without any shadow of a doubt, better without it. But then, they have no mental de-

pressions and exultations like man. They feel none of that tension of mind which man feels in this toiling, struggling age, and which is doubly required to meet the exigencies; to meet the extra work; to enable the mind to work at a push, to quicken the flow of thought, to impel the pen, to push the pencil, to stimulate the speech, to guide the hand. The writer who must, by a stern necessity, prepare a leader by four o'clock in the morning on the debate that had just closed; the artist who must, by a stern necessity, finish his long-delayed master-piece before that terrible first week in April; the orator lecturer, preacher, player, singer, who must appear before his audience at some inevitable hour; the surgeon who must perform with unflinching skill some surgical operation; the engineer who must do some daring deed of experiment or practice—these men—so runs the argument—what are all these to do in their great emergencies if they be not supplied with the stimulus to exertion which alcohol supplies? Let it be granted that the stimulus is bad. Is it not a necessity? That is the question.

2. Alcohol, it is admitted, may not be a food, but it is still necessary for another class of men: for men who are of excessive nervous temperament, and who are too anxious and fearful about themselves to venture to leave off what they have been long accustomed to receive and accept as a necessary part of their daily subsistence. The reasoners on the value of alcohol to the mind will agree readily enough with the statement that the wretched people who, upon being cast into prison, are suddenly cut off from all stimulants, suffer no injury from the de-

privation. But, they add, "these men and women of whom we speak are not prisoners; they are not of the same stolid, hopeless, sensual class; they are more susceptible to sudden changes, and the dread of deprivation and the sense of deprivation is therefore exceptionally severe, so severe it can not be borne." What, then, are all these to do? It may be true that alcohol does them some harm. Is it not, however, a necessity? That is the question.

3. Alcohol, it is admitted, may not be a food, but there are men and women who, by steady practice, have attained such an appetite for it, such a liking for it, that they can not by any effort do without it. They can not touch food with any sense or desire for it without alcohol. The food is insipid unless it is spiced with alcohol. The food will not digest unless it be commingled in the stomach with alcohol. Life feels a burden unless it be enlightened and enlivened by alcohol. Life is not worth having unless it be cheered, and, for a time, at all events, made passable by the sweet stimulus. If these for a time attempt to abstain, the merest sight of their old friend renews their desire and rekindles their love. They are like Robinson Crusoe's man Friday, who found the flesh of goats sustaining enough, but hankered to fall back on cannibal fare when he unearthed a dead enemy. What are all these to do? Alcohol most probably does them harm.* Is it not a necessity? That is the question.

4. It is admitted that alcohol may not be a food, but there are multitudes of persons who, understanding nothing accurately on this point, are determined not to alter their opinions as to the uses

or pleasures of alcoholic indulgence by reason of any new fact or suggestion. They have known the use of alcohol all their lives: their fathers and forefathers knew the use of it. They have become so habituated to the filling and mixing and emptying of glasses, the drawing of corks, the turning of taps, the holding-up of liquors to the light, the wishing good healths, the tasting of samples, and the talking of vintages, that, in the absence of such automatic contrivances, they could have no satisfaction or pleasure of existence. They have known people who have drunk freely every day of life, and have lived notwithstanding to an extreme old age. To depart from the drinking of alcohol is to break up a fine old social custom, to reduce hospitality, to lessen the capability of expending a good income in a free and generous way, to injure the interests of important commercial communities, to cast away as useless the great gifts of nature, and to condemn a good practice because, like all good things, it is open to abuse by the reckless and unwise. What are all these to do? Alcohol may have a bad side. Is it not to them a necessity? That is the question.

5. It is admitted that alcohol may not be a food, but is it not a luxury which at certain festive seasons may be enjoyed and even used with some advantage? This argument has more than once been placed before me, and it is a favorite argument of a select few who, following in the wake of Sir Walter Raleigh, insist that wine should now, as of old, do no more than minister to the feast. On such occasions it should be taken just to make glad the heart, no more. The joyous feasters should learn

the true bounds of safety. Thereby they are fortified, and are taught by their principle to obey a higher law than those obey who, weakly apprehensive of danger of excess, must abstain altogether. Better is it to face and wrestle with and conquer an evil than fly from it meanly. Those who meet to be merry must have something that will excite to merriment. What are they to do? Alcohol may not in the end be good for them. But, for their passing hour, is it not a necessity? That is the question.

6. Alcohol may not, it is admitted, be a food; but is it not true that there is a natural, instinctive desire, if not for alcohol, at least for some equivalent substance? This is an argument which many adduce and insist on as an article of belief. There is no tribe, say men of this school, there is no tribe so savage but that it has its stimulant of some kind. The Turk takes his opium; the native of Kamschatka his amanatine; the East Indian his haschish; the Styrian his arsenic; the Mexican his agave; the Indian of the Andes his yerba de nuacca; the primitive West Indian, whom Columbus himself discovered, his tabac. Is such an instinct, so universally and yet so diversely spread, to be ignored? What are people possessed of such an instinct to do without alcohol? Is it not to them a necessity? That is the question.

In adducing these arguments in favor of alcohol from the psychological side of the alcohol question, I am doing no more than repeat what is almost daily spoken to me on the subject. I might with perfect correctness introduce much more argument on the same side. I might bring forward the expressions of those very numerous persons who protest against any abstaining reformation at all, because such reformation would check and restrain by example and social influence their own gratifications. I might bring forward the expressions of the great indifferent on this question, who want to know what the noise is all about, and ask what it can signify to them whether a little more madness, a little more crime, a little more disease, a little more want, a few more sins of all kinds all used in each degree, should stand revealed as due to one prevailing, and, by consent of ages, all but universally recognized instrument? Why should such unpleasant subjects be disinterred, making day, as well as night, hideous?

These and others I shall let alone, that I may bestow more time on worthier objects: on those who have something more than base selfishness of nature to inspire them; on those who, in the many modes I have recorded, feel that they have, at the bottom of their resistance to abstaining temperance, the serious argument of necessity.

ARGUMENTS CONTROVERTED.

Touching, then, the first class of argument—the argument which declares for the necessity of alcoholic stimulation on the ground of the necessity of stimulus to feed forced growth of thought—the reply is as direct as need be. The argument is rotten even on its own basis. Forced growth of thought is itself a cankered growth, a fungus which springs up in the night to die and dry away in the morning, sinking before the light. Life in its fullness is such an ephemeron it is hardly possible to extract more than one or two really good things out of a devotion extended to them through all the active stages of the ephemeron. What, then, can be the true value of that work which is forced to the extent of striving to do something of lasting influence each day of life, and which, failing to do what it aims at by natural means, mainly seeks for aid from that which is unnatural, wearing, wasting, wanton, wasteful? In mental, as in physical action, wanton waste makes woful want.

But, setting aside this basic reason against development of thought by means of stimulation from alcohol, there is another falseness, in the actual results of forced work on the worker. The man who is driven headlong against invisible, all-resistant time, is actually not aided by the process of stimulation. If I reduce the pendulum correction or the regulating movement of a clock or watch, I make the instrument seem to tell the hours faster and seem to do more work. But I know it does not tell the hours so correctly as it would do if I let it work properly balanced—that it does not do more work unless it be more frequently wound up, and that, made to do more work by more frequent windings up, it wears out and becomes an old and useless watch so much the faster. It is precisely the same with respect to the body. If, by reducing the balancing power of the vessels which regulate the supply of the blood to my brain, I permit a more rapid current of blood to feed my brain, I may for a time think more rapidly and express myself with more apparent energy. It is clear, however, that under these circumstances I do but exhaust more quickly, require to be wound up more frequently, and wear out more speedily.

Nay, something worse than all this actually occurs to those who seek for mental vigor in the process of releasing the balance of supply of blood to the centers of thought. When the brain is in the whirl of rapid thought, induced by alcohol, or induced, indeed, by any mode of excitement, there soon comes a time when the very rapidity of motion is a cause of obscurity. The rapidity of nervous action is rebuked by negation of result. As in a "wheel of time," when the motion of the wheel is moderate, we discern clearly different colors, but see them all in one single color when the motion is increased, so in the wheel of thought, when it spins too rapidly, imagination, fact, memory, judgment, feeling, order, expression—all these primitive attributes, which make up the spectrum of the mind —run into each other, causing confused ideas, meaningless labor, irritable exhaustion.

I record these results as matter of daily experience in observation of men. Men are as much observable phenomena as less animate things, if you will but carefully observe them. Minds can be read as well as bodies by any skilled observer who will take the trouble to learn the method of reading, and will steadily maintain the practice. And the result of such accumulated experience is that those men who, in this sadly oppressed age, do most work, best work, soundest work, hardest work, and, in the end, quickest work, are the men who, avoiding stimulants under all contingencies and pressures, trust to rest and natural food for the power that is required to carry them most safely through the ordeal.

Yet another side of this reply to the argument of necessity, now before us. The result of accumulated experience shows that they who, by stimulation, force the growth of thought; they who daily relax the vascular control over their centers of thought; they who reduce that unconscious grasp which Nature, all-wise and wonderful, has placed in automatic concealment, and out of the capricious control of our constantly-changing wills; that they who indirectly defy Nature in this her imperative rule for healthy life, pay the forfeit for their temerity or ignorance. These are the men who break up, at their work; these are the men whose suns go down at noon; these are the men dying in this day at a rate alarming to contemplate. These are the men of whom it so often is said, "Whom the gods love die young." Pernicious falsehood! Whom the gods love die old; live out in usefulness and happiness their allotted circle; die without rending the hearts of any by unnatural strain of sorrow; die as they sleep, knowing nothing of the pain and conscious bitterness of death.

For the work that comes of the mind and that comes out under pressure no taste of alcoholic stimulation is necessary. Every such taste is a self-inflicted injury, and, what is more, an accumulating injury. The dose of alcohol which spurred the thought of to-day must be slightly increased to spur the thought of to-morrow to the same pitch.

So on and on the evil goes, until at last the simple, and, as it was called, harmless dose, rises to the poisonous dose; until, with unnerved limbs, faltering memory, dulled imagination, estranged feeling, enfeebled or even dismantled reason, the victim falls. Of all men, brain-workers are the men least able to bear up against the ravages of alcohol. Of all men they are the most liable to be deceived and played upon by this traitor, who enters the most precious treasury, the citadel of the mind. I hold that man as prematurely mad who defends the use of alcohol for himself on this ground of necessity. I hold that man as criminally mad who, knowingly, prescribes alcohol on this foundation.

Touching the second class of men to whom I have referred—those who are nervously affected in favor of alcohol and who fear to abstain—the argument that requires to be applied is of an assuring rather than of a disputative character. The influence of alcohol on natures of this class is exceedingly potent, and, as it happens that such natures are often conscientiously sensitive, and charged with desires to act rightly, they become exceedingly difficult to assure. If these feel, as is commonly the case, that the constant taking of alcohol is doing them an injury, that the enemy is becoming more necessary to their support, and is also doing them physical wrong, they for a time discard him. So soon as they give abstinence a trial, however, the void they experience is most painful to them, and a real anxiety. Then every symptom they experience, from whatever cause, they attribute to abstinence. Symptoms which they often experienced before, they now attribute to abstinence. They know also that they are making an experiment which places them under the marked observation of their relatives and friends, and every adverse remark is another cause of fear and dismay. When they have to perform a special and painful duty, for which they have previously been accustomed to fortify themselves by a glass or two of wine, they miss the stimulus with a feeling of positive terror as to the result of such temerity. I have known a clergyman in this state who felt he must actually die in the pulpit if he omitted the glass of sherry with which he was long accustomed to charge himself before leaving the vestry. I have known a doctor dread the ordeal of a serious professional duty in the absence of the usual artificial provocative to action.

In these states of mind many abstainers, during their novitiate, go to consult their medical adviser, and put such a case before him that he is led to sympathize with them, and, if he be not fully conversant with the position, to suggest to them that they should return to alcohol forthwith. They now return to the old path, backed, as they say, by medical opinion and advice. They declare for themselves, and others declare for them, that in their case total abstinence has proved a total failure, and thereupon the cause receives a blow which is as mischievous as it is unjust.

I admit freely that it is a most difficult thing to treat this mental state. It is so purely mental that it baffles the most careful treatment. If the physician meet it by prescribing alcohol, as alcohol it self pure and simple, in effective doses, he even then may not succeed. The mind of the affected will not care for alcohol in that form, but for the one particular form of wine, of brandy, or whisky to which it is habituated. In fact, the physician is combating a moral derangement, and his dilemma is most trying. If he maintain the soundness of the principle of abstinence, and give every assurance of safety, he often fails in carrying conviction, since he is arguing with the most subtle and obstinate of human frailties—fear. If he give way and yield his assent to the return to the assumed protecting and sustaining enemy, he constantly gives up his too willing patient to the danger of further encroachment, to confirmed adhesion to danger, and to certain injury.

And yet, ladies and gentlemen, in these cases, in all but the most exceptional instances due to physical disease, the course to be insisted on is, after all, clear, and that course is to enforce the abstinence. Nothing is wanting but time to assure and sustain the most nervous and timid nature in the absolute safety and advantage of abstinence. In a few weeks there is hope; in a few months there is victory. A few repetitions of trials of strength without alcohol confirm the effort, and with the certain confirmation the new habit of self-trust and confidence becomes the natural condition. Like one who, having learned to swim, has given up the belt or other artificial support, and wonders why he ever needed such unnecessary assistance, so the perfected abstainer wonders why he ever required sustainment from alcohol.

Touching the mental condition of those who are held to alcohol by the tie of appetite for it and fondness for the surreptitious cheeriness which it seems to impart, the same kind of argument against the indulgence applies as does to the condition of the timorous. Indeed, the two conditions are not infrequently in combination in the same person. It must, however, be said of them in whom the liking is strongly developed that they are almost invariably in actual danger. They have become the slaves of the tyrant. They tell you with mock triumph, what their own hearts assure them is false, that they prefer to live a shorter life if it be but merrier. In this stage they are just on the verge of that mental incapacity, by physical disorganization, from which nothing but total abstinence can save them. Most commonly they sink deeper and deeper, and die from organic disease.

Touching the fourth and fifth classes of persons to whom I directed attention—those who hold to alcoholic drinks with automatic consistency and prejudice of custom, and those who hold to them as a means for mere recreative gratification—their mental condition is of a kind that can only be reached by clear and often-repeated statements of the truth respecting alcohol. Many of this class are acting simply under the impulse of ignorance, or the feeling of good nature, and though they are slavish to prejudice, they are not inaccessible to reason. These have to be educated, the first by a long, the second by a short course, and they are now being educated hour by hour and day by day. This fact is apparent in every phase of social life.

At the dinner-table wine is no longer pertinaciously and almost vulgarly forced on every guest, as once it was; neither is every total abstainer a marked man, to be made the unhappy victim of rude jest because of his conscientious determination to live according to natural rule. The atrocious calumny against Nature that she sent wine for the use of man is certainly less frequently declared; and the idea that men who do not drink can not be merry of the merriest, as well as wise of the wisest, is being so determinately corrected by practical observations as to be passing into ignorant badinage.

Still, much information has to be instilled into the masses before a true and proper frame of mind is acquired in respect to alcohol, socially considered. That terrible habit of false hospitality which presumes that a man has not done by his neighbor as he would be done by until he has asked him "what he will drink," sadly needs reforming. The insane idea that every new task and every renewed rest must be supplemented and complemented by a glass of something strong, sadly needs reforming. That equally insane practice of transacting every bit of business by a preliminary draught of the great mental disqualifier for all business, most solemnly calls for reformation. The notion that everybody who is ailing or exhausted must at once be dosed with some stiff cordial, has to be banished not only from the heart, but from the mind. For these reforms we can only wait, and teach, and recast a mental constitution which, erring only from the heart, admits of definite improvement.

Touching, lastly, the argument of those who

maintain that the desire for alcohol rests on an instinctive basis, the reply is easy. The historical evidence which is adduced in favor of the instinctive view breaks down on all fours. There have been nations which have never shown the instinct described. The lower animals, which are mainly instinctive, have never shown the instinct. Those nations which have exhibited a predilection for some foreign agent influencing the natural life have exhibited no consistent method of selection of such an agent. Some have used a stimulant; others a pure narcotic; others a direct mental depressant. All have taken, by mere accident of place and mode of life, the agent which they have introduced into common usage. All, moreover, who have thus temporized with life have been but as the children of the world, whose childish instincts in matter of cooking, of dwelling, of fighting, of playing, the most rabid alcoholic advocate would scarcely care to follow. In short, this argument of instinct is mere excuse for sake of excuse, and when it is tried by the facts of current experience, with or without the history of the past, it is nowhere. The present experience, and I believe the most ancient experience also, is clear as daylight—viz., that the habit of drinking all strong drinks is an acquired habit; that all young children instinctively dislike such drinks and shrink from them; that much training is required to beget the liking for any one drink; and that no alcoholic scholar is ever so accomplished as to accept every drink with equal favor. What is more, it is obvious not only that Nature has provided no instinct in any young animal for alcohol, but that she has not herself provided the alcohol for the instinct. Measured by the perfection of her other designs, and her unerring mode of fitting one thing into another when she intends both to act together, it is, I think, inconceivable that she would have forgotten both the instinctive desire for a particular agent, as well as the agent itself, if she had designed that man should require the agent either for his wants or his pleasures.

DIRECT INFLUENCE OF ALCOHOL ON THE MIND.

This discourse on the action of alcohol on the mind would be incomplete if it did not add something respecting the direct influence of alcoholic indulgence, in its various degrees, on the mental powers, reasoning and instinctive. I would, therefore, offer a few concluding notes from derived practiced observation on this point.

I think I see three distinct effects of alcohol on the mind, which effects I shall term the superstitious, the demonstrative, and the destructive. They are as distinct as any of the physical effects which I have traced, and I daresay they rest on a physical basis, but they admit of study and description as mental phenomena, apart from the intricacies of their origin.

The *superstitious* feelings engendered or excited by alcohol have the widest range. They extend to the whole of the alcohol-drinking population, but are usually most pronounced amongst those of the population who are most moderate, or, to use their own words, most strictly temperate in their habits. These, at all events, express most clearly the effects

I am now denoting. They tell you, with a kind of regret, that while they are fully cognizant of the evils produced by alcohol, of the desolation produced by it, the pity is that such a potent cause of evil can not be safely given up. They themselves would give it up if they could, if they had the resolution, but to them it is so necessary. They can reduce it to any ridiculously small amount, but they must have a little, or they would break down. I was sitting at dinner, during the present season, by the side of a gentleman whose mind was fully imbued with this impression. "You see," he said to me, "I am almost, but not quite, of your persuasion, for that is my daily potion of wine, and that has been my potion for over twenty years." Thereupon he poured out in a glass about two ounces of a villainous compound which is publicly sold under the name of sherry. "Well," I replied, "that is not more than from three to four drachms of alcohol. It will, I confess, do you neither good nor harm, because there is really not enough to produce a physiological effect on one of your age and size." "Nevertheless," said he, "I couldn't do without it." "What effect has it?" I inquired. "What effect, for example, does that which you have just taken produce?" "Ah," he responded, "this is common wine, very bad wine indeed, and promises, I fear, to give me heartburn, as bad wine always does; a sort of acidity, I suppose, which such wine invariably causes in me. Still I couldn't do without even this. I should miss something; I shouldn't sleep without it; but what it does for me I really do not know. The worst it does is the heartburn and that is usual except at my own table, where I get the wine that I know suits me." And then he went off at a tangent to say that it was so sociable to be able to take a little wine; that when you are at Rome you must do as Rome does; that more people injure themselves by eating than by drinking; that this is an artificial age, in which artificial means are demanded; and that if such a magnificent gift of God to man as wine—including, I suppose, the sherry which every one at the table was heartily cursing—were to be cast aside, what next would be tossed away and despised? As a last and crushing fling, he threw at me the latest utterances which Mr. Worldly Wiseman—I beg pardon, I mean Dr. Worldly Wiseman—for since I last spoke of that worthy, I see he has taken up the doctor's degree in physic—which Dr. Worldly Wiseman has said in a professional point of view respecting alcohol, and from which he deduced that a daily dose of alcohol which would of a certainty shorten the lives of nine-tenths of those who indulged in it might, on my own evidence, be taken with impunity as well as pleasure. Certainly he had not read what I had written, but this is what he understood, and he believed that some understood the original facts of an author better than the author did himself.

This is a fair sample of the superstition, of the firm belief in the unreal—always weak, plausible, selfish, illogical—which alcohol excites in the minds of men and women who are accustomed to its use. The same superstition once hung about charms and amulets, and is hardly dead yet. In this superstition lies the secret power of that moderation fallacy by which the public body is inoculated with the persistent plague of drunken-mania. It is the origin of all the evil.

The *demonstrative* effects of alcohol are shown in the proceedings of those who confessedly or concealedly indulge in alcohol beyond what can be called, in any sense, moderation. Such persons are not, of necessity, drunkards; they may only be free in the use of alcohol, or reckless in its use. But, as if they were so many specimens of experiment, they are demonstrations of its effects on the mental as well as the physical constitution.

An analysis of the condition of mind induced and maintained by the free daily use of alcohol as a drink, reveals a singular order of facts. The manifestation fails altogether to reveal the exaltation of any reasoning power in a useful or satisfactory direction. I have never met with an instance in which such a claim for alcohol was made. On the contrary, confirmed alcoholics constantly say that for this or that work, requiring thought and attention, it is necessary to forego some of the usual potations in order to have a cool head for hard work.

On the other side the experience is unfortunately overwhelming in favor of the observation that the use of alcohol sells the reasoning power, makes weak men and women the easy prey of the wicked and strong, and leads men and women who should know better into every grade of misery and vice. It is not poor repenting Cassio alone who cries out in agony of despair, "O, that a man should put an enemy into his mouth to steal away his brains!" It is thousands upon thousands of Cassios who say the same thought, if not the same words, every day, every hour. I doubt, indeed, whether there is a single man or woman who indulges or who has indulged in alcohol who could not truthfully say the same; who could not wish that something he had unreasonably said or expressed under the excitation from alcohol had not been given forth.

If, then, alcohol enfeebles the reason, what part of the mental constitution does it exalt and excite? It exalts and excites those animal, organic, emotional centers of mind which, in the dual nature of man, so often cross and oppose that pure and abstract reasoning nature which lifts man above the lower animals, and, rightly exercised, little lower than the angels. Exciting these animal centers, it lets loose all the passions, and gives them more or less of unlicensed domination over the whole man. It excites anger, and when it does not lead to this extreme it keeps the mind fretful, irritable, dissatisfied, captious. The flushed face of the red-hot angry man, how like it is to the flushed face of the man in the first stage of alcoholic intoxication. The face, white with rage, and the tremulous, agitated muscles of the body, how like both are to the pale face and helpless muscles of the man deep in intoxication from alcohol. The states are not simply similar, they are identical, and the one will feed the other.

From this same mode of action, alcohol administers to the fears of mankind. The term "pot valor," vulgar as it is, how faithfully it expresses the truth. Before this paralyzing influence the reasoning power, which is the essence of resource and effort and continuous endurance, fails, and then the mere animal, beset with dangers he can not see how to escape from, sinks and falls. From the same mode of action, alcohol increases and intensifies grief, and maddens joy; makes life a wild excitement of wanton mirth, a deep, unfathomable sea of misery. The man who can enjoy no taste, no sight, no sound, no light, no shade of sense until he is primed to the perception by alcohol, loses half the joyousness and refinement of life. The man who takes into his senses the outward nature with the centers of his mind clear for the perception, has a double life; every perception is more finely caught and fixed, every sensibility is more finely and tenderly touched and cherished.

As men under the chilling northern wind shrink and sink more easily when they fly to alcohol for false support, so men under the chilling wind of adversity shrink and sink more easily under the factitious, tempting aid of the same agency. It is the sober in both cases, the all-abstaining sober who go through both trials most easily, and sur mount them least impaired.

And if I were to take you through all the passions that remain to be named, love and lust, hate and envy, avarice and pride, I should but show you that alcohol ministers to them all; that, paralyzing the reason, it takes from off these passions that fine adjustment of reason which not only places man above the lower animals, but, when celestially attuned, places him little fower than the angels.

The demonstrative evidence of alcohol in its influence on the mind is then most clear. From the beginning to the end of its influence it subdues reason and sets free passion. The analogies, physical and mental, are perfect. That which loosens the tension of the vessels which feed the body with due order of precision, and thereby lets loose the heart to violent excess of unbridled motion, loosens also the reason and lets loose the passions. In both instances heart and head are for a time out of harmony; their balance broken. The man descends closer and closer to the lower animals. From the angels he glides further and further away.

The *destructive* effects of alcohol on the human mind present, finally, the saddest picture of its influence. The most æsthetic artist can find no angel here. All is animal, and animal of the worst type. Memory irretrievably lost, words and very elements of speech forgotten, or words displaced to have no meaning in them. Rage and anger persistent and mischievous, or remittent and impotent. Fear at every corner of life, distrust on every side, grief merged into blank despair, hopelessness into permanent melancholy. Surely no Pandemonium that ever poet dreamt of could equal that which would exist if all the drunkards of the world were driven into one mortal sphere.

As I have moved among those who are physically stricken with alcohol, and have detected under the various disguises of name the fatal diseases, the pains and penalties it imposes on the body, the picture has been sufficiently cruel. But even that picture pales as I conjure up, without any stretch of imagination, the devastations which the same agent inflicts on the mind. Forty per cent., the learned superintendent of Colney Hatch, Dr. Shepherd, tells us, forty per cent. of those who were brought into that asylum during the year 1876, were so brought because of the direct or indirect effects of alcohol. If the facts of all the asylums were collected with equal care, the same tale would, I fear, be told. What need we further to show the destructive action of this one instrument of destruction on the human mind? The Pandemonium of drunkards: the grand transformation scene of that pantomime of drink, which commences with moderation! Let it be never more forgotten by those who love their fellow-men until, through their efforts, it is closed forever.

MODERATE DRINKING.

FOR AND AGAINST.

MODERATE DRINKING:

FOR AND AGAINST,

FROM SCIENTIFIC POINTS OF VIEW.*

When you are walking through a sculpture gallery, say in the Crystal Palace, or in the British or Kensington Museums, your eye lights ever and again on some all but living figure in dead marble or stone. You stay to look at that voiceless statue, and as you take in its features you ask yourselves: If it could only speak, what would it tell? If the lips had language, what tale would they unfold? I will undertake to say that in this audience there is scarcely a man or woman who has not experienced this sensation. It is, in a secret kind of way, the spring of the fascination that fixed you to look and admire.

Your minds are in this manner brought into communion with many faces and figures, and as they can not reply to your mental inquiries, you answer for yourselves, gathering your impressions from them in their dumb eloquence. You see that laughing face, and you think if it could speak now it might make me rend my sides with laughter Wny can't the laughing genius set me off? You

---

* A Lecture delivered in Exeter Hall, December 14, 1878.

wander on, and meet a face of quite a different kind; it is worn with care and sorrow; it grieves hopelessly over something lost; there is in its expression a shadow of a fixed, a horrible despair. Ah! say you, as you sigh in sympathy: If that dead silence could utter its story, how my soul would sink and shudder; how my eyes would weep, my heart palpitate, my breathing sob; and, glad that the statue is so silent and yet impressed with a sense of solemnity, you once more move away. In both cases you have been spoken to, to the heart. Your sympathies have been quickened, and feelings of the deepest character have been called forth by one influence—the influence of art on your finest, purest passions, on that which makes you sentient: sentiment expressed by and through art.

While the passion so inspired lasts, you move on again, and so you come upon another of these dead artistic forms of matter. What inscrutable figure is this? It has the face of a woman, the wings of a bird, the talons of a griffin. The face expresses everything, yet nothing that is explicable; in every view of it, it changes as if it could adapt its features to every subject, yet in no position does it suggest a realizable thought. There is no mirth in it, no sorrow no care, and still, though even care is absent, there is solemnity. Its ideal of motion gives it the appearance that on those wings, it could fly even beyond the confines of space if it willed. Its ideal of position and rest rivets you to the belief that by those talons of it, it can seize and hold everything it clutches, so that the very earth itself is in its ruthless grasp. To the ignorant this figure is a monster, ruthless as nature, and yet with a calm beneficence that seems to declare, You may trust me also like nature. You say, If that form could speak, what would it tell? It would excite no laughter, it would call forth no tears, but as solemnly as surely it would proclaim the truth. Once more you wander away, wondering at what you have seen. Your reason this time has been quickened, and feelings of the deepest character have been called forth by one influence. The element of wonder in your nature which makes you long to seize, to know, has been touched in you. Science has approached you this time through art.

All the riddles of this figure, says Lord Bacon, have two conditions annexed: laceration through and through to those who do not solve them, and empire to those that do. It is the Sphinx of the ancient, the Science of the modern world.

If from the gallery of the sculptor you transport yourselves into every-day life, you meet the same influences. These two powers of sentiment and reason, of passion and science, are in every sphere. They touch every question, and no question more than that with which we are now concerned. The custom of drinking intoxicants has been built up on passion or sentiment solely and absolutely. The laughing and the crying figures have been its chief commentators. They chiefly have been read, and their views proclaimed.

Until lately in the history of man the laughing genius has alone been listened to on this grave matter. The mournful, stricken genius has, it is true, never been silent, but he has been overpowered. At last his story, too, has been caught, and zealous listeners to it, burning with sacred fire of eloquence—like Father Mathew and John B. Gough—have echoed and re-echoed the terrible story told by the stricken, until the world has been obliged to hear voices louder than the shouts of the laughers and the yells of the profane. Passion at last has met passion in deadly contest, and as the contest still rages, the victory of the long-neglected sorrowful seems to hang in the balance. The pandemoniumites no longer have it all their way.

Meanwhile, what says that third authority—that silent, passionless Sphinx? She for ages past has watched the trial. Has she never, through any of her interpreters, spoken her mind? She has often spoken. She has spoken in parable; she has spoken in proverb; she has spoken in fact.

It is to her we appeal to-day; and as she is passionless and without prejudice, so let us be. Let us for the passing hour—

> "Retire, the world shut out, our thoughts call home;
> Imagination's airy wing suppress.
> Shut up our senses, let no passion stir;
> Leave all to reason, let her reign alone."

Thus may we learn what the silent, reasoning nature, Science, has said, and is saying, by parable, proverb, and fact, concerning the use of wines and strong drink by mankind.

SCIENCE IN PARABLE.

In early days the Sphinx spoke by parable. Bacchus, the god of the wine-cup, subdued the world to the furthest of the Indies; was drawn in a chariot by tigers; he was surrounded by deformed demons; was followed by the Muses; married the cast-off mistress of Theseus; was crowned with ivy; invented all such religious rites as were frantic, corrupt, and cruel; gained the power of striking men with frenzies, and tore to pieces Pentheus, the inquisitive, and Orpheus, the civilizer—the first because he dared to inquire into the evil work of the Bacchanalians; the second, because he dared to counsel and advise them.

All this is parable, yet parable grand in the extreme. That Bacchus should be the inventor of wine, says one of the profoundest interpreters of science, my Lord Bacon, carries with it a fine allegory, for every affection is cunning and subtle in discovering a proper matter to nourish and feed it—and of all things known to mortals, wine is the most powerful and effectual for exciting and inflaming passions of all kinds, being indeed like a common fuel to all. That Bacchus subdued provinces is equally true, for the affections never rest satisfied with what they enjoy, but with an endless and insatiable appetite after something further. Tigers are prettily fancied to draw the chariot, because so soon as any affection shall, from going on foot, be advanced to ride, it triumphs over reason, and exerts its cruelty, fierceness, and strength against all that oppose it. That ridiculous demons should dance round the chariot is also good, for every passion produces disorderly motions in the countenance and gestures, so that the person under the impulse of love, anger, insult, though to himself he may seem grand, lofty, or obliging, yet in the eyes of others appears mean, contemptible, or ridiculous. And, that the Muses should be found in the train is natural, because there is no passion without its doctrine to flatter it and become its handmaid. Further, says the same brilliant commentator, the allegory of Bacchus falling in love with a cast-off mistress, is extremely fine, for the affections always court and covet what has been rejected by experience; nor is it without reason that ivy is sacred to him, because the predominant passion of the mind throws itself like ivy round all human actions, entwines all our resolutions, and even overtops them. And that rank superstitions should be attributed to him is true, because every ungovernable passion is a short frenzy, and, if it take root, ends in madness. Hence, Pentheus and Orpheus were torn to pieces, because passion is extremely bitter on all curious inquiry, free counsel, and wise persuasion.

This is the allegory of wine invented while wine was young, and before its stronger allies, brandy, rum, gin, and whisky, were known. It is an allegory showing that all the custom of drinking wine is founded on passion or sentiment. It is an allegory that has been maintained without change until quite a recent page in the history of mankind.

SCIENCE IN PROVERB.

In such mode science has spoken in parable. She has spoken with equal clearness in proverb through her noblest representatives.

Through the wisest of them all, Solomon, the wise, she declared, "Wine is a mocker, strong drink is raging." Through another of her sons, Seneca, the Roman, she declared that to argue that a man may take wine and retain a right frame of mind, is as bad as to argue that he may take poison and not die, or the juice of the poppy and not sleep. She spoke through Demosthenes, the great orator of the Greeks, affirming "that to drink well is the property of a sponge, not of a man." By the true philosopher, Pliny, she told that King Antiochus, having forced his minions at a banquet to take excess of wine, they killed him, from which story she taught, through the same interpreter, the moral, that if we tempt others into error, the consequences fall back upon ourselves.

Through her favorite master, Shakespeare, she exclaimed, "Oh, that a man should put an enemy into his mouth to steal away his brains!" And so in endless proverbial sayings she has been ever speaking to all who would listen to her interpreters.

SCIENCE IN FACT.

I must not dwell longer on these utterances; my principal object being to exclaim what she has said and is saying in more modern times on the question of fact in relation to strong drink and its effect on the world of life. Let us take some of her more salient teachings first.

In the year 1725 she spoke to the Government of this country through the president of the College of Physicians of London, stating that "the fatal effects of the frequent use of several sorts of distilled spirituous liquors upon great numbers of both sexes renders them diseased, not fit for business, poor, a burthen to themselves and neighbors, and too often the cause of weak, feeble, and distempered children, who must be, instead of an advantage and strength, a charge to their country. Twenty-nine years later, she spoke again through the mouth of one of her most approved servants, the first inventor of ventilators, Dr. Stephen Hales. Through this illustrious philosopher she explained that strong liquors, though called spirituous, are so far from refreshing and recruiting the spirits, that, on the contrary, they do, in reality, depress and sink them, and extinguish the natural warmth of the blood.

You will see from these evidences, which could

be largely multiplied, that long ago Science spoke strongly by her best speakers on matters of fact relating to the use of strong drinks. You will note, moreover, that her utterances in that respect are very urgent against strong drinks. At the same time you will with fairness reply, " All that is true; but the argument is so far against excessive use." We all admit that argument; doctors admit that universally; statesmen admit it; statisticians prove that; clergymen who are not abstainers express that; nay, the very sellers of strong drinks, the gentlemen who sell wholesale, and the publicans who dispense for the gentlemen, they, too, admit the solemn, unanswerable truth, that strong drink kills. We therefore need no Sphinx to inform us of what is universally admitted. This, however, we do want to know. We desire to be informed what is to be said by Science on *the moderate use of these agents*. Let abuse of them go to the wall; let use stand forth alone, and let us hear what place this strong drink holds in relation to man and animals—what place it holds in nature—what good it is for man—what bad, when it is used in moderation. Let us have the for and against.

The request is justice itself. There can be no objection whatever to put the answer of Science to the " for" as well as the " against."

The most ardent of abstainers may venture thus far; nay, he must venture, otherwise his case is weak, though it may not be lost. In plain words, the reasons for the use of the strong drinks in a moderate way are so plausible, that if they can not be admitted and rebutted, all the reasons against it's use lose half their force. There is no escaping that irresistible conclusion.

WINE AND WATER.

Let us begin by looking at the interpretations of Science in her latest teachings as to the nature of strong drinks.

On this point all are now agreed who speak scientifically. For many ages wine was looked upon as a distinct drink, as a something apart altogether from water. Strong wine will take fire; water will quench fire. Wine has a color and sparkles in the glass; water is colorless and clear as crystal. Wine has taste and flavor and odor; water is tasteless and odorless. Wine is the blood of the grape and in some respects seems akin to the blood of man; water is of all things least like blood. Wine when drunken makes the face flush, the eyes sparkle, the heart leap, the pulses sharp, the veins full; water when drunken does none of these acts, and seems to do nothing but respond to the natural wish for drink. Wine makes the lips and tongue parched and dry, the drinker athirst; water keeps the lips and tongue and stomach moist, and quenches the thirst of the drinker. Wine when it is taken, sets all the passions aglow and dulls the reason; bids men enjoy and reason not; water creates no stir of passion, and leaves the reason free. Wine makes for itself a first and second and third and fourth claim on the drinker, so that the more of it he takes the more of it he desires; it is overwhelming in the warmth of its friendship; water sates the drinker after one draught; makes no further claim on him than is just consistent with its duty; leads him never to take more and more; and has no seeming warmth in its friendship. Wine multiplies itself into many forms, which appear to be distinct; it is new, it is old; it is sweet, it is sour; it is sharp, it is soft; it is sparkling, it is still; water is ever the same. Wine must be petted and cherished, stored up in special skins and special caves, styled by particular names, praised under special titles, and heartily liked or disliked, like a child of passion; water, pshaw! it is everywhere; it has one name, no more; it has one quality; it hurries away out of the earth by brooks and rivulets and rivers into the all-absorbing sea, where it is undrinkable; or it pours down from the clouds as if the gods were tired of it; it is no child of passion! Let the cattle, and the dogs, and the wild beasts alone drink water. Let the man have the overpowering drink, the blood of the grape—wine!

Alas! for this poetic dream. Science, poetic, too, in her way, but passionless, destroys in those crucibles of hers, which men call laboratories, this flimsy dream There she tells that, when one or two disguises are removed, even blood is water as to wine, that is mere dirty water—sixteen bottles or cups or any other equal measures of water, pure and simple, from the clouds and earth, to one poor bottle or cup of a burning, fiery fluid which has been called ardent spirit, or spirit of wine, or alcohol, with some little coloring matter, in certain cases a little acid, in other cases a little sugar, and in still other cases a little cinder stuff.

It is a pitiful fall, but it is such, and science not only declares it, but proves it so to be. A pitiful let-down, that men throughout all ages who have called themselves wine-drinkers have been water-drinkers after all; that men who have called themselves wine merchants have been water merchants; that men who have bought, and still buy, wines at fabulous prices have been buying, and still are buying, water. A dozen of champagne, bought at a cost of five pounds ten shillings, very choice—I am speaking by the book—consisted, when it was all measured out, of three hundred ounces, or fifteen pints of fluid, of which fluid thirteen pints and a half were pure water, the rest ardent spirit, with a little carbonic acid, some coloring matter like burnt sugar, a light flavoring ether in almost infinitesimal proportion, or a trace of cinder stuff. Science, looking on dispassionately, records merely the facts. If she thinks that five pounds ten shillings was a heavy sum to pay for thirteen pints and a half of water and one pint and a half of spirit, she says nothing; she leaves that to the men and women of sentiment and passionate feeling, buyers and sellers and drinkers all round.

ARDENT SPIRIT.

But if it be not her business to enter into this commercial undertaking or spoil its glory, it is her business to take up that pint and a half of ardent spirit which, split up through fifteen pints, gave all the zest and consequence to the thirteen and a half pints of colored water.

Taking this ardent spirit into one of her crucibles or laboratories, Science compares it with other products on the shelves there, and soon she finds its niche in which it fits truly. On the shelf where it fits she has ranged a number of other spirits. There is chloroform, ether, sweet spirit of nitre, and some other fluids, very useful remedies in the hands of the physician. These, she sees, are the children of the spirit, are made, in fact, from it. On the same shelf she has another set of spirits; there is wood spirit, there is potato spirit, there is a substance which looks like spermaceti; and these she sees are all members of the same family, not children, this time, of the ardent spirit, but brothers or sisters, each one constructed from the same elements in the same relative proportions and on the same type. Passionless, having no predilection for any one object in the universe except the truth, she writes down the ardent spirit as having its proper place in a group of chemical substances which are distinctly apart from other substances she knows of, on which men and animals live, and which are called by the name of foods or sustainers of life She says all the members of the spirit family are, unless judiciously and even skillfully used, inimical to life. They produce drowsiness, sleep, death. In the hands of the skillful they may be safe as medicines; in the hands of the unskillful they are unsafe, they are poisons. To this rule there is not one exception amongst them. There can be no demur, no doubt now on this particular point; it may be a blow to poetry of passion; it may make the ancient and modern bacchanalian look foolish to tell him that wine is a chemical substance mixed and diluted with water, and that beer and spirits are all in the same category; but such is the fact. In computing the influence of wine, men have no longer to discuss anything more than the influence of a definite chemical compound, one of a family of chemical compounds called the alcohols—the second of a family group, differing in origin from the first of the series, which is got from wood, in that it is got from grain, and is called ethylic, or common alcohol, pure spirit of wine.

Thus by the interpretation of scientific truth, we fix the agent that has made wine and its allies so notorious in the world.

ARDENT SPIRIT IN RELATION TO LIFE.

But now the world turns properly to ask another question. Admitted all that is said, why, after all, should the practice of mankind in the use of this spirit be had? Man is not guided solely by reason; passion may lead him sometimes, perchance, in the true path. Tell us then, O Science! why this ardent spirit may not still be drunken; why may it not be a part of the life of man!

To this question the answer of Science is straight and to the point. In the universe of life she says man forms but a fractional part. All the sea is full of life; all the woods are full of life; all the air is full of life; on the surface of the earth man possesses, as companions or as enemies, herds and herds of living forms. Of that visible life he forms but a minute speck, and beyond that visible life there is the world invisible to common view, with its myriads of forms unseen which the most penetrating microscope has not reached. Again, there are other forms of life; plants innumerable, from gigantic Wellingtonias to lichens and mosses, and beneath these myriads more so infinitely minute that the microscope fails to reach them. This is all life, life which goes through its set phases in due form; grows in health and strength and beauty, every part of it, from highest to lowest living grade, without a shade of the use of this strong spirit. What evidence can be more conclusive that alcohol is not included in the scheme of life?

And yet, if you want more evidence, it is yours. You try man by himself. Every child of woman born, if it be not perverted, lives without alcohol, grows up without it; spends — and this is a **vital** point — spends the very happiest part of its life without it; gains its growing strength and vitality without it; feels no want for it. The course of its life is, at the most, on an average of the best lives, sixty years, of which the first fifteen, in other words, the first fourth, are the most dangerous; yet it goes through that fourth without the use of this agent. But if in the four stages of life it can go through the first and most critical stage without alcohol, why can not it traverse the remaining three? Is Nature so unwise in her doings, so capricious, so uncertain, that she withholds a giver of life from the helpless, and supplies it only to the helpful? Impossible! She provides for the helpless at once a food and a drink — their mother's milk. Further, there have been many men and women, millions on millions of them, who have gone on through the four stages of life, from the first to the last, without resort to this agent for the support of life. Some men, forming whole nations, have never heard of it; some have heard of it and have abjured its use. In England and America, at this time, there are probably near upon six millions of persons who have abjured this agent. Do they fall or fail in value of life from the abjuration? The evidence, as we shall distinctly see by and by, is all the other way. There are, lastly, some who are forced to live without the use of this agent. Do they fall or die in consequence? There is not a single instance in illustration.

On all these points, Science, when she is questioned earnestly, and interpreted justly, is decisive and firm, and if you question her in yet another direction, she is not less certain. You ask her for a comparison of alcohol, and of man, in respect to the structure of both, and her evidence is as the sun at noon in its clearness. She has taken the body of man to pieces; she has learned the composition of its every structure—skin, muscle, bone, viscera, brain, nervous cord, organs of sense! She knows of what these parts are formed, and she knows from whence the components came. She finds in the muscles fibrine; it came from the fibrine of flesh, or from the gluten or albumen of the plants on which the man had fed. She finds tendon and cartilage, and earthy matter of the skeleton; they were from the vegetable kingdom. She finds water in the body in such abundance that it makes up seven parts out of eight of the whole, and that she knows the source of readily enough. She finds iron, that she traces from the earth. She finds fat, and that she traces to sugar and starch. In short, she discovers, in whatever structure she searches, the origin of the structure. But as a natural presence, she finds no ardent spirit there in any part or fluid. Nothing made from spirit. Did she find either, she would say the body is diseased, and, it may be, was killed by that which is found.

Sometimes, in the bodies of men, she discovers the evidences of some conditions that are not natural. She compares these bodies with the bodies of other men, or with the bodies of inferior animals, as sheep and oxen, and finds that the unnatural appearances are peculiar to persons who have taken alcohol, and are indications of new structural changes which are not proper, and which she calls disease.

Thus, by two tests, Science tries the comparison between alcohol and man. She finds in the body no structure made from alcohol; she finds in the healthy body no alcohol; she finds in those who have taken alcohol changes of the structure, and those are changes of disease. By all these proofs she declares alcohol to be entirely alien to the structure of man. It does not build up the body; it undermines and destroys the building.

One step more. If you question Science on the comparison which exists between foods and alcohol, she gives you facts on every hand. She shows you a natural and all-sufficient and standard food—she calls it milk. She takes it to pieces; she says it is made up of caseine, for the construction of muscular and other active tissues; of sugar and fat, for supplying fuel to the body for the animal warmth; of salts for the earthy, and of water for the liquid parts. This is a perfect standard. Holds it any comparison with alcohol? Not a jot. The comparison is the same with all other natural foods.

Man, going forth to find food for his wants, discovers it in various substances, but only naturally, in precisely such substances, and in the same proportions of such substances as exist in the standard food on which he first fed. Alcohol, alien to the body of man, is alike alien to the natural food of man.

ARDENT SPIRIT AND ANIMAL STRENGTH.

Some of you will perhaps ask: Is every use of food comprised in the building up of the body? Is not some food used as the fuel of the engine is used, not to produce material, but to generate heat and motion, to burn and to be burned? The answer is as your question suggests. Some food is burned in the body, and by that means the animal fire—the *calor vitalis*, or vital heat, of the ancients—is kept alive. Then, say you: May not alcohol burn? We take starch, we take sugar into the body, as foods, but there are no structure of starch and sugar, only some products derived from them which show that they have been burned. May not alcohol in like manner be burned and carried away in new form of construction of matter?

What says Science to this inquiry? Her answer is simple. To burn and produce no heat is improbable, if not impossible; and if probable or even possible, is unproductive of service for the purpose of sustaining the animal powers. Test, then, the animal body under the action of alcohol, and see your findings. Your findings shall prove that, under the most favorable conditions, the mean effect of the alcohol will be to reduce the animal temperature through the mass of the body. There will be a glow of warmth on the surface of the body. Truly! but that is cooling of the body. It is from an extra sheet of warm blood brought from the heart into weakened vessels of the surface, to give up its heat and leave the whole body chilled, with the products of combustion lessened, the nervous tone lowered, the muscular power reduced, the quickened heart jaded, the excited brain infirm, and the mind depressed and enfeebled. Alcohol, alien to the structure of man and to the food of man, is alike alien to living strength of man, and to the fires which maintain his life.

ARDENT SPIRIT AND CONSERVATION OF STRENGTH.

It will occur to you to make yet another inquiry relative to the action of this alcohol on the body. You will ask: If it be not a substance that supplies the material body with material, if it be not a substance that supplies warmth and power, does it not save expenditure of warmth and power, and so preserve? Does it not, to use a very homely simile, bank up the animal fire, and keep it in? If it should do that, then the nervous system and the muscular system may perhaps be so conserved that mental and muscular effort may, under trial, be maintained by it more determinately. The aid thus afforded may be artificial, but still useful. A crutch is artificial, and so is a wooden leg, but both are useful. What says Science on this point? Science replies again, clearly and decisively. She shows that so soon as the nervous system feels the effect of the stimulant, so soon as the will comes under its influence, so soon there is aberration in the direction of the will. There is excitement, there is deficient precision of directing movement of limb, there is lapse of presence of mind, there is limited endurance of effort. The vital fire is not being banked up, but banked out. With refined methods of research she turns to the muscular organs, those fleshy engines which produce the animal movements, and again discovers that from the moment these engines come under the influence of the alcohol, they fail in power; that from the first moment they are excited to that last moment when, collapsed and hopeless, they let their owner fall down helpless, our progress is steadily and inevitably toward that collapse, if the influence of the producing agent be not withdrawn.

Science goes further in her exposition on this part of our inquiry. She points triumphantly to every-day facts in open corroboration of her teaching. She places men engaged in severe labor of mind in two conditions: one set under the moderate influence, the other out of the influence of alcohol, and she declares the difference. She tells from direct experience that so little as one glass of wine is often sufficient, in fine intellects, to take away the sharpness of the intellectual power. She sees that in all great crises the clear mind of him who is free of alcoholic taint, is the mind on which dependence is most readily placed. She sees men who sometimes indulge in alcohol give up the indulgence during an emergency, that they may be readier for their work. She sees all classes of mankind making the first inquiry, in respect to those whom they have to trust: Are those we want sober men? Are they free of the feebleness of thought, action, and character that is induced by strong drink?

In continued illustration of her teaching, Science points to men who work with their hands in various labors, and places, and conditions. In temperate regions of the earth, she puts to the test men who march, who ride, who race, who swim, who fight. She matches those who take alcohol with those who don't, and she challenges the world to behold that those who don't are the winners. She takes a body of men to the arid regions of tropical lands; she leads them there, in different companies, on long marches, and divides them so that one company takes a measured ration of strong drink, while the other, content with its ration of simple water, don't; and she bids us see how easily, how healthily, how certainly those who don't, carry off the honors of superior marching power. Not satisfied with this test, she takes another set of men into the regions of thick-ribbed ice ; the extremest northern line where man has trodden. See you, she says to the brave men she leads there, see you at the distance only of a few hundred miles, like a journey from London to Edinburgh in length, or little more, is the goal of your ambition, the northern pole of the earth. Set out for it on foot, or in sledge, and try your way. To some of these she gives the moderate ration of alcohol, to some she don't. Now, who will win? The race is fairly started, and the men are away. Not one of them reaches the pole. They toil and toil, endure and endure. Some fail and fall, and yet they push on. At last, it is clear there is no hope of reaching the grand-stand, and that the few who can work must help the rest back to the ship. Of these few are some who do and some who don't drink ardent spirits.

The experiment is exciting, unexampledly fair in its method, crucial in its bearing. Who of those men has been nearest to the pole? who of them of those who do and who don't drink alcohol shall return least injured and strongest to the ship? One man did both feats easily, and he was of those who "don't." His name was Adam Ayles.

One step more in her great researches, Science sometimes puts men who work for her in a position which nothing but the most telling ingenuity could devise. In order to sink coffer-dams, she shuts up the workers under a pressure of three and even four atmospheres—sixty pounds of pressure on every square inch of body. In that pressure the very color of the blood is changed; the dark venous blood is made red, like the blood in the arteries. Under these extreme conditions she divides the workers into those who do and those who don't drink alcohol; and again the advantage rests with those who don't.

Thus far, then, without passion, without prejudice, Science tells us many facts. Wine, with all its allies, is water with something in it. That something a chemical body belonging to a family of chemical bodies, not one of which is a food—enters in no way into the grand scheme for the sustainment of life in the universe—enters into no part of the scheme for the sustainment of human life at the period when that life is most helpless, and requires most urgently every natural necessity. Through all stages of life, all men can live without this something; it forms no part of the body of man, nor of any animal; it makes no condition of animal organs, except what is of the nature of disease; it is not found in the healthy state within the precincts of the body; it compares with no natural form or standard of food; it supplies no means of warmth to the body, but reduces the natural warmth. Under every conceivable extreme condition of heat, of cold, of pressure, it reduces, under all prolonged and trying efforts, both the mental and the physical power.

WHAT ARDENT SPIRIT DOES.

Is nothing done to the body by alcohol, then? say you. Science answers: Yes. Directly the most appreciable influence from alcohol is felt, a great deal is done. All the minute blood-vessels that let the blood pass through them into the extreme parts of the body are reduced in power, so that they fill with blood, and the face gets flushed, and the brain gets flushed, and the lungs get flushed, and the breathing becomes quick, and the heart increases in its beating some four strokes a minute, or two hundred and forty strokes an hour, or at the rate of five thousand seven hundred and sixty extra strokes in an entire day.

I might tell of much more that would be done by larger quantities of alcohol in which even moderate drinkers indulge, but I keep to the mention of this small quantity, because it is the smallest that possibly can do what is commonly called "good." All who advocate the moderate use of alcohol, all who apologize for the use of alcohol at all, would tell you that they would not recommend any man or woman to use alcohol beyond the amount that produces these effects. They are the effects that would be induced by taking what the late Dr. Parkes calls the dietetic dose—namely, from one to two fluid ounces of alcohol; the effects that would follow the taking of one and a half pints of mild beer, containing five per cent. of alcohol, or half that quantity of French wine, containing ten per cent., according to his great authority. To produce this first effect, all moderate drinkers plead for alcohol. They ask for no more. They admit that if more be taken, some worse effects will follow. But for this gentle stimulation, this mild warming-up surely they may be granted a salvo there.

This is the knotty point of points. There is not a sane man or woman in the world who has any knowledge on the subject at all, who would plead for the habitual use of alcohol beyond this stage of its action. To carry it a stage further, so as to get into confusion of thought, with failure of lip, angry passion, thickness of speech, headache, nausea, a little too free communication of sentiment, or conversation rather too fast to be perfectly cool in expression—oh, fie! why, that would be passing into the second degree of alcoholic influence. Not to put too fine a point on it, it would be an approach to what is called, not intoxication exactly, but elevation, moral or physical, I can not say which, but elevation of some kind, which would be decidedly wrong and off the board.

ALCOHOLIC STAGES AND "RULE NISI."

I confess there is a great advance of opinion—a concensus of opinion, I think, is the right term—on this part of our subject; but there is not a sufficient advance. A man or woman sitting down, or standing up if you like, to drink wine or other stimulant, always starts on the way that leads through four stages toward an easily realizable destination. Stage one is that gentle stimulation called moderate excitement or support. Stage two is elevation —whatever that may mean—it is not elevation of character; of that I am satisfied. Stage three is confusion of mind, action, and deed, with sad want of elevation. Stage four is complete concatenation of circumstances: all the stages perfectly matured; the journey completed, with the traveler lying down, absolutely prostrated in mind and in body. The destination is reached, and found to be a human being dead drunk and incapable.

I repeat, whenever a person begins to take any portion of alcohol, he starts on that journey; starts just as distinctly with the first drop swallowed, as he would start with the first step he would put forward in a walk from the pure region of Hampstead Heath into the outfall of that Babylonish sewage which greets the smiling Thames at Barking Creek. The knotty question then is this, Ought a person to start on that remarkable journey of alcoholic progress at all? Should he try any stage? Every one says, venture not on the last three stages on any account; but some say, live and go happy, day by day, through the first; walk the first fourth of the way, and you will be the better for it. It is a nice exercise. It makes your heart light; it refreshes your mind; it quickens your secretions; it assists your digestion. The wisest men of all ages have daily walked this stage on the alcoholic highway toward the point of concatenation of circumstances. In this first fourth of their way, with an occasional venture a little further when the companionship was good, they have given the world its wit, its humor, its poetry, its greatness. Suppose they have lived a little shorter time from the exercises, they have done more work in the shorter time than they would have done in a longer time under duller circumstances; so that the advantage, on the whole, is with this moderate indulgence in alcohol. Indulgence just a fourth of the way on toward danger; never further, except on rarest occasions; and then certainly not quite half-way—to the foot of Mount Elevation at furthest, and no further, for sake of body and mind alike.

This, in plain language, is the argument of the moderate school of thought. It is met point blank by the abstaining school, which calls out with all its sympathetic might: Take not a step on that highway. It is the devil's highway! It is the grand model of his engineering skill; it is wide, it is open, it is straight, it is smooth, it is filled with jolly companions every one, it is fenced with pleasures, it is rich in historical reminiscences, but there is this peculiarity about it, that there is not an inch of it, not a hair's-breadth of it safe. Therefore keep off it altogether. It is the devil's highway!

We listen to these opposing voices. The first are seductive, and sound even as if they were voices of men of science and knowledge. The second are fierce, solemn, earnest, but not voices of philosophic ring. They are pathetic, persuasive —perhaps in some moments terrible; that is all.

What, O Science, say you to this contention?

Be passionless as ever, but speak and tell us your mind.

Listen carefully to the whole argument of Science as she tells her mind fairly and faithfully. She tells you nothing whatsoever about the devil and his devices, but that there is, as claimed, a certain degree of moderation which does not seem to be attended with much evil if it be closely followed. She grants that the moderate of the moderates may have a *rule nisi*. She says to a man of sound health: If you are in first-rate condition of body, if you can throw off freely a cause of oppression and depression, if you are actively engaged in the open air, if you have nothing to do that requires great exactitude or precision of work, if you are not subjected to any worry of mind or mental strain, if you sleep well, if you are properly clothed and are not exposed to excesses of heat or cold, if your appetite is good and you can get plenty of wholesome food— if you are favored with all these advantages, then you may indulge in Dr. Parkes' moderate potation of wine, or beer, or spirit. You are strong enough to bear the infliction, and may, without any great risk, enjoy it. But these favorable conditions are all necessary. If you are limited in respect to exercise, if you are of sedentary habits, if you are much worn or reduced in mind, body, or estate, then that small amount of alcohol is adding to all your troubles, and you will leave it off if you are wise.

I can imagine with what pleasure some of the world of pleasure may receive such tidings as these. The salt of the earth, and the salt is good, can then enjoy its luxury, just as it can keep a carriage, a livery servant, a horse, or any other unnecessary, but pleasant extravagance. It can take wine in moderation. What more is required? Science, in her most Puritanical utterances, gives, so far, her consent.

It is quite true, but take her consent with her provisions equally true and very solemn.

Science says, you who can afford the luxury may use it with the perfect understanding that it is a luxury. Positively, solemnly, it is never a necessity, and if the expression of truth be absolutely rendered, you are better and safer without even that moderate indulgence.

What is the danger?

The danger is that attaching to all luxuries: that they being unnecessary, are apt, first, to lapse into self-imposed necessities; next, to become tyrants and bad masters, and to set up bad examples by which many, who are not fortunate even among the easy and luxurious, fall.

A learned man, who is, I assume, a man of science, has, however, bidden us ignore this matter of setting examples. It betrays, he thinks, weakness and want of logic. If there are a number of weak creatures male and female, who by first following moderate example, are led to go further than that example, and who fall into perdition, let them fall, That is their lookout, and examplers are faultless. Stint your own enjoyment to save a man from drink! As well take your warm overcoat off your own back to save a beggar from death by cold. That may be philanthropy, it is not science.

Stop, says Science, not quite so fast there. I said, ages ago, by one of my wisest servants, also a physician, a sentence which another immortal man, who was not one of my disciples, happily reiterated: "Be not deceived; God is not mocked. Whatsoever a man soweth that shall he also reap." I really meant by this sowing, the mere casting into the susceptible soil the smallest seed that will bring forth a harvest; and if you, by your example, sow perdition, in the purest physical and worldly sense, you and yours will reap perdition. This is in the order of nature, from sowing and to reaping; but, adds Science, there is apart from such results as these, another. When you, luxurious man, in your luxurious resolve, have made a self-imposed necessity, you have created a condition of body which, being unnatural, is calculated to feed itself. So you have sown again, your own body being the susceptible field, and in it you may reap the harvest. You have set up within yourself a desire which nothing but the most zealous exercise of your discriminating and resolute will can meet and keep under subjection. You must, therefore, be ever on guard. Trespass but a little on your reso

.ution, and your false desire gains power with the most perplexing decision. In this way, continues Science, some of the very strongest and best of my own sons have been tried and overcome. She directs our minds to one of these, whose illustrious name is the boast of this country, and she gives you his own confession word for word. The case she explains is that of the great man who first discovered, by experiments on himself, the effects of inhaling laughing-gas — Sir Humphry Davy. No one can accuse him of want of will, or skill, or knowledge, or goodness. But he made it a habit, gradually acquired, to inhale this intoxicating gas, until at last he declared that he could not look at a gas-holder, could not even watch a person breathing without experiencing an all but irresistible desire to indulge in this form of intoxication. Who are you then, she inquires, that can resist these subtle influences from intoxicating agents? How know you that you are powerful enough to oppose self-inflicted necessity? There was no one who ever lapsed into danger who did not begin by little and little to learn, first to desire, and afterward to feed desire. Wisely, sedately, without the least feeling, I warn you not to create that desire, and then can you never be betrayed.

And to this warning Science once again adds her cautious instruction. It is true, she repeats, that men who are favorably placed may seem to escape injury from the moderate use of strong drink. But still, on this point, she has a word of information. She proves, from hard facts, that even those who are moderate, live less longer lives than those who abstain altogether. She holds up nine years of actuarial calculations of a provident institution, in which there were two classes of insurers—one class which drank moderately, another which abstained altogether. She shows that in the general section, including those who were moderate drinkers, 2,002 deaths were expected to occur, and 1,977 actually did occur, or within twenty-five of the expected number. She shows that in the abstaining section 1,110 deaths were, by the same mode of calculation, expected to occur, but that actually only 801 deaths did occur, or 309 less than the expected number. Truly, she exclaims again, by the voice of her esteemed interpreter, Dr. Parkes, "the difference in mortality of these two classes is quite extraordinary."

Thus you learn that Science, when she comes to matter of fact, though she admits a possible excuse for moderate drinking, does not favor it; and when she brings us face to face with some other figures, showing the results of the habit that springs from moderation, she strikes us almost dumb with the severity of her warning. Lesson upon lesson is here piled before us from her hard, but faithful voice. Listen to some few of these.

If a man becomes intemperate at twenty years of age, he will only live 15½ years instead of 44 years

If a man becomes intemperate at thirty years of age, he will only live 13⅔ years instead of 36 years.

Amongst men who are engaged in the sale of intoxicating liquors, the temptation to intemperance tells with such force, that 138 of these men die in proportion to a mean of 100 following seventy other occupations.

Out of every 100 persons who were taken into Colney Hatch Asylum in one year, forty were taken from insanity, directly or indirectly produced by alcohol.

Out of 900 inquests held per year by the coroner for Central Middlesex (Dr. Hardwicke) on persons who have died violent deaths, deaths requiring an inquest, 450, or one-half, are due directly or indirectly to the effects of drink.

In England in the year 1876 as many as 1,120 deaths were directly recorded against drink, the persons dying in drink; while the deaths, direct and indirect, due to the same cause, recently most ably calculated by Dr. Norman Kerr or Dr. Morton, are 14,710 wholly due and 24,577 partially due to alcohol; a total of 39,287, and the lowest possible estimate.

We have advanced now a second step in our readings of science on the subject of strong drinks. In our first step she denounced all these drinks as necessities; in the second step she permits them as luxuries; with all due notice of the consequences that attend the indulgence. In this matter she does not directly prohibit, because she does not consider it her province to interfere with the free will of man, but she issues advice which is true to the letter, based on facts which are true to the letter; and that advice is practically prohibitory, if it be honestly followed.

DRINK AND NATIONAL DEVELOPMENT.

There remains still one other subject for her to speak upon—a subject which is thought by many to bring out the stronghold of moderation. Let us have the subject set forth and the answer supplied. It is said that the use of wine and its allies has been the source of the power of the most powerful nations. It is said that the wine-cup has been the fountain of that wit and poetry and artistic wisdom, if I may use the term, which has made the illustrious men of the world so illustrious and so generally useful as they have been to the world. Take away the wine-cup, it is argued, and the whole intellectual life must needs become flat, stale, and unprofitable. It were indeed a pity if this were the look-out of total abstinence. A second deluge of water, with not so much as a graceful dove and an olive-branch to cheer the trackless waste. It were indeed a pity of pities if this were the final look-out of total abstinence in the intellectual sphere. Can it be that all intellectual energy and hilarity must die out with the abolition of the wine-cup? My friend, Dr. Farr mourns that the very eloquence and fire and soul of a dinner of city aldermen, with the mighty Lord Mayor at the head of the table, and Gog and Magog bursting with intellectual admiration, would under such a revolution all go out together—

> "And, like the baseless fabric of a vision,
> Leave not a rack behind."

At first thought, certainly it makes one's blood run cold to think of such a catastrophe. Let us see if things are really so bad. What does Science say on this awful topic?

Science, ever fair, says that some nations and wonderful peoples that have lived have been wine-drinkers at certain periods of their history. But she draws also this most important historical lesson, that the great nations were, as a rule, water-drinkers purely until they became great; then they took to wine and other luxuries, and soon became little. Up to the time of Cyrus, the Persians were water-drinkers. They became all-powerful, and then also became such confirmed wine-drinkers, that, if they had some great duty to perform, they discussed the details of it when inflamed with wine, and rejected the judgment or revised it when they had become sober, and *vice versa*. Surely this was the acme of perfection as a test of wine. Curiously it didn't answer. With its luxury, Persia succumbed—fell into hands of less luxurious conquerors, and, like a modern rake, found its progress anything but promising in the end. The Greeks in their first and simple days were clothed in victory over men and over nature. They grew powerful; they sang and danced, and all but worshiped wine; but it did not sustain them in their grandeur as it ought to have done if the theory of such sustainment be correct. The Roman rule became overwhelming out of the simplicity of its first life. It rose into luxury and made wine almost a god. But Rome fell. Wine did not sustain it. It is all through history the same. There is not an instance, when we come to analysis of fact and circumstance, in which wine has not been to nations as to man individually, a mocker. It has been the death of nations. It has swept down the nations as it sweeps down men in the prime of their life and in the midst of their glory.

POST HOC ET PROPTER HOC.

When we face the question of the influence of wine on the individual greatness of great men, Science in candor again admits that there have been illustrious wine-drinkers. The statement is unanswerable. But when to that statement is added the rider, that the men were great because they were wine-drinkers, she demurs at once. She asks the man who makes that statement, How do you know? How can you know what those great men would have been if they had never tasted wine or other strong drink? You are reasoning, she says, on the principle of "*post hoc et propter hoc*"—after this and therefore this—a common and convenient plan, especially amongst physicians and politicians, of which she gives the following very practical illustration:

A gentleman, well-to-do and happy in his worldly possessions, having dined rather heavily and very late in the evening, fell asleep in his chair before the fire, and woke after a long doze with a severe pain in his stomach. His wife administered her simple domestic remedies, but as her skill seemed to fail, she persuaded the sufferer to put on his thick ulster and walk down to a fashionable physician in the city where they lived and get his learned advice. The physician in question had an enormous reputation. He was reputed to be eminently sound and practical. He was skilled in all pathies, and had been dubbed by a well-known wit whom he had "cured," "the eminent Omniopath." He had a saying, which each day of his life he repeated to his patients some four or five times at least, which stamped his soundness. It was a borrowed saying, but it answered—

> "Drink deep, or taste not the Pierian spring;
> A little knowledge is a dangerous thing."

And of this spring he was believed to drink so deeply, that some said he sat up all night at the source of it taking it in like a fish. The sufferer in the ulster coat had no fear, therefore, though it was very late at night, of not finding his adviser awake and ready for an emergency. His expectations were realized. He found the learned man in his study, and at his usual exercises connected with the classical spring. He told the reason of his late call and related the history of his suffering. The doctor grasped the case in a minute, explained the nature of it, summed up the possible dangers, if the worst came to the worst, and then proceeded in due form to prepare for the prevention of the worst by writing a prescription. The prescription was for one small pilule, which was to be taken by the patient the moment he arrived at home. All thanks and admiration the suffering man departed, and now his next care was to get that prescription made up. He called, therefore, on his way home at the house of a chemist and druggist. He was not so fortunate here. The drowsy owner of this establishment, caring nothing about classical springs, had gone to rest and was fast asleep. It required three or four vigorous pulls of the night bell to pull him out of bed. At last a window in the second floor above the shop opened, a head and shoulders came out of it, and a voice, not very soothing in its accents, asked what was wanted. "I want you," said the sufferer in his blandest and most winning manner, "to be kind enough to come down and make up a pilule (emphasizing the pilule) for me. It is only one pilule, and it will not take you a minute." "Sha'n't come," was the curt reply; "if it's nothing but a pilule you can do without it." "But I can't," was the answer. "Then you must get it somewhere else," were the words that came back to the sufferer. "Where else shall I go?" was the imploring inquiry. The answer dropped like a shot, and the window went down with a rattle that was almost terrific. When the sufferer regained his temper he remembered, by recalling the maps he once drew at school, that the place he was directed to go to was somewhere in the Holy Land. It was clearly too late to go there, and as the walls of the place had been leveled some three thousand years or so, the chances were twenty to one against finding a druggist on the spot, even if he got there; so he took immediately the wise course of going home to his wife. The wife was naturally indignant at the conduct to which her husband had been exposed; but being a shrewd, observing lady, she detected that he was very much better, and by her advice, instead of worrying himself any more about the prescription for that night, he went to bed, slept soundly, and in the morning woke as well as ever he was in his life.

By arrangement, on going into town next day, he called on his physician, and joyfully reported a clean bill of health. The doctor's eyes gleamed with triumph. "'Drink deep'—no, I don't mean that; I mean 'A stitch in time saves nine.' That pilule—that one little pilule, hardly more than a globule, saved you all the impending trouble."

"But," replies the patient nervously, "excuse me sir, I never took it," and then he told the sad story of the drowsy chemist, and the altercation, and the place he was told to go to, and the advice of his wife, and the complete story.

You will expect that the physician was abashed. Not a bit of it. The Empress Josephine was not more ready at a moment's notice to step into the carriage of her Imperial Master than that physician was with his explanation. "You, sir," said he, "are an idiosyncrasy. You are an exception to all rule, and by that you prove the rule. That medicine was used by Dioscorides and the other Greek physicians; it was used by the immortal Galen and the Roman physicians; it was used by Amando Sancto de Joannes and the other mediæval physicians; it was used by the learned Michael Albertus in the last century; it was used by all these eminent men in cases such as yours, and in this day I have myself, with many more, resorted to it in hundreds of the same cases to yours, without, I had almost said, a single failure. You, it is true, got well without it; but where would the other sufferers have been if they had not had it? No, sir, the exception proves the rule, and you are fortunate in what has happened. Be thankful it is no worse." The patient listened, as all patients should, with becoming modesty, but still astonished and bewildered. He was for a moment inclined to ask whether all the other sufferers might not possibly have got well as he did without the pilule But he stood in the presence of a tremendous authority. Moreover, he had got the prescription for that remarkable pilule in his pocket; and, what is more, he had paid for it. So silently he went his way, mingled once again with the crowd, believed in the pilule after all, swore by it, and was never tired of descanting on his own singular constitution, which put him even beyond the necessity for the exercise of an experience that well-nigh had descended from Æsculapius himself.

You smile at this illustration of the *post hoc et propter hoc*. Science does not smile. You think that physician knew better than what he said. Science says probably not. To err is human, and the narrative is supplied for one purpose only in relation to our subject, and that is to suggest to the minds of those who so readily and confidently assert that this great man and that great man would not have been what he was had he not taken wine, the self-question is not that *post hoc et propter hoc*. How can any one tell what the great man would have been if he had abstained from wine altogether?

In the writings of some men of genius there are passages obviously written under the influence of wine, which passages, for the sake of those men of genius and for the world, we would we could blot out forever. If under some better influence the inspiration of these men had been in those moments of writing devoted to purer and finer thoughts, would the result have been less worthy?

Science replies on this point by inference only. The men perhaps thought so themselves in their sober hours. Nor wrote they anything, nor did they anything, of truly noble character under wine. In the whole history of man, find, if you can, a truly noble deed done under the excitement of the wine-cup.

CONCLUSION.

And thus are we brought to our last step on the question before us. The past history of mankind yields no demonstrable proof that nations and men have owed their power and their ability to wine or any strong drink, moderately or immoderately taken. Suppose we leave the verdict there as something wanting proof. No one can say that is unfair.

From this position we may turn to modern life, and test anew for the truth. If those who say that wine moderately used, is, in spite of all its dangers, necessary to the sustainment of current power, intellectual and physical, then it follows, as plain as night follows morn, that we who abstain are intellectually, physically, morally inferior to those who call themselves moderate drinkers. Is it so? The proof lies with those who make the proposition, and who by inference declare in face of day their own superiority. Let them — I say it with my whole heart—let them by their superiority prove it. For my part, I am content to leave the proof with history.

To conclude. From my readings of Science she gives no countenance to the use of strong drink in any sense, except medically and under scientific direction. She faithfully records its evils; she honestly exposes its dangers; she exposes the gross and vain fallacies by which it is supported; and if, in her absolute fairness, she admits it under certain arbitrary restrictions as a luxury, she condemns it as a traitorous evil.

It were pleasanter far to apologize through Science for indulgence in alcohol than to speak through her as I have done to-day. But my business in this world, in the short time I have to live in it, is to dare to speak what I believe to be true, irrespective of all personal pleasures and of all personal penalties—to dare to speak as a votary, rather than a follower, of fashion in scientific service. Thereby, in speaking on the subject that has now engaged us, I may unintentionally offend some natures. I hope not, but this I fear is the fate of all votaries, and must be accepted as such. I recall one votary, who, in introducing the light of a new and purer faith into the world, in the course of his career once exclaimed: "If an offense come out of truth, better is it that the offense come than the truth be concealed." With all gratitude to its author, that statement deserves to be echoed and re-echoed by every one who represents the cause I have ventured to plead, and never more in this country than now. It requires no depth of diagnostic skill to detect how serious is the diseased condition of this country at the present time—how dangerous are the combinations of afflicting causes. Luxury blindly fattening itself for easy prey; want eagerly watching how it may rush to relieve its misery; and both fed by an agent which, with equal facility, ministers to the slothful indifference of one and the sleepless passion of the other. In such a time as this, is it an offense to attempt to exorcise from our midst an agent so maddening, so devilish, so deadly? If it be, let the offense come; for then also is it an offense to wish that the future history of our still self-enslaved land may be a history of soberness sanity, health, happiness, and spotless freedom.

THE
MEDICAL PROFESSION
AND
ALCOHOL.

THE MEDICAL PROFESSION AND ALCOHOL.

AN INAUGURAL ADDRESS

By Benjamin Ward Richardson, M.D., F.R.S.,
President of the British Medical Temperance Association.

> "Be stirring as the time; be fire with fire;
> Threaten the threatener, and outface the brow
> Of bragging horror. So shall inferior eyes,
> That gather their behavior from the great,
> Grow great by your example."

OUR national poet made these lines address themselves to a living power he had in his mind which he wished for his dramatic purpose to excite into vigorous action. The words meant an instigation to sharp, decisive, and real warfare against an armed threatener. To-day in relation to actual war no such words are necessary; but there are struggles—warfares, if we like to call them so—to which the words, and the thoughts expressed by the words, wondrously apply. The civilized world is just now in open hostility to a threatener which, of all others, has, time out of mind, been most deadly ruinous, cruel, and devastating. A threatener, grafted on to a superstition, self-inflicted by man on man, that he, out of the whole circle and chain of living creatures, must have for his life and sustainment a thing to drink so foreign to his nature that he must learn to endure it before he likes it, and then suffer endless penalties for the liking he has acquired. In the fifty years which I have lived this superstition has been, by direct and indirect means, the cause of death to at least two millions of human beings in our country alone. What war, what conqueror in the histories of the histories of the world, ever destroyed forty thousand persons a year in one country every year for forty years; what plague, pestilence, or famine ever committed such havoc?

Nor is it a question only of death that is to be considered. There are the consequences also to the survivors. There are the diseases, the griefs, the shame, the disgrace, the helplessness, the homelessness, the poverty, the crime, the whole of the domestic anarchies incident to the mortality. These must be added to the triumphs of the merciless threatener, the Juggernaut of civilization.

I am by profession a healer of men. I solemnly swore on entering the splendid profession to which I belong, I solemnly swore as my brethren of the same calling have each and all solemnly sworn, that I would consider it a part of my holy duty, as long as I lived, as a capable rational being to practise it, to respect, of all things, life; to relieve pain and disease, to alleviate, and to the very height of known skill, according to my gifts, to stave off death from my fellow-men. Can I, in conscience, in the remembrance of so solemn an obligation, be anything else than a foe to so mortal a threatener as that which slays forty thousand of my countrymen per year, and accompanies the act with all the accessory ferocities and evils attendant on such wholesale destruction? I ask any member of the body of Medicine, who is under the same obliga tion, if he can reconcile the tolerance of this practical and merciless threatener with the conscientious fulfillment of his binding obligations? What men of any class are so encompasssd with an obligation touching the lives and interests of their brother men?

One of the objects why the society of medical men which meets together now has been formed, is to threaten the threatener, and, as the poet would continue—

> "To outface the brow
> Of bragging horror."

For this superstition is, of all superstitions, a bragging horror of the truest kind. No man at table lifts his glass defiantly to his neighbor to encourage him to the same, or to laugh at him for noncompliance, without having the consciousness that the act is simple bragging, and that the end of it, as a lesson, is, in the strictest sense of the practice of it, mere horror, which he could not look at were it put before him in all its wholesale woe.

We, as a society, are a small body. We number a hundred at most, all told; so that I am, by the pleasure of the members, as their captain, a mere centurion in the army of medicine. Still it is a notable fact that there should be one hundred medical men joined together with the rest of the abstaining community to make war against the threatener. We assume at this moment to exist only as a nucleus. We wish chiefly to exist that we may attach all others of the same profession to join with us. We would that every man who calls himself a healer were "stirring as the time" were "fire with fire," and that his example, so potent for good or evil, should be stamped for good in this great contest.

And this, I think, is indeed a point to win—even beyond the winnings of science through him—that, whenever a medical man is fairly and fully brought over from the fanatical superstition of this Juggernaut of civilization, he is at once an example of examples to all around him. The example of the clergyman is, no doubt, of the greatest moment; but that, even, is not like the example set by the doctor. The clergyman is open to challenge from hour to hour, on the doctrine of necessity. He may urge all that he can on the moral side of the question; he may appeal in the most fervid and eloquent terms to the sympathies of his auditors; but when they approach him on the ground of necessity, when they say to him that they cannot exist without the aid of alcohol, when they, as intelligent persons, reason with him on scientific grounds, then they are, or may be, a match, or more than a match, for him. In like manner, the head of a family or of an establishment may declare his own views, set forth his own example, insist on his command being obeyed, and even enforce those commands; but he will have a diminished influence when he comes to close quarters in argument with those who are of the same standing and right as himself; while he is liable to be branded as a mere opiniated man, and a tyrannical man, by those who obey because they fear, and do not believe.

Moreover, there are times when all who may be

staunch believers in total abstinence see cause for doubt in their own minds. Some one near to them, some one for whom they feel they hold a responsibility, declares that, in a pressing emergency, the stimulus of strong drink is necessary; and what is then to be done? How can the unlearned man deal, even with a drunkard, under such circumstances? He hesitates in the crisis; and gives way, it may be, to a good-natured impulse, which is as likely to be ruinous as it is likely to be useful in its after-effects.

But when the medical man is brought on the field he is in a different position altogether. It really is not necessary for him to enter on the moral side of the question at all. It is hardly necessary for him to appeal to any sympathetic argument. On that side of the Temperance question he finds the battle won for him. There is no one whose opinion is worth considering who doubts the morality of perfected temperance; no one who hesitates to admit that, under the absolute reign of temperance, poverty, crime, disease, would lessen, and happiness increase. The medical man may, therefore, stand with effect purely on his own ground. He speaks with authority on the question of authority; he reads with precision the pleadings for the supposed sustaining agent, and detects without hesitation whether they be real or the mere unnecessary desires of a perverted and distempered brain. How strong his position! in proportion, how solemn his duty! Other men may laugh, he cannot; other men may sigh, he need not. He is there the wise man, the arbiter who is educated to know, and who is referred to as knowing. Just a word from him in the right direction how it may save those who are deceiving themselves, and, in that self deception, deceiving others more determinately. If our society, as a nucleus, could get the whole of the profession to proceed with it so far, in the exercise of the legitimate influence of medicine, and no further, what an aid it should bring to the work of the great reformation that is in progress I need not tell to those who, with anxious minds and hearts, are watching the professional tone and sentiment for the slightest breath of its sympathy. The act of all medicine thrown into the scale of perfected temperance; the example, of which the poet speaks, thrown into the scale of perfected temperance! It is one of those aspirations so much to be hoped for; there seems to be no labor too great to realize it. no honest prize too heavy to win it.

In estimating this success, we are bound, moreover, to look at it from the negative as well as the positive point of view. They say, in politics, that one vote gained is equal to two, because the winning side wins what the other side loses. In the contest on which we are engaged to win, one doctor is a far greater winning: because, if the influence of the physician or surgeon on our side be for good, the influence of but one against us is far more potent for evil. A doctor whose example turns the scale ever so little toward intemperance; a doctor who treats this question as a joke; the doctor, moreover, who devotes his energies to his calling of saving life, and who, with forty thousand of his fellow country folk dying yearly around him from one cause, and who, toward that cause, exhibits indifference or carelessness, or apathy—what pretensions has he to be a healer? Where is his honor, to say no word of his feeling? Is it honor to swear fealty and not to obey? What if some other great cause of mortality—say of consumption—were at work, slaying its thousands annually, and that cause were as well known to him as this cause—would he toward that be equally indifferent? Would he hand it about, partake of it himself, give it to his children, laugh at those who are wearying to sweep it away, or tell the afflicted from it that it is a necessity? I am sure he would scorn to do any such thing.

As a society we want to bring these things home. We know they are not ignored intentionally, but we feel that they are ignored unintentionally; and we hope that, if they can be only canvassed fairly by our brethren, they will soon be recognized as truths deserving the choicest judgment. We offer no reflection on the past, for we admit that in the past there was a common error pervading medicine in relation to the physiological action of alcohol, a common blindness as to the pathological evils springing from it, and a common misunderstanding or ignorance as to the extent of the evils. We remember how in our pathological studies our masters indifferently noticed the lesions admittedly produced by alcohol as they were observed in the dead, while they devoted their energies to define with the utmost nicety the lesions which immediately caused death. I recall one of those devoted.

teachers, whose memory I shall ever cherish, who, at nearly every research in the dead-house, would end the most careful description of the conditions that were the actual cause of the fatal disease with, "Gentlemen, there are the usual known other lesions, with which I need not trouble you, because they come under one head—whisky."

We admit all these past mistakes; we know how blind not we alone but all the world has been, and we come at present purely to review the past with the intention of improving the future; of asking if there be not some common ground on which we can all work, and, stirring with the time, be indeed "fire with fire."

There is much already that is uncommon amongst us, as a fraternity, in respect to the alcohol question. It is astonishing what we have gained in a few short years in the way of positive knowledge on the subject. How, having got into the natural lines of inquiry, we have, even in opposition to our prejudices, found one proof of action confirm and support other proofs. Fifteen years, or at most twenty years ago, the true physiological action of alcohol was a speculative discussion unsupported by any reliable experiment, and therefore of the most contradictory order. Now there is so much evidence of its mode of action that dispute gives way to accepted fact. That the ultimate action of alcohol in the animal temperature is to reduce the temperature that alcohol relaxes organic muscular fibre; that alcohol produces four destructive physiological states of the body; that alcohol reduces oxidation; that alcohol interferes with natural dialysis; that alcohol induces, even taken in small quantities, a series of morbid changes and diseases which were not formerly attributed to it; that alcohol prepares the body for destruction by external shocks and depressions which are thus made more fatal; that alcohol belongs to the same class of chemical substances as chloroform, ether, and the anæsthetic family; all this is practically now on the accepted record, with the final admission, when we are speaking and thinking seriously, that man, like his lower earth-mates, and like his own children, can, in health, live and work and play as well—not to put a finer point on it—without a trace of alcohol as he can with it.

"I agree," writes a medical friend to me—a friend who will not go so far as to allow himself to belong to a totally abstaining society even of his own brethern—"I agree with you that the lower animals are better without alcohol. I agree that children and young people are better without alcohol. I candidly confess I do not know when a young person should begin to partake of it, or at what age of life any person who has never tasted of it should begin. I agree with the ancients, who had a law on the subject that the whole female sex would be vastly better without it, and that those women bring up the healthiest children who never touch it. I agree that a man in a good condition of health is better without it. I have been to see Carver shoot, and I am forced to the conclusion that a glass of wine would almost of a certainty spoil all his sport; nay, to please you, which is always a satisfaction, I will honestly state that I do not believe any man who trusted in the least to alcohol could do what Carver does, with such almost superhuman precision. I quite admit what you relate in one of your lectures, that in towns and communities of abstainers, like Johnsburg, health, comfort, happiness, and wealth are all advanced far beyond what they would if the wine-god made his entrance there. All these confessions I make, but but still I can not join you."

My friend is a representative, I believe, of nearly the whole profession of Medicine that thinks on this question seriously. Strange it is that with such ad vance of thought there should be so much of hesi tation as to the logical course to pursue!

Another physician I could name has recently read Dr. Cheyne's well-known essay on "Health and Long Life," published in 1725, and thereby he is sorely perplexed. Cheyne puts before this reader some curious arguments. Cheyne says, "That no man is afraid to forbear strong liquors in an acute distemper, what quantity soever he might have drunk in his health, and yet any sudden change in his humours would not only be more dangerous then than at any other time, but also would more readily happen and come to pass in such critical cases. But," he continues, "the matter of fact is false and groundless; for I have known and observed constant good effects from leaving off suddenly large quantities of wine, and flesh meats too, by those long accustomed to both, and never observed any ill consequences from it in any case whatsoever. Those whose constitutions have been quite broken and running into dissolution, have lived longer and been less pained in sickness by so doing; and those who have had a fund in nature to last longer, have grown better, and attained their end by it."

This experience of a very wise old father of medicine perplexes my doubting modern friend the more, because, to the letter, it represents his own practice and his own experience. In all cases of acute disease he has, from custom, forbidden, as a first direction, wine and every other stimulant; and in most cases of diseases of all kinds—liver cases, stomach cases, brain cases—he has followed the same plan. What is more, he has found it a good plan, and, as Cheyne says, he never has seen anything but ultimate good from it. And so he asks himself—if it be good to cut this agent off in disease because the body is diseased; and if it be true, as all seem by consent to declare, that in health the body does not require the agent, when does the body require it, even from the point of view of a doctor who, in spite of it all can not join such a society as this?

Another of my brethren, who is, in like manner, in doubt, communicates his view in equally striking terms. He says, referring to one of my lectures: "The best service you, I think, ever made was in your pulling us all up on the question of the degree to which alcohol should be carried in its administration, and in insisting that it should never be carried beyond the first stage or degree of its action. I see" (he adds) "that one of the writers in the *Contemporary Review* repeats the same lesson, and lays it down as a rule that whenever alcohol is taken to the extent of doing more than causing flushing of the face, and a little excitation of the heart and brain, it has been given or taken in such sufficiency that to go further would be to go into danger. I entirely agree with this advice sometimes, my friend, but the difficulty with me lies in carrying it out in practice. How do I know what quantities of different wines or spirits to order for people of different ages and constitutions so as to produce just this effect and no more? The drinks are varying quantities, the drinkers more varying still. To carry out the rule, I must first make a physical analysis of every drink I prescribe, and then make a mental analysis of every person I prescribe for. This is absurd. Again, I find that the constitutions treated are like the movable feasts, never twice alike. If I can produce the precise tint of flushing to-day, in a man, by six ounces of sherry, or three ounces of the finest whisky—the Encore whisky, for example, which is said to be the purest—I am told in a week or two that the quantity had lost its effect, and that I must change the drink or give a little more. Then I shake in my shoes, lest by yielding I should encourage my patient to rely on the drink, to increase it and become a tippler. So," he concludes, "the question, as I see it is surrounded with difficulties. The theory is perfect, the practice an impossibility. I do not want, certainly, to induce people to get into the second stage of alcoholism any more than you do, and would like to prescribe alcohol to cause a given effect, as I prescribe chloroform, chloral, mercury, iodide of potassium, or quinine; but the thing is not to be done unless, like you and your friends, I go over to total abstinence and use the good gift as if it were a mere drug; a step which, in my opinion, is just as intemperate as the intemperate misuse of the gift." It is very strange indeed to hear these reasonings, reasonings against reason; and yet I rather greet them. They are signs of an awakening conviction that at the bottom of the argument some fanatical sentiment, some ingrained looseness of principle, is felt and almost repented of. By standing steadily together, though we be but a hundred, we shall, I think, in time easily conquer such objections as these.

It is a fact, openly confessed by those who are not with us, that we are logical, and only too rigid in our method. So we are charged.

Let us not at the same time, in pride of logical status, contend that those who are not with us have no other arguments save of the kind above quoted. There are other arguments, and with one or two of the best of them I propose, in all candor, to deal for a few minutes of time.

There are some who say that if we are logically right, we are losing ground by insisting too forcibly even on our rightness. This is a world of give and take, and the wisest rules will be relaxed by the wisest men. The old author of the work on "Health and Long Life" helps his argument when he says, "The reflection is not more common than just that he who lives physically must live miserably." The truth is that too great nicety and exactness about every minute circumstance that may impair our health is such a yoke and slavery as no man of a free spirit would submit to. "'Tis," as a poet expresses it, "to die for fear of dying. On the other nand, to cut off our days by intemperance, to live miserably for the sake of gratifying a sweet tooth, is equally beneath the dignity of human nature." Well, we all admit this to be true, and we would relax our rigid rule about wine if we felt that to take off wine were "to die for fear of dying." Our contention is, that to leave it off is not to assume but to cast away a yoke and a slavery which no man of a free spirit would submit to. Our argument is that the wine drinkers are the yoke bearers, we the free men; and that their indulgence, in this instance, is beneath the dignity of their nature, while the casting off the yoke is for the happiness, not less than the health, of all mankind whom it affects, now and to come.

There are others who argue that the world itself is not prepared to receive the truth from the professors of medicine, even if the arguments against the use of alcohol were all accepted. They say that faith would be lost in them by their patients if the luxury were too hastily forbidden; they insist that they could not live by practice expounding such extreme views, and they assure us that free will is one of the potent influences to be conciliated even in matters of life and death. I admit at once the speciousness of this argument. I have written an essay dealing on free will in relation to physic. I have a keen appreciation of the power of free will, but I still see one other side, perhaps two, even to this objection. First, if medical men were united, free will in the many against them would have little chance; secondly, in this matter, if I mistake not the signs of the times, the tide of free will is going rather against them than with them in opposition to the use of alcohol. At all events, if popular free will has not set up in full tide against alcohol, popular free doubt has, and that is next thing to it; so on this mere subject of expediency (and it is nothing else) our society has no need to do more than keep up its colors and stand by them triumphantly.

The idea that alcohol is necessary to enable men to perform extra mental or physical work has so utterly come to grief, it is really not necessary that I should put it forward, even as a remnant of superstition against us; but it has been suggested, leaving the present ground of history altogether, giving up, in despair, all attempts to reply to those unanswerable modern proofs against the old fallacy, which Arctic explorers, men of great strength and physical skill, incessant minds, and the most laborious literary scholars so richly supply; it has been suggested, I repeat, that, in some inscrutable manner, alcohol has been the feeding-mother of great nations, that it has sustained racial tenacities and vitalities, overcome mighty adversaries, and been, in short, both a herald and a conqueror on the side of civilization. For our parts we, who dare to doubt this conclusion, want to know on what facts the conclusion is based. We are willing to learn, but we insist that those who preach must prove. Who can say what any great and mighty nation would have been to-day if wine had never been? By what evidence can the destinies of nations in favor of a good destiny be traced through wine or strong drink? We can see some facts in history in relation to the effects of human acts plainly enough. We can see, for instance, that Constantine most probably destroyed the Roman empire by moving the seat of government from its old basis to a new city that should be marked by his name. But where is there any corresponding fact bearing on great events and making of nations, wine being the factor? Suppose we turn to some facts, such as they are, in history, and they point circumstantially all the other way. Nations the mightiest have risen while they were abstaining nations; have fallen when wine became their luxury. Herodotus gives us the record of all-powerful Cyrus receiving from a small Ethiopian prince a bow, with this message; " Tell Cyrus that when he can bend this bow, which is mine, or find a Persian to do it, he may come and conquer Macrobia." And the historian relates, with evident satisfaction, that these Macrobians, who were the finest of men, so that they stood a head above the Persians, and were a truly noble race, were distinguished from the Persians in that they drank no fluid stronger than milk, while the Persians reveled in wine. There is yet another bit of evidence against a hypothesis of alcohol as the nursing-mother of great nations. Through all tribulations, through all vicissitudes, through all persecutions, what nation has maintained its vitality like the Jewish nation? Has alcohol been to this people a nursing-mother? Baron Haller, dealing with this topic in the last century, gave the secret of the cause of this vitality all in one word—*sobrietas*.

There is one other line of objection taken against our work, which is the last I have space to refer to, but which is first in its bearing on our success. The objection relates to the possibility of successfully treating disease in some forms of it without the aid of alcohol. Opinion in the profession itself has greatly changed at various times on this subject, independently altogether of the subject of temperance. Before ever the temperance question was dreamed of, medical men, and schools of medical men were in conflict from time to time on the right and wrong in using alcohol in disease. The Greek and Roman physicians were moderate in their employment of wine. They used, it is true, various kinds of wine; they used salted wines; they used acid wines; and in many ways they used wines purely as medicines, not confounding the general with the special use at all, and, as a rule, proclaiming against their general use. The Middle Age physicians were almost as cautious as their predecessors, and although, after the time of Albucases, in the eleventh century, they became acquainted with the use of spirit of wine—ardent spirit—they do not seem to have employed the ardent spirit to any extent, if at all, for internal use in the treatment of disease. They used the spirit chiefly for tinctures and for dissolving resins and gums. After the time of Stahl the doctrine of the phlogistic theory, and of the antiphlogistic treatment of disease led to the all but abandonment of stimulants in the treatment of disease, so that during last century we had many illustrious physicians who, on theory, let stimulants stand aside; while some others joined in the objection to the use of those agents from more general and, I had almost said, for more generous sentiments as to their danger to mankind. The illustrious Haller, Boerhave, Armstrong, and particularly Erasmus Darwin, were earnest in their support of what we now call the principles of temperance, and the illustrious representative of the name of Darwin to this day maintains the principle in unbroken line. Then, just about one hundred years ago, there occurred for a time a revulsion of feeling, owing to the attempted establishment in Edinburgh of what was called the Brunonian system of medicine, founded by one of the most erratic, generous, and unhappy men and classical scholars medicine ever possessed, John Benson Brown, who strove to institute a system of medicine based on the internal administration of stimulants and narcotics—chiefly wine, or rum, and opium. In his physiology he classed the stimulant and the narcotic together as stimuli, and held up the practice of their free administration, as the all but universal cure. Disease was to him always a relaxation or loss of vital power, and the cure of disease was by and through the conserving elevating stimulant. In 1780, Brown was for a second time elected president of the old Medical Society of the Edinburgh University, and to such fury did debate run there that a law was passed for expelling students who challenged other students to mortal combat. Cullen, and all the leaders of the Edinburgh School, opposed Brown, who, in time, came to London, where he died, in his fifty-second year, of apoplexy, after having taken a large dose of opium, to which stimulant narcotic he was accustomed. That he exerted an influence in favor of the stimulating method of treating disease is without any doubt; it suggested a bad idea which ministered in its badness to one of the weaknesses of mankind, and he himself, no doubt, with all his genius, fell upon his own sword. In the early part of the present century the debate as to the value of wine in disease continued, the practice at least lapsing into a compromise, the rule of which still continuing I am myself able to remember. The rule was that, in acute disease, phlogistic disease, the remedies to be used were to be strictly antiphlogistic or depressing, by which rule all stimulants were rigorously excluded; but when the fury of the phlogistic attack had been subdued, and the sick man, by bleeding, tartar emetic, and purgatives, had been reduced to death's door, then it was the thing to bring him up again by gently pouring in wine or other stimulants with an improved dietary. In the profession of medicine these were halcyon days; for the people they were rather too systematic to be advantageous, and they met their end by the hand of Dr. Todd, who, seeing the evil done by the depressing system, and not the evil by the recruiting system, pushed his theories to the extent, practically, of saying that all disease was depression of itself, and therefore, required to be treated boldly, and, from the outset, with a stimulant. I, for my part, imbued in early life by the lessons of a venerable practitioner of medicine of the antiphlogistic school, was never led away by the enthusiasm of Todd, whom I knew very well, and who was always most kindly interested in my experimental work. But I have always felt that Todd did great service in dispelling the old dogma of the violent antiphlogistic line, and only erred in not stopping at that point. His revulsion back to Brunonianism was for a time, no doubt, a serious disaster; but the very mischiefs it wrought were, in the end, a gain to the cause of temperance. By exaggerating the tendencies of mankind to intemperance, it struck a note of alarm in the hearts of conscientious physicians, and made them anxious (as the eminent Dr. Fothergill in his latter days expressed) whether, in curing the sick by wine, the physician might not be giving him the first lessons in fatal inebriation.

Since the time of Todd the tone of the profession has been one of conflict and sobering down, in these last days, to the idea that stimulants are only temporary necessities in disease, and that men in good health require none. The old antiphlogistic mania has departed, and its Brunonian sequence is following the same course.

With this improved mode of thought the profession, no doubt, is lending itself to the spirit of the age. What we want is that it should do more. Confessedly in the march of those simple and grand men who, in their noble simplicity and greatness of nature, led the way to the redemption of the drunkard from drink, the profession has lost the lead. We may regret this; but, as it is too true, regrets were vain. It has not, in this respect, been worse than its learned friends. The Church of all banners lost its lead; the law has not yet moved in a single form of organization into the ranks of the veterans. But, at last, the Church of all banners has taken up its place, and we are organized to go with it. Our aim now should be to cast off all things that so easily beset us, and step boldly into the van. We are held back mainly by one conservative feeling—I do not say that in derision, for medicine, to be sound, must always be conservative; we are held back by the idea that alcohol is a necessity, not for health nor for the healthy, but for our work in the treatment of disease. We are none of us in this society out of sympathy with this sentiment, though it be but a sentiment. We all claim the right to use alcohol if, in our hearts, we believe we save life by it, save suffering, or lessen affliction. We merely contend —and this is the point we want our fellow-laborers to recognize—that it must be used *secundum artem*.

As a therapeutical agent, I have never excluded alcohol from my practice. But this is what I have done for nine years past: I have, whenever I thought I wanted its assistance, prescribed it purely as a chemical medicinal substance, in its pure form, in precise doses, in definite order of time; as I have prescribed amyl nitrite, or chloroform, or ether, so I have prescribed alcohol.

By this method I have an absolute experience of the clinical use of alcohol, which, I think I may safely say, does not belong to many other prescribing physicians. There are thousands of physicians who, in the same time, have probably prescribed alcoholic fluids a hundred times to my single time; but if they were to be asked the precise doses they have ordered, the actual purity of the substances they have ordered, they would be quite unable, in most cases, to answer at all. So many ounces of wine, so many ounces of brandy or whisky, really means nothing at all that is reliable. Therefore an absolute experience of alcohol, and that only, is a novelty. When I order alcohol, I prescribe so much of it as I think or know will produce the desired effect, directing the specific gravity of the fluid to be ·830, which is not absolute alcohol, absolute alcohol being ·795, but which is sufficiently near to be reliable. This is the alcohol commonly retailed as absolute alcohol, and is made without the expense and trouble of removing the last portion of water.

Used medicinally in this manner, the therapeutical action of alcohol may be soon reduced to a positive method. There is no ambiguity of action about it at all. It is as easily manageable as chloroform, and is as definite in result as mercury, or iodide of potassium. The differences of statements as to its influence in disease are, in fact, one and all due to the unscientific and utterly fallacious mode of ordering it as wine, or spirit, or beer, without regard to quantity, quality, or admixture; for when it is ordered in that way the percentage of alcohol is unknown, the fact that there is no other alcohol save the ethylic is unproven, and the other disturbing agents that may be present, in the way of ethers and acids, are not calculated for, though they may be very important.

From the simple method and scientific course pursued, I may say that when alcohol is prescribed for the sick in a positive mode in relation to quantity, quality, and purity, so that nothing but the action of ethylic alcohol is brought under observation after the administration, the phenomena which follow are singularly corroborative of the physiological facts which have of late years been made known as to its action on healthy bodies. It is probable indeed that the influence of no other medicine in the pharmacopœia can be more correctly read by the light of physiological learning than alcohol. The chief difficulty that attends the administration for securing positive results lies in the circumstance that so many persons have accustomed themselves to the use of it in varying quantities, there is no standard dose applicable to the community at large for ensuring the precise degree of action that may be desired. We are often in the same condition in respect to this drug as we are in respect to opium, when on rare occasions we have to treat a person who is addicted to the daily use of opium.

When, however, we have under treatment those who are not accustomed to alcohol, the results are regular and decisive. Then the dose of half a fluid ounce, by measure, of ·830 ethylic alcohol administered to an adult is, as a rule, sufficient to produce a brief temporary action. The action commences within ten minutes after the fluid is taken, and the first sign of its action is detectable in the circulation. The action of the heart is quickened, the rate of quickening being distinct even when the pulsation is previously quickened from disease. The rate of increase runs, as a rule, from five to seven pulsations per minute, and even in cases of permanently slow pulse the rule is maintained, as I found in the instance of a member of my own profession, who has a permanently slow pulse of thirty-five. With this rise in the pulse there follows the temporary elevation of surface warmth, and all the other signs and subsequent effects of that ephemeral fever from alcohol with which we are so well conversant; a fever which, in some respects, resembles a mild ague, and in other respects a hectic. By the use of alcohol in this pure form we learn with much accuracy its effects when it is administered in minor doses so as not to produce any objective effect; but it is presumed to conserve metamorphoses of tissue, or quicken local circulations. On the whole I am not inclined to deny the use of alcohol in this strictly scientific sense. I could do very well without it, since there are other substances which take its place that are less persistent in their effects, and are not so prone to create a constitutional appetite for themselves; but as a remedial agent of a third or fourth class value it deserves to be retained in the arcanum of physic.

I think I have shown now, in all that is present and practical, that there is a reason for the existence of this nucleus of abstaining medical men; that the nucleus has its work laid out; and that the affection and adhesion of other members of the same profession, of which it forms so small a part, is for all sakes a realization to be hoped for and expected.

The illustrious Descartes, in one of his prophetic

moods, ventured to predict that all the great movements of the world of thought, in physics, in morals, and even in government, would at some future day be evolved out of the medical sciences. It was natural for the founder of the Cartesian philosophy to predict in this wise. With him there were but two principles in nature—" I think, therefore, I am "—" and nothing exists but substances." The combination made up man, a spiritually materialized organism, who must, with his material surroundings, come, in course of time, more and more particularly under the cognizance of those who study the attributes and structure of man, and the effects of the external forces and materialities upon his existence, habits, and character. To Descartes the social status of the Physician strengthened this conception. In his time there were no general rivalries of thought and learning to oppose the particular thought and learning of the strictly professional man. Between the philosophical scholars, and the commonalty there was a gulf which seemed to be impassable. The few learned were so distinct they held the whole province of knowledge, and when they spoke others did but wonder and listen ; listen to Réné Cartes himself as to an oracle. Why should they change?

Had Descartes lived to this hour he would have seen that the gulf between the learned and the unlearned was anything but impassable, that it might be broad but was not too deep to be crossed successfully, and that the ultimate fate of the world was probably for it to cross *en masse* into the domain of learning, to settle there and make the domain as common property as ever was claimed by an overwhelming force that knew how to march and to conquer.

Perhaps, therefore, in this day the great metaphysicist might not be inclined to take the same sanguine view as that which he expressed so convincingly in his own day. He would see, with deep satisfaction, his theory of the extension of matter into infinitude brought, by such men as William Crookes, into experimental demonstration; but he would not see any particular sect of men belonging to medicine taking under their supervision the whole physical, metaphysical, and moral administration of the world. So far from seeing this, he would be a witness to a decline from any such commanding position. He would see all the learned professions bordering on a state of discontinuity. He would observe that men and women of all classes were beginning to know and think for themselves without the aid of any professional adviser, or, when calling in the aid of such adviser in great emergencies, being extremely inquisitive at the moment and extremely critical afterwards when the fruits of the advice, good, bad, or indifferent, were declared. More remarkable still, he would see in our modern civilized circles an universal educational life growing up amongst the young which, like hardy vegetation on good old soil, was threatening to uproot everything before it and to establish a new face and destiny.

Stranger still would it be to the father of the Cartesian philosophy that in no point were his calculations so far out as on the point of the progress into power of his favored professional community. He would see the grand interests of that profession poorly recognized; he would fail to discern that classical scholarship which was so distinctive a feature in the medical celebrities he knew; he would discover no exercise of political influence beyond what was held by the community in general; he would be pained to hear amongst the half-educated ruling classes not unfrequent remarks of disparagement as to the social and scientific distinction of his favored brotherhood; he would witness with sadness and amazement the fact that, in deference to a whimsical folly of the age, some of the best men amongst the brotherhood were frittering away their lives at some contemptible little section of their noble craft, to which section they were mercilessly, piteously specialised: and, worst of all, he would gather that by this process of dividing, dividing, dividing, the whole body was, by wide-spreading, being brought into danger of utter disintegration.

And yet, gentlemen, there was after all nothing but what was natural and probable in the prophecy of Descartes. It is perfectly true that we, as a brotherhood, are or ought to be engaged in studies and pursuits so sublime and so intimately connected with every incident of this mortal life, that we should be in every sense a first power amongst mankind. So closely connected are our pursuits with the heart and soul of all that lives that if we had no ambitions, no passions, no desires, we ought by our very work to stand in the first ranks of mankind. Respect, profound and persistent, should be paid to our work if not to our workmen; and yet our best work is, as a rule, known only to ourselves.

At last, in this social position of our body politic and scientific,—a position not heartily accredited by men of pure science; not over warmly admitted by the republic of letters; scarcely thought of by the artistic world, although our artistic working is of the most refined order; sometimes frowned at by the Church; resorted to by the masses as a necessity they would gladly avoid; and all the while keeping within our own sphere as if we had no connection with the outer world except by the practical tie of professional interest,—in this position, I repeat, we come at last face to face with one of the great revolutionary incidents in the present grand—surpassingly grand beyond anything of which we have any record—revolutionary epochs of human history: I mean the supreme effort which is now being made, with every prospect and certainty of ultimate success, to rid the world of the slavery of superstition, folly, sin, sorrow, madness, and death that has for ages past been imposed upon the world by the use of alcoholic drinks.

Never in our course as a profession have we been brought face to face with the public in a more serious or solemn manner. We are brought face to face with the public on a question which it will have solved though it solve it independently of us altogether, and that a question which is singularly, and in the name of health, emphatically our own. The question is not whether man can live without the use of alcholic drinks, but whether we can, by our voice and authority, justify the thoughtful section of the public in its attempt to prove that men can not only live without such aid, as the lower creation lives, but can live as healthily; whether men who have been accustomed to take stimulants until they have acquired a lower organization than was meant for them, can give up the habit with safety as well as advantage; and, lastly, if it ever be necessary that alcohol or some similar agent be positively called for in emergency, whether we, as men specially fitted for the task, can not come to the assistance of the public, and by our skill meet their difficulty without encouraging a habit which is fraught with danger to the individual, and with endless suffering to the nation—to the world.

We who constitute this society are all of us men who, in the active exercise of professional duty, are living witnesses of the truth of the proposition that men engaged as we are fulfil our allotted tasks without recourse to alcohol as a sustainer or a part of our life's feast. We join hands in this matter with the rest of the abstaining community, and we join with it in the belief that we perform our work more steadily, more cheerfully, more easily, more healthfully, than we did when we indulged in the factitious delusion and practice of seeking sustainment from alcohol. We extend from this experience our lines of observation and inference. We argue that, as we are no more and no less mortal than our even Christian, what we can do can be done also by any member of our profession. We, therefore, have a logical basis of argument, and can move heart and soul with those who strive to redeem the world from one of its worst slaveries But, then, we are a mere isolation. Out of twenty thousand in the ranks of medicine we number a two-hundredth part, and the rest, what does it say, that voice of two hundred to one?

I will not indicate, at this moment, what the representatives of that great voice should say. I will only urge that the mode in inspiring reliance on their utterings by the public mind and conscience —is, that they should speak definitely, aye or no, to definite questions. When they are asked if alcoholic drinks are a necessity for healthy life, they ought to be able to say, with the proof on their lips, aye or no. When asked if the confirmed alcoholic, of any age, can give up his stimulant without injury, they ought to be able to say as clearly, aye or no. When asked by an earnest man or woman, who wishes to reclaim either a single individual or a community, whether they can help in the emergency by meeting an assumed necessity, they ought to be able to say aye or no, with a precision of statement worthy of their learning and their vocation. We stand, all of us, on our mettle when these questions come forward to be answered. The public, that regards so little our politics, that cares so much less for our routine work, that ignores our finest triumphs of skill with so much stolidity, tests us here. These (say they) are the men who, of all others, ought to say definitely aye or no. Here is a great public question, essentially their own. Let us test them and try them. If they are not able to answer questions so simple and straightforward more distinctly than we are, what good are they? As to that two-hundredth part, they may be mere enthusiasts, and their saying may be prompted by their sympathies rather than by their reason; we want to know what the majority can satisfactorily tell us.

I do not overstate the matter in the least in these remarks. The profession of medicine has lost sufficient already by its attitude toward this vital, urgent question. Remaining as it does a few years longer, it will lose beyond recall the confidence it still retains; for time will yield the answer it ought to give without reference to its final judgment, if that judgment be long delayed.

With all respect, therefore, but all earnestness, we say to our brethren everywhere—

"Be stirring as the time, be fire with fire."

nor do we fear to add the corollary of the poet:

"So shall inferior eyes,
Which gather their behaviors from the great,
Grow great by your example."

THE
LIBERTY OF THE ABJECT.

THE LIBERTY OF THE ABJECT

An Address delivered at the Anniversary of the London Auxiliary of the United Kingdom Alliance.

Mr. President, Ladies, and Gentlemen:—Some friend of mine, whom I have known for many years as an acquaintance rather than as an intimate friend, met me ten days ago on the Metropolitan Railway, and said, "So you are going to be with that Canon of Westminster again on the platform. If you go about with canons and prelates much longer we shall expect to see you in the Church, and looking out for a bishopric." "Well," I said, "if it had been my fate to be in the Church I have no doubt I should have lived or tried to have lived so worthily that I might even have looked out for an archbishopric, though I never got more than a curacy; but I don't remember to what you refer" —for this meeting had passed for a moment from my memory. "Why, you are going to the Memorial Hall—you two Liberals, as I suppose you call yourselves—to plead against the liberty of the subject." "I beg your pardon," I said, "we are not going to do anything of the kind; we are going to plead for the liberty of the abject." "That's another way of putting the question," said he. "I never thought of that." A few days afterward I met him again, and he said, "Do you know that idea of 'the liberty of the abject' sticks to me? It is uncommonly like saying 'the devil in solution, and my boys have got hold of it, and if you make that your text I am not quite sure that I sha'n't go to hear you speak." He may be here. It has occurred to me that, as we are going to hear about local option in Canada from Mr. Manning, I had better let that rest with him, whilst I use this accidental text in order to fortify your minds when persons rise up and talk to you upon the question of the liberty of the subject. Now we don't in any way interfere with the liberty of the subject in our proposed measures when we think of liberty in its true sense. That distinguished and thoughtful philosopher, Mr. Tony Weller, speaking to his son on a very important subject, said, " There are vheels vithin vheels, Samivel." That is true; and there are liberties within liberties; and that which we contend for in respect to liberty is this, that we are preaching against a liberty which is created and for a liberty which is eternal. There is the broad distinction. There is an old story re-told by my friend Professor Polli, of Milan, told before, but told again by him, in reference to a physiological question, that in ancient times there lived an old man called the "Old Man of the Mountain," and that old man, by some strange spell which he exercised over his followers, could send them here and there to do whatever he liked, making them brigands to-day, murderers to-morrow—anything that he wished. Well, those men would go about, I dare say, declaring that they were at liberty; and, perhaps, if you had gone and endeavored to stop them in their career they would have said, "You are interfering with the liberty of the subject." We say, "No, not at all! because you yourselves are not free. You are under an influence which leads you to do deeds which are not for the benefit of mankind or yourselves, which are dead against human liberty, and for which you can scarcely be called responsible." That is the position in which men stand with regard to this "Old Man of the Mountain," alcohol. They stand obeying orders to do that which is not liberty, and then they become the abject, and we stand to reclaim the abject. We enter our prisons. Some of the abject are there picking oakum; others walking the endless wheel; others tied to the pillar to be whipped; some thinking of their last moments and the approach of the executioner. We ask, "What brought these men here?" and the reply, by the mouths of our judges themselves, is, in nine-tenths of the cases, "that glorious liberty which England gives to her children to allow them to debase themselves till they come to these conditions." Is that the liberty of the subject? We say —that is the slavery of the abject. We go amongst the sick, and find there, amongst those who are passing through various stages of pain and disease, no less than 40,000 a year going in a certain way to death. We ask, "Why are these dying and suffering in this manner?" and the answer, faithfully spoken, is, "Because of the liberty which this country gives to produce all this disease and misery." That is the liberty of the subject truly, but it is the misery of the abject! And when we come to particular cases we find, as the chairman has said, that those who are nearest to the debasing influence of alcohol are those that are most afflicted. If you could in imagination see the Angel of Death sweeping over a large town till, as Mr. Bright once said, you can almost hear the motion of his wings and watch him ready to pounce upon those victims nearest to his grasp, where would you see that Angel of Death going in the largest proportion? You would see him going 138 times to the houses of those who sell strong drinks while he went to 100 houses where these drinks were not sold. Can there be a more awful problem put before us than this—the rescue of these abject from their slavery? But we go a step further. We look at this liberty in relation to what may be called the pleasure of the thing—the "merry moments" which the Old Man of the Mountain allows to his followers. You walk into the dens of East London and look there at what is called "pleasure"—dancing-saloons lighted up with the most gaudy frippery, men sitting there, and dejected and enslaved women dancing up the center and making a scene, the whole by and by going in one giddy whirl—in one wild, furious circle; and then the break-up and the leading away of those wretched women to the worst of all slaveries the mind can conceive. Call that the pleasure of the Old Man of the Mountain! Call that the liberty of the subject! Yes, it is the liberty the nation gives to its subjects to indulge in that which produces such unspeakable misery. If you were to follow these people to their homes (as I have done recently), and see the children sitting half-dying on the door-steps, the women waiting for the infuriated man called "husband" and "father," then you would indeed think that the liberty of the subject was something that deserved to be reconsidered in connection with the liberty of the abject. Ladies and gentlemen, we don't in our own time think of this time as we do of past times. We look back to past times and say, "How horrible things were then!" There is a great scholar and antiquarian friend of mine who has spent many thousands of pounds in collecting the history of London and pictures relating thereto, and there are no more remarkable pieces of knowledge than those which can be obtained in looking over his plates of London—exhibitions of Bartholomew Fair, Tyburn, the Savoy, the Prisons, and the like. One night, when I was looking through that collection, I was horrified by one picture. I, a man accustomed to see death in all forms, accustomed to see the dead, turned pale at one picture. It related to a debtors' prison. There was a punishment which the recalcitrant debtors within 100 years of this time sometimes illegally underwent· they were put into a cell in which a dead body was allowed to lie, and when it could be retained there no longer another was put in its place! We exclaim in horror, "Could such a thing be 100 years ago?" It could, and if in 100 years hence some man should stand as I stand now, and only refer back any week to the admirably conducted *Alliance News*, and take up one column, "Fruits of the Traffic," and commence to read of the horrible crimes committed in the name of this demon of drink in one day, he and his audience would be not less horrified by the record there given of our time than we are by the record of the debtors' prison 100 years ago. We turn to others of the abject. We turn to a better class perchance of men—to men who, in their despair, brought down to the lowest depths of mental shame and degradation, are contemplating the loss of their own lives—nay, the taking of them by their own act—under the influence of this Old Man of the Mountain. It is not many months since a respectable-looking man called at my house in the greatest state of distress through drink, and he said, " You stand between me and Regent's Park Canal. I am on my way to it unless you can reason me out of the step I am going to take." I succeeded that time. For two months he became an abstainer and a different man altogether; but one day, the influence of the Old Man still pursuing him, some friends met him, dared him to taste the drink, and the result was, that two weeks afterward a coroner's inquest revealed that this man had brought himself to the very fate from which I had once rescued him. What was the cause of that? The liberty of the subject—the liberty which this country gives to these men so to indulge that they shall use the liberty to their own self-destruction. We pass to the mad-house, and what is the story told us there? The story is that 40 per cent. of those who are led into the hopeless chains of confinement in the lunatic asylum come in from one cause—this permission, this liberty of the subject to indulge unchecked in that which produces the misery of the abject. And so with regard to the work-house. When we move into that we find that in a large per centage of cases just the same tale is told of the liberty of the subject becoming in this respect the bondage of the abject. We must work steadily on toward the one great end of declaring the liberty of the abject. The learned Canon [Canon Farrar, who was presiding] in the pulpit and on the platform and in the study must and will continue his work. The others who have so ably spoken must and will continue their work. You must continue yours. I must continue my work—and if you give me your support I will try and extend it, for I will stand by the side of Mr. Whitworth in Parliament, if I can, and confirm by my vote that which I have said in my speech. We have a great many prejudices to overcome, and I will tell you a bit of history, which shows how prejudices ought to be met when they are brought forward even in high quarters. In June, 1752, the illustrious Franklin sent up a kite, caught the lightning from the clouds, and showed that lightning and electricity were the same; and thereupon he suggested those splendid lightning-conductors which you see on the tops of our churches and public buildings. This was a great discovery, and was soon adopted in our country; but in 1772 there was much dissatisfaction here in respect to America, and philosopher Franklin himself was very much distrusted. Thereupon an Englishman started another kind of lightning-conductor which differed from Franklin's in this respect, that it had a blunt end instead of a sharp point. King George III., very desperate against America, went in immediately for blunt-ended lightning-conductors for his palaces. The Royal Society did not agree, and the King sent for the president, Sir John Pringle, and said, "You must use your influence with the Royal Society to introduce blunt-ended lightning-conductors." Sir John replied, "Sire, it is my inclination as it is my duty to obey you, but I can not reverse the laws and ordinances of nature." "Then you had better resign," said the King. But Sir John didn't resign, and the sharp points remain to this day as evidence of the value of keeping closely to an opinion when it is founded on the laws and ordinances of nature. We sometimes have to face this great potentate, Public Opinion, and it sometimes pulls us up to the bar of public-house opinion, and would, if it could, make us give way. It says, "All your sharp points of argument should be given up. Your lines are right, but put blunt ends to them." We must stand out against that. We must keep up our bright, sharp points, and we shall certainly win, and in that winning, ladies and gentlemen, we shall touch no man's freedom. We may say, in the words which Sheridan Knowles has put in the mouth of his hero, Tell: we would have every man—

> "Free as our torrents are which leap our rocks
> And plough our valleys without asking leave;
> Or as our peaks which wear their caps of snow,
> In very presence of the regal sun."

But this freedom, this liberty, must not be a created liberty. It must be so pure, so natural, that the very spirits of the just made perfect might declare of it, "It is eternal, it is justified, it is sanctified."

WHY I BECAME AN ABSTAINER.

Dr. Richardson, of London, author of the celebrated "Cantor Lectures on Alcohol" and "The Temperance Lesson-Book," gives his reasons for abstinence in an address in Sheldonian Theater, Oxford, from which we take the following:

"Let me say, that at the commencement of the labors which brought me to the conclusion above stated, I had no bias in favor of or preconceived opinion respecting alcohol.

"Like many other men of science, I had been too careless or too oblivious of those magnificent labors which the advocates of temperance, for its own sake, had, for many previous years, through good report and evil report, so nobly and truthfully carried out. But for what may be called one of the accidents of a scientific career I might, indeed, to the end of my days, have continued negative on this question.

"The circumstance that led me to the special study of alcohol is simply told. In the year 1863, I directed the attention of the British Association for the Advancement of Science, during its meeting at Newcastle, to the action of a chemical substance called nitrate of amyl, the physiological properties of which I had for some months previously been subjecting to investigation. My researches attracted so much attention that I was desired by the physiological section of the association, over which Professor Rolleston most ably presided, to continue them, and, in the course of pursuing them, other chemical substances, nearly allied to that from which I started, came under observation. Amongst these was the well-known chemical product which the Arabian chemist, Albucasis, is said first to have distilled from wine, which, on account of its subtlety, was called alcohol, which is now called ethylic alcohol, and which forms the stimulating part of all wines, spirits, beers, and other ordinary intoxicating drinks. To the research I devoted three years, from 1863 to 1866, modifying experiments in every conceivable way, taking advantage of seasons and varying temperatures of season, extending observation from one class of animals to another, and making comparative researches with other bodies of the alcohol series than the ethylic or common alcohol.

"The results, I confess, were as surprising to me as any one else. They were suprising from their definitiveness and their uniformity. They were most surprising from the complete contradiction they gave to the popular idea that alcohol is a supporter and sustainer of the animal temperature.

"I. That it is an entire fallacy to suppose that alcohol, in any of its forms as intoxicating drink, is the gift of God to man.

"II. That if the habit of drinking intoxicating beverages is never indulged, it is never felt as a want.

"III. If this habit be indulged, the difficulties ot throwing it off are tenfold increased.

"IV. You may further teach by history and example—but always better by example—that the hardest work, mental and bodily, is best carried out without the stimulating effects of this agent which so many look to for support in all their labors.

"V. That alcohol has no claim, in a scientific sense, to be considered as a sustainer either of bodily or mental life or work.

"VI. That in alcohol there is nothing that can build up any tissue or supply any force.

"VII. That in approaching the subject of temperance, and in showing the uselessness of the most mischievous of all agents within the reach of men, you are promoting a good which extends beyond your own time."

THE EFFECTS OF ALCOHOL.

By DR. BENJAMIN W. RICHARDSON.

AN ADDRESS AT EXETER, ENGLAND, SEPTEMBER 28, 1880.

I STAND before you as a sanitarian. I can have no object whatever in defending the temperance cause except in my own solemn convictions of its importance as one of the basic facts of sanitation, and as such that we should give it our support. I have also to stand on other ground. One of the restless spirits of our country in the latter part of his life was constantly putting this question to himself, "What will men say of me when I am dead?" Well, every man who works in this world has that to say, "What will men say of me when I am dead?" And that occurs to me in reference to what I speak and write now, "What will afterward be said?" and thus I would only leave behind me that at which I have arrived as the result of honest conviction after inquiry. In that spirit I want to address you to-day. I wish for no professional brother to believe it because I say a thing bearing on this question, though my studies may have been longer than his, but I would invoke his honest judgment. He has the most perfect right to think and act in his professional thought and capacity on this as on all other subjects; but I want him, if possible, to see both sides. And here is the mistake which often occurs in men of science, that they look only on that side of the temperance question in which they have been educated. I know that is quite possible and often most natural, and I shall give an instance by and by to show you how my own mind was influenced in that way. One medical man has stated authoritatively and officially with regard to alcohol that it is "a food, a stimulant, and a sedative." He was perfectly justified in expressing that opinion; but I want the profession to take the other side and analyze such a statement as that. If a thing is a food it is not a stimulant, for a food is something which sustains; and if it is a stimulant it is not a sedative, or where is its tranquillizing power? Therefore this seems a contradiction in terms. If I go to a clock and wind it up, I give it food in that winding. If I shorten the pendulum I make it go quicker. I use that which becomes a stimulant there, but it is not a food that I have then applied I have put nothing into it. If I stop it, that is a sedative. I have stopped it. I can not say these three things are all one. Just so with alcohol. If I take alcohol I don't take food; I take something that quickens my circulation. I do not take a sedative (unless, indeed, I use the word in a different sense to what it is always understood). I take something that may exhaust me afterward, and in that sense make me weak and feeble, but that is not a sedative. And so I would ask medical men to consider these three words, look at their meaning, and see how they apply as used. To say them of any one substance seems to my mind altogether illogical and out of the question. Recently I have been studying (as a student again) the works of the masters in my profession on one particular subject —that of the degenerations to which the body is subjected during life—those slow changes which come on, making the animal organs different from that which they are naturally; and I have been reading without the slightest selection the authorities on the causes of these great degenerations—degenerations of the heart, of the liver, of the brain, and of other organs of the body. I take up the works of those who have had nothing to do with this question, who are simply great pathologists, and I say this, that there is nothing so striking in all that history as the circumstantial testimony which these men bear to this one agent (alcohol) in the production of these degenerations. We find other agencies referred to, but only accidentally, as it were, and in regard to particular points; but on questions of pathology this has an all-pervading influence. "This degeneration is likely induced by alcohol—that degeneration springs from the too free use of spirit—that degeneration from whisky—that from gin"—and so forth; and you find these men by consensus of opinion, plainly in reference to this question, writing down a series of degenerations springing from that one cause, which put together would make a volume of the largest possible kind. Now, I say, presuming that alcohol is a food, a stimulant, and a sedative (let us suppose it to have the whole of these effects), I would like to ask a professional friend who would read through these histories in the same way as I have done, whether he could afterward conscientiously say that even advantage should be taken of this food, stimulant, and sedative to use it for the production of so much disease as is here traced to it as a cause?

On the question of work, too, there are two sides which should be put carefully and constantly forward. It is common to say that we give this substance for the work which comes out of it; and we total abstainers say that there is no truth in that—that there is no work to be got out of it at all. A large number of other men of science say there is. I want them to look at the question now in regard to work, and consider the other side of that. And here I will tell you an incident in my own life which shows how men may be biased against what is good sound common sense and judgment for many years.

In the early part of my life I practiced medicine at Mortlake, and I had under my care a very famous rower—a champion rower—and that man once consulted me professionally. He was a little below par, and he came to me to ask me what he should do. He was training then for a race, and I recommended him to take so much wine in the day. He flatly declined. That was about twenty-five years ago, before the temperance cause was so prominent as it is now. "Well," he said, "I can't take anything of that sort, for I shouldn't win my race if I were to take what you say." "Would half a pint of wine a day make a difference?" "Certainly," he said. "In what way?" "I will tell you. I once won a race and regained all my honors in a very curious manner. I had against me a competent rower,—a man as good as myself—and it was a great occasion. It was a grand match, and I was not very well on the particular morning. I went to the post to be started, feeling that the Fates that day were against me. Most curiously, I lost the toss, so that I got the wrong side of the river, with the sun in my face, and I felt that the race was all up with me; but as my opponent was getting into the boat a friend of his, and a supporter, took out a spirit flask and gave him a nip of whisky, and I said, 'That is as good as the sun to me;' and then, not quite satisfied, he gave him another, and I said, 'That is equal to the right side of the river for me.' Now I will tell you, in rowing you want these things: You must know precisely where you are going, and if anything springs up you must be quite ready for it, and you must not take any notice of the cheering going on, and you must have presence of mind in all that occurs." "Then," I said, "it seems to me that you want precision, decision, presence of mind, and endurance." He said, "Those are the four qualities. We went on a little, stroke for stroke, so that it was quite musical. By and by there was a little jingle in his stroke, and I said, That man is not precise. That is a little point for me. We went on toward Chiswick, and when we got opposite that place there was something floating along which looked like a capsized boat, and it started us both for a moment. It was a question to know which side to take, and I immediately decided and gained a good point in that way, and as we went along I found that my opponent was embarrassed by what was taking place around him. Finally he began to flag. I didn't flag, but improved, and I won the race by a boat's length. Those two glasses of whisky, I believed, turned the scale against my opponent on that occasion, and for that reason I will never take any stimulants while I am training." I often laughed with him about this, not believing it for twenty years, but when I came to my scientific research, and to look into the action of alcohol on muscular fiber and on mental action, I found that that man was absolutely right, and I had been going on for twenty years in blind ignorance and prejudice, and there was the plain truth, if I had had the common sense to receive it from a common-sense man.

I was able to convey a considerable amount of conviction to an intelligent scholar a little time ago by a simple experiment. I was in his house, and he was extolling wine and singing its praises. He sang:

> Life is chequer'd o'er with woe,
> Bid the ruddy bumper flow,
> Wine's the soul of man below.

He sang that to me every morning in order, as he said, to rouse my flagging spirits. I said, "You sing that song well. Why not begin with wine at breakfast, and give it to your servants?" "My dear friend," he said, "I couldn't get through the day. I should be as seedy as possible. I couldn't; and as for my servants, if I gave it to them I don't know what would happen." "Then, when do you take it?" I asked. "When the cares of day are over, then's the time for a few glasses of wine and a night-cap." "Will you," I said, "be good enough to feel my pulse as I stand here?" He did. "Count it carefully. What does it say?" "Your pulse says 74." I then sat down in a chair. "Will you count it now?" "Your pulse has gone down. Your pulse is now 70." I then laid myself down on the couch, and said, "Will you take it again. What is it?" "It is 64; what an extraordinary thing." "What is the effect of position on the pulse? When you lie down at night that is the way nature gives your heart rest. You know nothing about it, but that beating organ is resting to that extent, and if you reckon it up it is a great deal of rest, because in lying down my heart is doing ten strokes less per minute. Multiply that by 60, and it is 600. Multiply it by eight hours, and within a fraction it is 5,000 strokes different, and as my heart is throwing up six ounces of blood at every stroke, it makes a difference of 30,000 ounces of lifting during a night." "That is a curious fact; but what has it to do with me?" "When I lie down at night without the alcohol that is the rest my heart gets, but when you take your wine or grog you do not allow that rest, for the influence of alcohol is to increase the number of strokes, and instead of getting this rest you put on something like 15,000 extra strokes, and the result is you rise up very seedy, as you yourself have said, with the result of a restless night, and unfit the next day for work until you have taken a little of the wine which fills the ruddy bumper, and which you say is the soul of man below." His wife said, "That is perfectly true. The night is attended with a degree of unrest and broken sleep which I can hardly describe, and which gives me very much anxiety." That had an influence. He began to reckon up those figures, and think what it meant lifting up an ounce so many thousand times, and in the result he became a total abstainer with every benefit to his health, and, as he admits, to his happiness. I would like those who speak of alcohol as something to be taken at night to give a night's sleep and rest and comfort, just to take the opposite side of the question into consideration, and see how these two positions fit in together.

I should like every one who is interested in this question, and not prepared to move with us on our side, to consider the matter in regard to premature decay. I would ask every man who is enjoying the wine-cup and proposing his friend's health, and all that kind of jovial thing, just to remember amongst his circle of friends how many that he knew in boyhood have now advanced to middle age, who, without being drunkards at all, have fallen insidiously stricken by this foe. I think a more solemn question could not be put to a body of middle-aged men than this. They will, I am sure, be astounded at the number of men that they can reckon up, who, instead of passing to a fine old age with all that vigor of character and power of speech, have in the midst of their very usefulness, and when the wisdom which they had acquired by their experience should have been most pronounced, sunk simply into what I can but call an untimely grave. And when that is considered, do they think that the use of this "food, stimulant, or sedative," should be so largely employed as to lead to such dire and such entirely unnecessary results?

PUBLISHED BY THE NATIONAL TEMPERANCE SOCIETY AND PUBLICATION HOUSE, NO. 58 READE STREET NEW YORK. PRICE, $6.00 PER THOUSAND.

TWENTY-ONE
HISTORIC LANDMARKS.

By B. W. RICHARDSON, M.D., F.R.S.

WHEN one is given to speaking night after night, as I am doing, on Temperance, it is very difficult to find fresh matter and a new line of thought to develop, or to get a thought which would lead to a discourse; but the very happy suggestion which the Rev. Stenton Eardley made to me of giving an account of what has been done in twenty-one years by the Temperance movement did afford me an opportunity of looking back and trying to ascertain, from the direct personal knowledge which I have of this great queston of Temperance, the course that has been followed in my department of it, and the results at which we have arrived. I have noted down twenty-one points, upon each of which I will offer a few observations. There are twenty-one salient points in which great advance has been made in relation to education among the masses, and indeed all classes, on this subject.

I.—ALCOHOL AND ITS PURCHASERS.

First of all I remember that twenty-one years ago it was a very common notion—one of the most common of all notions—that wine, beer, and spirits were things quite distinct from water. The common impression was that when these things were taken they were distinctive agents of themselves, that there was no water connected with them according to ordinary acceptation, and even through our better classes this view was constantly expressed. A gentleman sitting at table would tell you that it was the best champagne he provided, no watery stuff, and that he had given £7 a dozen for it. You were under the delusion, if you took this man's word, that this was no watery beverage, but something different. You found the poor man at the inn smacking his lips and saying, " This is no water; it is good malt and hops." So a person taking a glass of spirit which burnt his lips and throat thought it all the better the hotter it was, "because," he would say, " it is furthest removed from water." There is no doubt a great advance in the public knowledge on this one topic. We, as men of science have so impregnated the public mind with the facts of this question that there are very few who do not know that this which is sold as beer, and wine, and spirit is always largely water. The bottle of champagne which costs so much per dozen, when it comes up for investigation, what does it turn out to be? It turns out to be a fluid of which, if you take one hundred pints, ninety pints are water—a large sum, £7 per dozen, to pay for a fluid of this kind If you turn to the beer which the man is drinking at the inn you find the same story. I remember about twenty-one years ago Mr. Ray wrote a very remarkable and able book on the malt tax. His idea was that the Government was greatly defrauded, not by the great brewers, but by the retailers, who sometimes charged their beer with water, thus reducing the tax. He went about London from day to day collecting at various places bottles of beer, which he brought to my laboratory for analysis. I remember the result of that inquiry was to find that as a general fact (sometimes there was a little excess of spirit) that beer sold conveyed to the man who bought it from ninety-four to ninety-five parts in the one hundred of simple water. So with regard to spirit. In sherry there will be three parts of water to one of spirit; in brandy, the strongest spirit, fifty of water to fifty of spirit; and now I think, through the length and breadth of the land, we are making an impression, and those who are not engaged in this question of scientific research can use this argument as forcibly as we can, and perhaps more so, that people who think they are paying these large sums of money for something exceedingly choice are after all unwittingly, and in a very unfortunate way, water buyers and water drinkers.

II.—Alcohol—What is it?

Then another point has been brought out. When the idea of spirit was brought forward, and we talked of the strength that was in beers, wines, and spirits, it was thought that this one particular alcohol or spirit was the only thing of its kind. Men of science knew better, but the general impression was, and is to some extent still, that the substance which we call spirit is a thing alone of itself, that it stands as though there was nothing else like it. Now, I hope we have pretty fairly imbued the nation with the fact that this spirit of wine is only one of a great family; that there are an immense number of alcohols—dozens, in fact—some derived from wood, some from wheat, the potato spirit, and so on—all bodies of the same chemical family, and not in any way distinct, except by the simple accidents of taste, and weight, and a few other physical varieties, from that alcohol which we drink. As Professor Gladstone has pointed out, it is a mere accident that this came into common use—this alcohol from grain. It might have been any other alcohol that came first into play. We now know that this is not one of the special things coming to us as a distinctive thing, but as one of a family, and has only come into use or habit, as it were, by accident.

III.—ALCOHOL NOT A FOOD.

Another point. I do think we have fairly brought out what is the positive effect of this particular alcohol we take in this sense—that it can in no way be considered a food. We have shown that foods are substances that either make up the great mass of the body like water, which exists to about seventy-five per cent., or substances which build up the tissues like albumen, egg, cheese, meats, etc They are substances that burn in the body like fat, and oil, and starch, and sugar, which go to produce animal warmth, and keep up the vital fire, or substances which go to make up the bony structure. We have shown that alcohol does not belong to water, and there is nothing in alcohol chemically which it can represent in regard to meat substances, and the same with the structures which fill up the skeleton of the body. Thus, when we ask whether this agent can be classed with the foods which keep up the animal warmth, we find that its imbibition reduces the animal temperature, and prevents the creation of those products which come from the burning of the body. Therefore, so far as alcohol is concerned, we can positively affirm that it is no food at all, that it produces exceptional effects upon the body, but it is no more a food than chloroform and ether or anything of the kind are foods.

IV.—Alcohol and Practical Abstainers.

Again, we have traced out that this agent acts just as do other such agents. Men of science have come by a common consent to this position, that there must be a certain point when the quantity must not be taken beyond that point. There is not a single physician living, who is a thoughtful man, not a man of any moment in the scientific world of thought, or of literature bearing on science, or in debate, who would not tell you candidly and honestly at this day that there must be a very strict border drawn as to where this influence must stop. Twenty years ago men did not think of a limited quantity at all. "Oh!" says the man who wishes to please all parties and preach moderation—to those who abstain and those who take a little—" you may take a little, but it must not exceed the physiological quantity," no more than you can by your good health dispose of without injury to yourself. "You may take one and a half ounces of alcohol, if you like, in the twenty-four hours." That means a very minute quantity indeed. It would be represented by two or three glasses of ale. "You may take that in the twenty-four hours, but you must not exceed that quantity. If you do, then you run the certain risk of slipping into disease." Now we have brought the matter down to a very fine point indeed, and some even reduce the quantity still lower. One of the most distinguished men in this kingdom, who was presiding where I was speaking the other day, said that when he went out hunting or to public gatherings the most he could take was a teaspoonful of this spirit. I said, " Practically you are an abstainer." "Yes," he replied, "but that just prevents me declaring myself." There are thousands who, knowing these facts, actually take a small quantity to avoid being called abstainers, waiting until the cause gets greater strength and power. Still, this is a hopeful position.

V.—Alcohol and Athletics.

Twenty-one years ago it was a common belief that men did more work when they took a little drink—not a little, for I think I am wrong there, but when they began with a little and went on, and great feats were performed constantly by men when they were taking the drink—they thought the taking of the drink was the necessity for the feat. Science showed that there was no strength got by alcohol, that it was perfectly impossible that that which did not build up the tissues of the body, did not supply water, warmth, or vitality to the body, could give strength to the body, and numbers began to try it independently of science, and so two favoring currents set in. Now, what are the facts? To all men who are going into training for rowing, racing, long walks such as Mr. Weston takes, firing, and the like, whatever they are going to do with regard to training for these pursuits, they discover the advantage which they get if they altogether abstain from the use of this degrading and debasing physical agent.

VI.—ALCOHOL AND BRAIN WORKERS.

Another advance has been made with regard to mental work. I remember the time when it was considered necessary to write at night that a man must prime himself with a glass of wine or spirit. Here again our scientific works come into play, and we have been able to show positively that nothing is so injurious to mental work and capacity as for any one to lace himself up with strong drink, under the idea that he is assisting himself. All our medical authorities in this day proclaim that the general fact, and they proclaim it from the reasons which are most fearfully standing out day by day in the most glaring colors, and on the most unmistakable lines. The very best of men (such is the evidence) have fallen, from this idea, that being engaged in mental or artistic work, they would gain assistance from that agent which, of all others, is to them the most enticing and the most perilous. It is this class that most readily succumb. Their nervous tension is great, the brain is great. The brain is an organ rich in fluid. The little excitement is for the moment very pleasant, but it is not an ex citement that can be kept up by repeating the least quantity; more must be taken each time, and then the whole system in these men becomes absolutely saturated (and the term is scientifically correct) with this destructive agent; and so they fall, and in my time I have seen artists of the highest class, musicians of the highest class, writers of the highest class, and the best members of my own profession, and the clerical profession, and the legal profession, fall in spite of themselves, in spite of all you can say to them, because upon their susceptible, refined, nervous organization this is of all others the most deadly, the most mortal of poisons. This impression has had its influence all through society, but whether there is a great reaction in favor of the simple lines of nature or not, this is quite certain: that the evidence that should lead to such reaction is now fairly and fully before the world, and it has been put before it by the labors of those who have worked on the scientific basis during the past twenty years.

VII.—Alcohol and Climatic Extremes.

Twenty-one years ago, except amongst the total abstainers themselves, it was believed that to meet the vicissitudes of cold and of heat it was necessary that a certain amount of alcohol should be taken; and so our ships went out to the Arctic regions charged with spirits to "assist" the men, and our soldiers were sent out to India charged with spirit rations to give to the men. Look at the extreme absurdity of this practice. If the men that went due north had this alcohol to warm them, the men that went to tropical climes could not want it for this. Did they want it to cool them? What is the evidence? We have proved that under cold there is nothing so bad as this spirit, and that it is as it were death added to sleep, and when the temperature of the body is raised by extreme warmth, then there is nothing so bad as the tension produced in the blood by this light vapor of alcohol. We have shown through science what is the effect of alcohol on heat and cold, and have shown that in both cases it must from the nature of its action be ruinous to health and life. That has had a good effect. We now know that those men who have been total abstainers have lived best, worked hardest, suffered least, and come home soundest. We know that in the tropics those men who have taken least have fought the hardest battles and made the best marches; and those who have taken none at all have been better off still. In tropical weather we have found that the mortal disease which kills so many, and which is called sunstroke—that the people thus stricken are not all persons in perfect health, but those who have prepared themselves for the effect of the sun direct upon them by the introduction into their system of this agent.

VIII.—ALCOHOL vs. WATER.

Twenty-one years ago it was supposed that persons could live for a certain length of time upon alcohol, and one of the hardest nuts we have had to crack has been to meet this statement. It was very common to give to persons weak and feeble, wine and strong drink, and they lived upon that, as it

seemed, so well that nobody could be convinced for
many years that this was not good in certain cases
of weakness and exhaustion and want of other fluid.
As we have thought over the matter, the facts have
come out, that what is most wanted by these starv-
ing people, that which keeps them alive, is not the
alcohol, but the water that is commingled with it.
This person who is said to take a bit of rusk, and
with that so much gin and water or champagne,
has not been living by virtue of the alcohol or spirit,
but by virtue of the water that has been taken with
that limited fare, and we have come to a positive
conclusion and knowledge that a man may go on
for days and weeks, and may live as it were upon
himself, if you will simply supply him with a sufficient quantity of water. Take the case of the Welsh
miners. They were placed in a cell, away from all
the world for many days, and deprived of all food.
If they had had as much as a few ounces of brandy,
only an ounce per man, all those who are opposed
to us would have cried out, "Behold what a little
quantity of alcohol has done"; but, as if the experiment had been intended for the scientific development of our cause, there was not a drop of anything
containing spirit among them, but there was in that
dark cave at the feet of these imprisoned men a little spring or rill, and they laved at that, and drank
it, and upon that they lived through long trial.
They lived comparatively well, and they came out
almost unscathed—a proof, beyond any that could
be brought to light by experimental research, that
it is possible to live for a long period of days under
the greatest imaginable excitement and anxiety of

mind, in the greatest possible melancholy, on this one fluid which has been distilled in the rivers and in the clouds for our use and for our life. I have myself known an instance where, for fifty-three days, life has been maintained solely on water. To those unfortunate people who, for some reason or another, are unable to take food at all, and who can only drink small quantities of fluid, there is nothing so injurious as the administration of stimulants in any form. For months they will live on water and milk, and live a comparatively comfortable life, but touch them with this stimulant, make the waste go on faster, make their hearts beat quicker, and then directly they are as if they had had to perform a work of labor for which they had no strength. These people who are said to have lived on alcohol have in reality lived on the water in spite of the alcohol.

IX.—Alcohol as a Medicine.

Another point. I recollect twenty years ago that alcohol was considered the grand panacea in diseases. For my part, though I had not then become a total abstainer, I had always stood aloof from this method of treating all descriptions of disease, and particularly diseases of an exhaustive kind, with large quantities of alcohol. In my student life I observed in cases of fever—and I had a great deal to do with it in the epidemic of 1847—that the free administration of alcohol always produced a great deal of excitement first, and then depression, and then sleep, and a delirium which did not seem to be very different from the delirium of drunkenness, and yet under the influence of masters who said this was necessary, a student was obliged to accept that that was the right treatment. Later in life, when I began to practice for myself, and found a very distinguished physician praising this treatment in all directions, and a number of disciples following this man, I was obliged to hold aloof, and be somewhat unpopular because I would moderate the quantity of spirit that was being given; and then gradually the truth began to dawn upon me and others that the thing was all wrong, and through the great efforts made by a very few men, in the first instance, what is the result?—that the whole of this heroic line of treatment of disease, not of ounces of spirit, but of pints per day, has been altogether given up. The idea of the brandy treatment of fever has passed nearly away. To Dr. Gairdner, of Glasgow, we are greatly indebted. With a boldness which few men under the circumstances would have evinced, he eliminated these stimulants from his wards one by one. He found persons come there sick with the disease and die at the rate of thirty-six per cent. In from two to three years, by steadily and with truest conservatism reducing the quantity of alcohol until he brought it to a minimum, or to nothing at all, he gives results of deaths at the rate of eight or nine per cent. We are all struck by this, and you will find wherever you go—France has not caught the contagion—that this treatment of disease by large quantities of drink has passed into oblivion, never, I hope, to rise again, and passed away with results at which every one wonders, with results in recoveries which never could have been hoped for if by a slow and gradual process from that which was—yes, I will say it boldly—vicious and dangerous, and even fatal, a different system had not been carried out.

X.—ALCOHOLIC DISEASE.

Twenty-one years ago we attributed but little to alcohol as a cause of disease. We said that there was a disease called gin-drinker's liver, and that this was attended afterward with dropsy, and led to a certain fixed mortality. We heard also of *delirium tremens*. We heard of *mania a potu*, as the French call it, or "dipsomania," as we call it. You will, however, find now that the word alcoholic has become an adjective in disease. Men speak of alcoholic phthisis or consumption. I was the first to discover that there was a particular form of consumption very fatal in its character which was peculiar to persons who indulged largely in alcohol, which was specifically alcoholic consumption. That has been accepted, and later on other forms of disease—liver disease, heart disease, paralysis, apoplexy, various forms of dyspepsia, premature old age and death. You will say a man has got alcoholic paralysis; he has died from apoplexy, the result of alcohol; he is prematurely old from alcohol—that is the evidence you get now; but you did not get it twenty-one years ago. The facts had always been these; all history had told the facts; but they had not been analyzed and traced to their true source. We had not known that it was from the influence of this one particular agent that all this vast mass of disease was springing. A professional brother, going farther than I would have gone, has even said that in walking his hospital for twenty-five years he has been led to the conclusion that sixty to seventy of the cases of disease which came there were cases of disease brought about either directly or indirectly by this one agent.

XI.—Alcohol and the Physiological Minimum.

Another point. We have known always that when a man or woman sat down at table, and began to take wine too freely, there is a stage of excitement, another stage of more excitement, another stage of wasted excitement, and coldness and pallor, or darkness of the face, and a final stage, when the body lies helpless, or, as we should call it, dead drunk. That was known as regards the first effects of alcohol. What did we now learn? We know that the slow, insidious effect of alcohol upon persons taking it day by day and year by year at last gives us great populations who, not being intoxicated in this special or acute form, are still its victims in the same way. We know there are populations who can go about and just take the "physiological quantity" which brings them up to the first stage; and then numbers who begin rather early in the day, and go from bar to bar and place to place, are perpetually in the second stage; and others who go on day by day, and never go to bed thoroughly sober, are in the third stage. And when we go into our asylums and hospitals we find the victims of general paralysis, who are unable to help themselves, who are practically speechless, and practically dead drunk from the permanent use, and this because they have advanced in this slow, insidious manner into the fourth stage, in which they are ripe and ready to drop into the grave. Of this great population this fact is standing well out before the world, and the more fully it is now declared, the more certainly will, I think, the common sense of mankind come to bear upon it, and say we will not be representatives in the sole form of what you may call death by drink, any more than we will be the degraded representatives of it in the acute form at the table when the glass of wine is commenced, up to the time when there is perfect insensibility.

XII.—Alcohol and Longevity.

Another point. Twenty-one years ago these facts about disease and short life from drink, not being so recognized, our insurance companies were blind to them; but now so keen are they on this question of the effect of drink upon the persons who come to be insured, that on the lives of those who sell strong drink there is actually an extra tariff, and the question asked by the insurance companies is the question of sobriety, for the company knows that there is nothing so fatal in a general way, or so likely to lead, not simply to disease from the agent itself, but springing up and intensifying by its employment other diseases, as the free use of this particular destructive national enemy.

XIII.—Alcohol and Mortality.

Another point. We have figures in regard to the mortality in reference to this agent which are startling, and which twenty-one years ago we should never have conceived as possible. Lately we have got much more refined examination of facts than formerly. There has been a difference of opinion as to the real mortality from the use of strong drink. Dr. Farr, who thought that the mortality was very much overrated, has since said that forty to fifty thousand a year die from what he calls "tippling." Dr. Farr before he resigned his post was so good as to allow me (being then engaged in delivering a course of Cantor lectures on the mortality in industrial occupations to the number of seventy) to examine the returns, and this came out, as a startling fact, that there were variations from 70 to 138, 100 being the standard—that is to say, if the mean mortality of the whole of the occupations in the years examined was 100, then the most favorable occupations went up to 70, and those that were least favorable came down to something considerably over 100. We find that when we get to one occupation we get to the lowest but one. Amongst those engaged in the sale of spirits we find 138 deaths to the hundred to the mean of population. The grocers who before they had the license to sell spirits were standing in a most favorable place on the scale—86 to 100—since they began to sell the drink have begun to go down, and show a higher mortality. Then you see what an important point we have scored—that just in proportion as this agent is approached by the multitude which deals with it, just in proportion does that vast multitude begin to die with the rest of its fellows.

XIV.—ALCOHOL AND INSANITY.

Then as regards insanity. Exactly in the same way as the body ceases to exert its proper power under this agent, so the mind begins to go. There is great difference of opinion as to the amount of mental disease produced by alcohol. Twenty years ago the subject was not under discussion. Now it is, and our commissioners are reporting upon it. There is a difference of opinion, but it is generally admitted that there is a very large amount of insanity produced by drink directly or indirectly. Dr. Edgar Shepherd declares that forty per cent. of the persons who come into the great asylum of Colney Hatch are brought there by the direct or indirect effects of drink. The Royal Commissioners say that the direct effects are represented by fourteen per cent. It is difficult to get at the direct and separate them from the indirect effects. Suppose it were only that, see what an important point it has brought forth. I hold in my hand the record of 232 cases published by Dr. Mason, of Fort Hamilton. Dr. Mason shows from the persons who have been under his own care that it is not the poor and the badly educated, but that all classes are affected through this agent, and are represented in his asylum. He says: "We have at present amongst our patients clergymen, lawyers, physicians, and representatives from all classes of society who once held remunerative and responsible positions, but who now, voluntarily in many instances, seek the shelter and restorative aid which our asylum affords." He goes on to say how this inebriety is brought on and produced by the drink, and he would put as mental alienation from drink the statistics far higher than Dr. Shepherd. You see what a lesson this is to us, that there should be not only the physical, but the mental death so distinctly brought out by the use of this agent.

XV.—ALCOHOL AND HEREDITY.

Another point, and it is a sad and impressive one. We know that twenty years ago we had no kind of knowledge of an exact nature with regard to the effect of *heredity in drink.* Dr. Connolly, the late Sir John Forbes, and Dr. Carpenter had hinted and pointed out the relationship of drink to certain forms of hereditary disease, but we had no conception of how marked is the influence of alcohol to produce disease by heredity; that is to say, not only in the person directly affected, but in the offspring of that person. We know now as certainly as possible that the thoroughly inebriate man or woman having children, impress those children distinctly with the diseases which spring from the use of this particular agent, and here we have Dr. Mason again coming forward and telling us " the inebriety of parents should be regarded as one predisposing cause of insanity in the children. The principal cause is the inebriety in the parents—92 of 116 cases in our asylum have such a parentage." Think of that, and if anything could impress the mind more solemnly than another it is this: think of the future generations in reference to the present. Think of the important, solemn truth that you unwittingly, by indulging in this one particular agent, may be the progenitor of abuse in another generation, which shall be affected in a similar manner, and that that may go on for age upon age always with the still-continued increase of the same form of disease, intensified perchance and multiplied perhaps a thousand and a million fold. I do not know anything more solemn than what I have just said in regard to this great question. Here, like as a forest may begin from the implantation of a single plant, so from the beginning of the taking of this agent the mischief may progress from generation to generation, until at last, if such efforts as ours are not put forth, this world might indeed—I am using the words of truth and soberness—become one gigantic inebriate asylum.

XVI.—Alcohol and Crime.

Again, we have had brought out before us in a manner never before the relationship of alcohol to crime. Our judges now are alive to this subject. Some have said that 90 per cent. of the cases come from this cause, and this very day the papers contain a charge by Mr. Justice Kay, in which he says judicially—" I know by my experience that 50 per cent. of the crime of the kingdom springs from this cause." We have come down to individual forms of moral offence. Just think of this. I am president of a society called " The Medical Temperance Association." There are 300 of us banded together as Total Abstainers—physicians and surgeons in large practice—not to make a propaganda of Total

Abstinence, but to meet amongst ourselves (strangers are welcomed), and discuss the points relating to Total Abstinence which are most interesting to us in the treatment of disease. A little while ago the question came up as to the treatment of dipsomania. That being a public question we opened our doors generally. We had a very remarkable discussion on this subject, and what struck me as I was presiding was that everybody who spoke dealt with one moral aspect of the question. We speak when talking of a disease of its "diagnosis"—in other words, an explanation of the disease from its symptoms. We were all of this mind, that one of the most diagnostic marks of drink-craving, that which distinguishes it as a mental characteristic from all other things is, that the drink-craver is always a falsehood teller, that there is no actual case where a person affected with the drink-craving has been known to speak the truth, that we never can believe a word they say, and many of us are of opinion that the tendency to untruthfulness descends to the children of those people. See how solemnly strange it is that a physical agent should be taken into the body which should after a time so destroy all moral sense of right and thought of responsibility, that the very foundation of morality is actually so changed that the person becomes as it were naturally and habitually the child and representative of falsehood. These are facts which were not known twenty years ago, and which must in the end tell largely as they are made known in the promotion of our cause.

XVII.—ALCOHOL AND PAUPERISM.

We have declared that alcohol prepared and taken on a large scale is a source of starvation—that to take large quantities of this is to starve. We have known that all through our history. Our painters have shown that. Our Hogarths and Cruikshanks have sketched it. All who have depicted drunkenness have connected it with want and penury. We get beyond that. We see that nations that are going to suffer severely are nations that destroy the produce which is given to them for the supply of their natural wants, by appropriating it to unnatural productions. For instance, in Ireland—one of my friends has brought me a book on the culture of land in Ireland, and has shown that 75 per cent. of the cereal produce of the country goes for the production of one grain—barley, which goes in its turn for the production of one destructive drink—whisky. Let us take that to our minds; and that is only one illustration of which many more could be given; but we have here this broad fact before us, that directly we begin to take food for a false purpose, we take from ourselves that which nature wished us to have, and starvation, misery, and penury are the natural results. Perhaps some one will say, "We can get corn and food elsewhere." But we can only do it by the extension of our principles elsewhere, because if the opposite were to prevail then those countries sinking into the same abyss would perform the same act, and the whole world might in course of time be brought into one gigantic famine.

XVIII.—Alcohol and Prison Life.

We have gained a piece of information we had not twenty-one years ago. Twenty-one years ago it was common to say, "What the Total Abstainers say is right enough, but we are accustomed to the use of strong drinks, and are unable to leave them off; it is dangerous to leave them off. You must not break lightly a habit. You must be moderate." On that point we have a grand experiment going on in our model prisons. We know that those unfortunates who are locked up are locked up directly from this agent. When my mind became turned toward the action of alcohol upon the body I said, "Here is a crucial test about the leaving off." I inquired of all the prisons—"Do you let these people down drop by drop, and gradually reduce it?" "No," I found was the response. As the prison door closes the tap closes, so far as they are concerned. Then I asked, "Do they suffer in any way?" The answer was "Never.' But wherever I made inquiry into prison discipline of life I have never once found an instance where it could be shown that the sudden leaving off of their drink by these people was a cause of any disease or any kind of defect whatsoever. In America and Canada we have had some experience. Dr. Buck has recently published some experiments he has conducted. In 600 cases he has removed suddenly strong drink, and he says his asylum was never in better condition, and that he has never had the least occasion to suppose that the slightest injury was inflicted. For the cause of the moral side of this question this is a fact of supreme moment for you to bear in mind.

XIX.—ALCOHOL AND HISTORY.

We get to see that through history there is a great deal to be learned in regard to what have been the failures of nations. Historians now are beginning to look up, and say there were great wars at various times—how did they spring up? Who were the men that led them? They look at those great wars that led to the American Revolution. Who were the statesmen? Why, they were the statesmen who were always in wine. Look at the great riots and troubles that have arisen. What was their origin? Wine and strong drink. Even Alexander the Great is spoken of as "Alexander the Drunkard," and it is known that he died intoxicated. Historians will soon be able to pick from the history of the past that which was sober and that which was drunken in the history of mankind and of nations.

XX.—ALCOHOL AND LEGISLATION.

We have scored a point in legislation. Twenty-one years ago no statesman would have dared to have thought of legislation as touching the English Juggernaut. On the contrary, he would let our people roll under its wheels, and be killed wholesale, and think nothing about it; but now it is the ambition of statesmen to lead the van, and by and by Sir Wilfrid Lawson would have more compeers, perchance, than he liked, were it not that his heart is as sound as his head.

XXI.—Alcohol and Ourselves.

Lastly, we have given up the notion pretty generally — those who are men of science and of thought—of alcohol as a necessity. That general expression of alcohol as a necessity has passed from our minds by the accumulated evidence derived from so many sources. We speak now of this as a plague, and we say it produces fever, and it kills; we speak of this as a pestilence, for we say that it infects, and spreads, and devastates. Twenty-one years ago we used to hear in our churches the minister say: " From plague, pestilence, and famine, from battle and murder, and from sudden death " —and we used to hear the congregation give the response—" Good Lord deliver us." Now, by the knowledge we have, we say yes, and plague, and pestilence, and famine, battle, murder, and sudden death are all more or less linked up with this one agent; and we declare that if we could say, and not only say, but insure ourselves that we were delivered from this one agent, then the rest of our deliverance were indeed at hand.

www.ingramcontent.com/pod-product-compliance
Lightning Source LLC
Chambersburg PA
CBHW020300240426
43673CB00039B/660